Language, Languages and New Technologies

DUISBURGER ARBEITEN ZUR SPRACH- UND KULTURWISSENSCHAFT

DUISBURG PAPERS ON RESEARCH IN LANGUAGE AND CULTURE

Herausgegeben von/edited by
Ulrich Ammon, René Dirven und/and Martin Pütz

Band/Volume 87

PETER LANG
Frankfurt am Main · Berlin · Bern · Bruxelles · New York · Oxford · Wien

Gerhard Stickel
Tamás Váradi
(eds.)

Language, Languages and New Technologies

ICT in the Service of Languages

Contributions to the
Annual Conference 2010
of EFNIL in Thessaloniki

EFNIL
European Federation of National Institutions for Language

PETER LANG
Internationaler Verlag der Wissenschaften

Bibliographic Information published by the Deutsche Nationalbibliothek

The Deutsche Nationalbibliothek lists this publication in the Deutsche Nationalbibliografie; detailed bibliographic data is available in the internet at http://dnb.d-nb.de.

Cover Design:
© Olaf Gloeckler, Atelier Platen, Friedberg

ISSN 0934-3709
ISBN 978-3-631-63536-0

www.peterlang.de

Preface

This is the fourth yearbook of EFNIL, the European Federation of National Institutions for Language that endeavours to preserve and further develop the linguistic diversity in Europe and to enhance the plurilingualism of the Europeans. One of the activities of EFNIL is its annual conference that is each time devoted to a topic of special importance for the member institutions and their national tasks within the European context. The present volume renders the texts of the papers read at the annual conference 2010 in Thessaloniki. This conference was hosted by the Greek member institute of EFNIL, the ΚΕΝΤΡΟ ΕΛΛΗΝΙΚΗΣ ΓΛΩΣΣΑΣ, the Centre for the Greek Language. The conference dealt first of all with the use of new information technologies for language research, language documentation and language learning. Besides general contributions to the theme, several reports were given by member institutions on concrete uses of information technologies for linguistic purposes in different European countries and at the European Parliament. In this volume, the texts of the brief introductory statements are followed by the general contributions and then by the partly enlarged reports from the various countries.

The contributions to the closing panel discussion were devoted to a different issue, an issue that has been discussed again and again by the members of EFNIL as well as within European language politics: the various readings and uses of the symbolically loaded term *national language*. The editors hope that this part of the book will not only stimulate the further discussion in international linguistics but also find the interest of persons involved in national and European language politics and policies.

We thank again Ulrich Ammon and his colleagues for accepting also this volume for their series. And we thank Joachim Hohwieler, Katalin Vargha and Mark Newson for their efficient help in preparing the book for the printers.

Vorwort

Dies ist das vierte Jahrbuch von EFNIL, der Europäischen Föderation nationaler Sprachinstitutionen, die sich seit ihrer Gründung 2003 für die Bewahrung und Weiterentwicklung der Sprachenvielfalt in Europa und für die Mehrsprachigkeit der Europäer einsetzt. Zu den Aktivitäten von EFNIL gehören jährliche Tagungen, die jeweils einem Thema von besonderer Bedeutung für die Mitgliedsinstitute und ihre nationalen Aufgaben im europäischen Kontext gewidmet sind. Der vorliegende Band bietet die Texte der Vorträge, die auf der Jahrestagung 2010 in Saloniki gehalten worden sind. Gastgeber war das griechische Mitgliedsinstitut von EFNIL, das ΚΕΝΤΡΟ ΕΛΛΗΝΙΚΗΣ ΓΛΩΣΣΑΣ, das Zentrum für die Griechische Sprache. Die Tagung befasste sich in erster Linie mit dem Einsatz neuer Technologien für Sprachforschung, Sprachdokumentation und Sprachunterricht. Neben generellen Beiträgen zum Thema wurden mehrere Berichte von Mitgliedsinstituten über die konkrete Nutzung von Informationstechnologien in verschiedenen europäischen Ländern und auch beim Europäischen Parlament gegeben. In diesem Band bieten wir nach den Texten der kurzen Eröffnungsansprachen zunächst die generellen Beiträge und dann die zum Teil ergänzten Berichte aus den verschiedenen Ländern.

Die als Schlusskapitel wiedergegebenen Beiträge zur abschließenden Podiumsdiskussion waren einem anderen Thema gewidmet, einem Thema, das die Mitglieder von EFNIL wie auch die europäische Sprachpolitik immer wieder beschäftigt: die verschiedenen Lesarten und Verwendungen des symbolträchtigen Ausdrucks *Nationalsprache*. Die Herausgeber hoffen, dass auch dieser Teil des Bandes nicht nur zur weiteren Diskussion in der internationalen Linguistik anregt, sondern auch das Interesse von Akteuren in den nationalen und europäischen Sprachpolitiken findet.

Wieder einmal danken wir Ulrich Ammon und seinen Kollegen für die Aufnahme auch dieses Bandes in ihre Reihe. Joachim Hohwieler, Katalin Vargha und Mark Newson danken wir für ihre tatkräftige Hilfe bei der Vorbereitung des Buchs für den Druck.

Bevezetés

Ez a negyedik évkönyv az EFNIL (European Federation of National Institutions for Language) történetében, amely arra törekszik, hogy megőrizze és továbbfejlessze Európa nyelvi változatosságát és támogassa az európaiak többnyelvűségét. Az EFNIL központi tevékenységi körébe tartoznak az éves konferenciák, amelyeket minden alkalommal egy, a társintézmények és azok európai kontextusban tekintett nemzeti feladatait érintő fontos témának szentelnek. A jelen kötet a 2010-ben Tessalonikiben megrendezett éves konferencia anyagát tartalmazza. A konferencia házigazdája az EFNIL görög partnerintézete, a ΚΕΝΤΡΟ ΕΛΛΗΝΙΚΗΣ ΓΛΩΣΣΑΣ (A Görög Nyelv Központja) volt. A konferencia elsősorban a nyelvkutatásban használatos új információs technológiák felhasználásával, valamint nyelvi dokumentációval és nyelvtanulással foglalkozott.

Emellett a témához kapcsolódóan a kötet néhány jelentést is tartalmaz, amelyekben az egyes partnerintézetek beszámolnak az információs technológiák nyelvi célú felhasználásáról, különböző európai országokban és az Európai Parlamentben.

A kötetben a rövid bevezető nyilatkozatok után következnek a konferencián elhangzott előadások, majd az egyes országokra lebontott jelentések.

A záró kerekasztal beszélgetés már más témáról szólt. Egy olyan témáról, amely újra és újra megvitatásra kerül az EFNIL-en belül ugyanúgy, mint az európai nyelvi politikákban. Ez nem más, mint a nemzeti nyelv szimbolikusan terhelt különböző olvasatai és használata. A szerzők remélik, hogy a kötet ezen része nem csak ösztönözni fogja a nemzetközi nyelvészetről szóló értekezéseket, de felhívja a nemzeti és európai nyelvekben jártas politikákkal és eljárásokkal foglalkozó szakemberek figyelmét is.

Köszönjük még egyszer Ulrich Ammonnak és kollégáinak, hogy elfogadták ezen kötetsorozatot. Köszönet illeti még Joachim Hohwielert, Vargha Katalint és Mark Newsont mindazon segítségért, amelyet a kötet nyomtatásra való előkészítésében nyújtottak.

Mannheim / Budapest
Gerhard Stickel / Tamás Váradi

Contents

a) Opening

b) General reflections

c) Reports on various countries

a) Opening

John Nikolaos Kazazis

Welcome address

In the tradition established at the EFNIL conferences, according to which each meeting focuses on a fundamental research or practice issue of great value for language and language policy, this 8th Annual Conference concentrates on Language, Languages and New Technologies: ICT in the Service of Languages. The theme will be approached through a series of general overview lectures delivered by expert guest speakers and in brief reports by delegates of member institutions.

The titles of the papers show clearly that a safe distance is generally kept from the *scopuli* of both technophobia and technomania. Indeed, the speakers obviously endeavour to read dispassionately the current state of things in the area of Information and Communication where new data and technological developments radically transform the landscape as it was known in the past; where especially under the influence of the multimedia technologies, and the global supremacy of the English language, the entire cycle of the perception and production of oral and written speech (and subsequently of *reading* too) is changing all over the world. Literacy is being redefined. Whereas, however, the massive impact of this ensemble of semiotic systems on the reconstruction of meaning is gradually becoming better and better understood by the linguistic community, one does not fail to be overwhelmed by the overabundance of English language digital environments in the Internet, while similar environments for the "less spoken languages" are far and between. The pressure on these languages is hard to sustain.

Under these circumstances, the question rises how we can best harness the technological horses into the chariot of language research and education to achieve best results for all languages. In the Centre for the Greek Language, in an effort to carve a clear policy to match this new reality and to practically intervene in the official educational language policy, we developed various digital environments for the Greek language, which have been proven very popular with both the educational and research community. It is, however, our experience and firm believe that here cooperation among our institutions is most desirable in order to move towards a common European policy –a policy that will define problems, set priorities and discuss and propose solutions. It is in this spirit that we are more than happy to host this important Conference in Thessaloniki.

Προς τον καθηγητή Γεραρδο Στικελ, προς όλα τα μέλη της διπλής οργανωτικής επιτροπής και προς όλους εσάς που εργαστήκατε εντατικά για να πετύχει η διοργάνωση αυτή εκφράζω τις θερμότερες ευχαριστίες και την ειλικρινέστερη ευγνωμοσύνη μου. Σας εύχομαι ένα συνέδριο επιτυχημένο από κάθε άποψη, και άνετη και ευχάριστη την παραμονή σας στη Θεσσαλονίκη. (To Professor Gerhard Stickel, to the entire organizational committee from either side and to all of you who worked hard to make a success of this event I offer my warmest thanks and most sincere gratitude. We wish you a most successful conference and a comfortable and pleasant stay in Thessaloniki.)

Antonios Rengakos

Welcome notes

The growing impact of ICT on the study but also on languages themselves sets an unprecedented challenge for what aspires to be the vision of the European Union, i.e. the promotion and development of multilingualism on the basis of a balanced and equal valuation of all languages. This conference concentrates on three, critical areas of research, aiming at exploring possible solutions against a potential side-effect or by-product caused by ICT: the use and exploitation of the medium of technology for the promotion of a market-oriented agenda for the sake of globalization; the transformation of language and languages into commodities instead of dynamic entities that can contribute to the multilingual and multicultural mosaic of modern Europe.

Within the framework of such a complicated environment, in which the 'game' of the linguistic market is determined by the tendency of 'strong' languages to impose themselves on 'weak' ones, the technologization of languages should develop in a cooperative spirit towards a 'European' *ethos* of communication. For example, we should aspire to make the internet –this contemporary informational highway– a real 'contact zone' between languages and cultures, rather than a means of (re)confirmation of linguistic and cultural hegemony. In fact, boosting multilingualism through the internet should become the critical turning point in the increasing crystallization of cultural and linguistic homogeneity.

In conclusion, I think we all agree that the thoughtful integration of technology in the sociocultural reality of our times constitutes a pressing demand, especially because its use is interwoven with the development of new forms of grammaticality.

Hoping that this most promising conference will bring about new insights on at least some of the issues it has set out to discuss, I welcome EFNIL and its distinguished guests to Thessaloniki and wish everyone a fruitful exchange of exciting ideas.

Gerhard Stickel

Αυοιγμα / Opening

Κυριε Προεδρε,

Αγαπητες και αγαπητοι συναδελφοι,

Κυριες και Κυριοι:

Με την ευκαιρια της εναρξης του ετησιου Συνεδριου της ΕΦΝΙΛ, της Ευρωπαικης Ομοσπονδιας Εθνικων Φορεων για την Γλωσσα, σας χαιρετιζω ολους στη Θεσσαλονικη.

Ειναι η ογδοη φορα απο την ιδρυση του Οργανισμου μας στη Στοκχολμη που συναντιωμαστε σ ενα επισημο Συνεδριο.

Οπως και στο παρελθον διαλεξαμε μαζι με τους συναδελφους που μας φιλοξενουν ενα θεμα Που εχει ιδιαιτερη σημασια για τις εργασιες μας: Γλωσσα, Γλωσσες και νεες Τεχνολογιες.[1]

We all use tools and methods of ICT in our daily work and would get frustrated or desperate if somebody took away the personal computer or laptop from our desk or the advanced mobile phone from our pocket. The older ones among us have in the course of our professional life experienced several radical changes of the material conditions for our professions as lexicographers, grammarians, dialectologists, sociolinguists or language teachers since the time when we mainly used books, typewriters and card files for our work. Maybe, some are still secretly using card files because they do not trust the durability of digital data carriers. I still remember the attempts during the sixties of the last century to have linguistic routine tasks done by huge machines that droned with their 8 or 12 tape units in large halls. We fed them with Hollerith cards or paper tapes that first had to be punched on other clumsy machines. As a result we got our processed data printed in coarse characters on large leporellos.

At that time, the big main frame computers and the available software were also first of all made for numerical computing. It took quite a while to develop programmes for the processing of non-numerical data, that is, words and texts. I remember that two of my colleagues needed several days to write a programme for arranging words in alphabetic order. That was 45 years ago. Now every little laptop or notebook computer has such programmes as small components of its rich standard software. In the old times of linguistic data processing, the input and storage of larger texts also meant real physical efforts, because besides the huge number of punch cards or tapes for the input, the magnetic tapes of the computer also had to be exchanged again and again or moved from one unit to the next. Now the input and output facilities have become multimedial and highly

[1] Mr. President, dear colleagues, Ladies and Gentlemen:
I salute you at the Annual Conference of EFNIL, the European Federation of National Institutions for Language. Since the foundation of our organization in Stockholm, this is now the 8th time that the members assemble for an official conference. As in previous years, we have chosen – in agreement with our hosts – a general theme that is of special importance for the research and administrative work in our member institutions: "Language, Languages, and New Technologies".

flexible. There was even hope for paperless research and other office work. However, practice showed that the consumption of paper increased considerably due to comfortable high quality printers. The storage capacity of computers for linguistic data has increased enormously and is continuously growing. This has led, among other things, to the development of a new linguistic discipline, that is, corpus linguistics. Unfortunately, the legal conditions for the storage and computational processing of printed and oral texts have not quite kept up with the progress made in computational and linguistic methods. Our conference also offers an opportunity to discuss this issue and to look for feasible solutions.

Besides the rapid progress in the development of ever smaller and more powerful computers, the introduction of new communicative tools and channels by the interlinking of computers, by the Internet and the world wide web, has caused great changes for our work in traditional fields of linguistics. They affect the methods of research in the various disciplines of pure linguistics as well as the tools and ways of applied linguistics such as translation and interpretation, language teaching, learning, and testing. Perhaps, we are not even aware of some of these effects. Most of the EFNIL delegates assembled here are trained linguists or philologists. As far as I know, only a few of them, few of us, are experts in computational linguistics or other fields of ICT. Therefore, I think, many of us (including myself) have not yet grasped all the opportunities and possibilities that recent developments in ICT offer for our work. We also have only limited information on the advanced uses that some of our member institutions are making of ICT. Thus, I presume, that we all are eager to hear from our colleagues about their use of ICT including specific explorative projects in their institutes and to learn from the invited guest speakers about new developments in ICT and their actual and potential relevance for the study, the learning and the use of our languages.

The topic "language and new technologies" has one additional aspect that will, perhaps, also be treated in some of the contributions to this conference: This is the influence that ICT has or can have on languages proper, on their phonological, grammatical and textual structures. We can all observe that the use of computers, the Internet and mobile phones has lead to changes of verbal communication: from the emergence of new types of communicative interactions, that is, new text and dialogue types and conventions, to grammatical innovations down to new spellings and, perhaps, even phonetic peculiarities. I am not quite sure about phonetic changes but would not be surprised if they were discovered. These changes mean that the new IC technologies do not only offer new tools and methods for linguistic research and linguistic applications but also cause new forms of language use that itself again becomes the object of linguistic investigation.

At this conference, however, the changes of verbal behaviour by ICT can only be a minor issue. The general overviews and principle reflexions of our guest speakers and the reports about the concrete use of ICT in several of our member institutes will, probably, focus on the instrumental qualities that ICT has or could have for the activities in the service of our languages. At this conference, most of us will be learners rather than teachers. But I think that the expert speakers will also have some gain from the questions we will ask them and I hope that the reports we will hear will stimulate new cooperative projects among EFNIL members.

Let me conclude with thanks to our Greek colleagues and friends for so carefully organizing the conference and for the generous hospitality offered to us.

And let me add special thanks to Vasiliki Dendrinou (Bessie Dendrinos as we call her), member of the EFNIL Executive Committee, who proposed the important and attractive theme of this conference and who also had an essential part in the preparation of this event. I am confident that at the end of the general assembly tomorrow afternoon we all will have ample reason for repeating and confirming these thanks also to Maria Theodoropoulou and her team.

Now, let's get to work!

Danke sehr, Merci beaucoup, Many thanks etcetera, and, of course: Sas efxaristo!

b) General reflections

Sabine Kirchmeier-Andersen

Language technology for language institutions. What kind of technology do languages institutions use – what kind of resources can they provide?

Abstract (English)

In this paper I will examine the use of language technology (LT) in national institutions of language. After a short review of the typical tasks of language institutions and the basic aspects of language technology and its relevance for language institutions, I will discuss which types of technologies are currently put to use, and which types may be useful in solving the tasks of language institutions in the future. The empirical basis is the current language policy of the Nordic countries and a survey of language technology and language resources in the Nordic language councils in 2008. Finally, I will make some suggestions for how language technology and language institutions can profit from working together to meet the linguistic challenges that lie ahead.

Abstract (Danish)

I denne artikel undersøger jeg brugen af sprogteknologi i sproginstitutioner. Efter en kort gennemgang af de opgaver der typiske for sproginstitutioner, og af sprogteknologiens grundlæggende aspekter, diskuterer jeg hvilke slags teknologier der for øjeblikket bliver taget i anvendelse, og hvilke former for sprogteknologi der kunne være nyttige for sproginstitutioner i fremtiden. Det empiriske grundlag er den nuværende sprogpolitik i Norden og en undersøgelse af sprogteknologi og sprogresurser i de nordiske sprognævn som blev gennemført i 2008. Til sidst vil jeg fremsætte nogle forslag til hvordan sprogteknologi og sproginstitutioner kan drage nytte af at samarbejde for at blive bedre rustet til fremtidens sproglige udfordringer.

1. The tasks of language institutions

The central or national institutions of language in Europe are mainly concerned with research, documentation and policy making relating to the officially recognized standard languages within the states of the European Union. Whereas the tasks of European language institutions may vary considerably with regard to how much weight is put on language research, teaching, standardization and giving advice, Nordic Language institutions have quite a number of similar tasks. The core activities are to monitor language development, that is changes in the corpus of the language mainly regarding lexis and grammar, to provide orthographic standards and to give advice on language use in private and public institutions. Most institutions also follow the development of the status of the language and provide information about the contexts in which the language is used in order to support the development of language policies. Other important activities are research, publishing and information to the public on language issues. Some institutions work on a strictly monolingual basis, whereas others, depending on the linguistic situation in their countries, provide services for multiple languages such as bilingual dictionaries or grammars. Although spoken language receives some attention, the main focus in most institutions is on the written language.

Monitoring language development means tracking the negotiation of norms in language communities and the development of neologisms. It is a huge task which traditionally has been carried out by hand – e.g. by reading through lots of carefully selected texts extracting quotes that are stored in large archives, or by recording and transcribing spoken language – the classical work of the philologist. Today, new technology is being put to use in various phases of this process: archives have become databases, quotes are extracted via a scanner or taken directly from the electronic version of the text from the internet and supplied with metadata to facilitate automatic search and further processing.

Even though language institutions have been collecting large amounts of texts and corpus linguistics and language technology play a more important role, the task of identifying a new word or phrase or a new sense of a word in most cases is still carried out manually. Today, people interact with written texts via sms, email, chat etc. much more than just 10-20 years ago, and the development of their languages has changed accordingly. Many language institutions would like to extend the language that is monitored to include a much larger variety of written and spoken texts, for instance from the increasing numbers of conversations in the social media, but do not have the resources to do so. The introduction of language technology might be a way to cope with this development.

2. How can language technology help?

Language technology is usually described as computer programs that work with written or spoken language as input or output, i.e. speech or text – "a kind of artificial device that is created to augment our abilities" (Sproat 2010). Various applications have been developed over time, e.g. spelling and grammar checkers, machine translation, information retrieval, computer assisted language learning, speech synthesis and speech recognition just to mention a few (cf. figure 1). Often language technology is integrated into other programs or applications such as robots, databases, user interfaces etc. There is an overlap with multimedia technology – integration with computer games, toys and teaching applications. There is also some overlap with artificial intelligence and knowledge technology, e.g. both use ontologies and taxonomies that describe relations in the world and facilitate automatic reasoning.

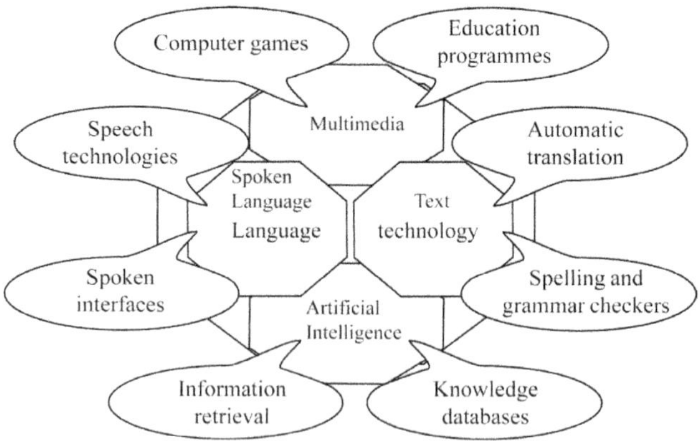

Fig. 1: Applications of language technology

Language technology today has two basic methods to perform its tasks: rule based and statistical. The rule based methods use formalized linguistic rules encoded in computational dictionaries and grammars that enable the computer to analyze or generate natural language in a number of well defined steps. If the systems are used for translation, there will also be translation rules defining the correspondences between two or more languages. Statistical systems on the other hand derive heuristic knowledge from a large collection of texts or transcribed speech which may be enriched with various types of annotations. The heuristics are then applied to new texts. Recent approaches tend to combine the two methods in order to further improve the performance of the system.

Regardless of the choice of method, LT-programs are composed of two elements: one or several software modules, such as databases, language analyzers, speech recognizers etc., and language data such as text corpora, speech data, dictionaries or formalized grammar rules (cf. figure 2).

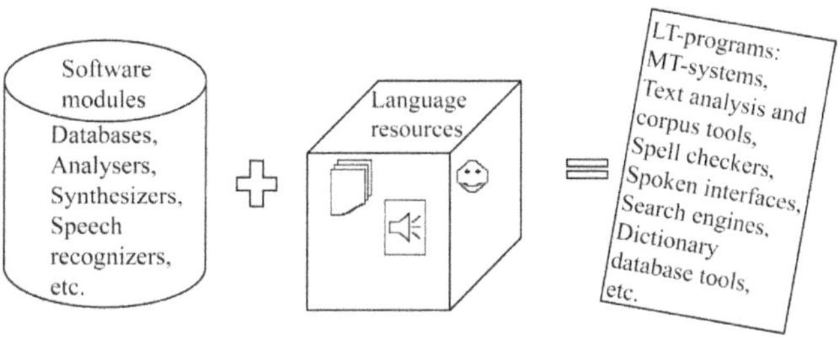

Fig. 2: Basic components of language technology

In sum, language technology is about developing various software modules that can be applied to language data in order to create a number of LT-programs or tools that can aid us in performing various tasks where the knowledge of language is involved.

Even though this description of the basic methods is very brief, it is sufficient to reveal various points of interest for language institutions: first of all a common interest in dictionaries, grammars and large collections of linguistic data, i.e. recorded speech and texts. This can be characterized as mutual interest, i.e. both groups could profit from each other if information and data could be exchanged. Secondly, language institutions could profit in various ways from the automated methods and tools developed by language technology. This is probably best illustrated by some examples.

The first example concerns tracking the distribution of the use of competing similar or synonymous words or expressions in a language, in this case the English "exit poll" vs. the corresponding Danish expression "valgstedsmåling". Going through a large newspaper corpus to produce a graph as the one in figure 3, showing the occurrences of the two words over time, is a time consuming task which can be done faster and easier through the use of language technology and at the same time giving valuable information when it comes to discussing lexical developments and language planning. Such graphs are quite informative and are well suited to illustrate linguistic observations to a large public audience.

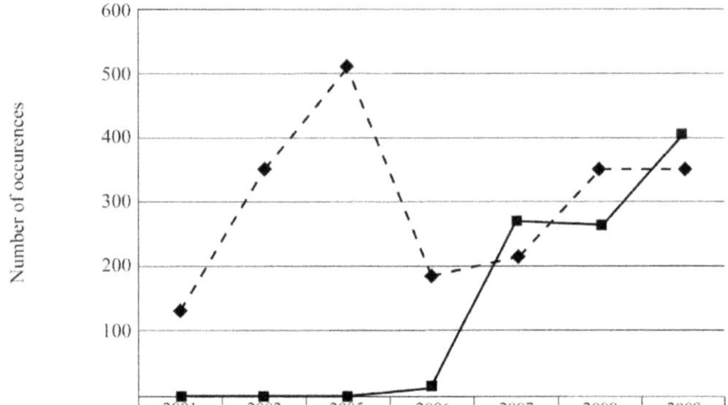

	2001	2002	2005	2006	2007	2008	2009
exit poll	133	352	508	188	214	352	352
valgstedsmåling	0	0	0	13	272	265	406

Fig. 3: The frequency over time of the words "exit poll" and "valgstedsmåling" in a corpus of Danish newspapers.

The second example concerns the collections of records of answers to questions from the public about language to the Nordic language councils. Norway, Sweden and Denmark keep track of the 8,000-10,000 questions that are received at their information desks every year, as this gives valuable information about the language problems that arise on a day to day basis. Not all questions are worth keeping. Out of the approx. 500,000 questions that have been answered by the Danish Language Council since 1955 around 10,000 have be recorded in a database for future reference because they concern new linguistic phenomena that have not previously been described. Many of these answers are also made available for the public on the internet.

The three Scandinavian languages are closely related. There is frequent contact between the information services, and the possibility of searching through the databases of questions to find answers to similar problems in the other languages has long been an important point on the agenda. Since there is considerable orthographic and lexical variation between the languages, and since questions often are connected to certain words or expressions, a simple text based search is not useful. Therefore a common taxonomy of linguistic terms was developed in order to enable thematic search across the languages. Answers on, for instance, morphology of nouns in relation to definiteness can thus be retrieved for all three languages at the same time, although the answers deal with completely different word forms. Advanced language technology is used to facilitate the development of a Nordic taxonomy of linguistic terms and to enable search across languages.

The third is a recent experiment at the Danish Language Council, the development of a new tool, the wordtrawler – a computer programme that automatically scans newspaper texts for neologisms (Halskov/Jarvad 2010). Each month the system collects and processes 20 million words of text and identifies new word strings by checking them against all dictionaries and wordlists that are available at the council, including the ones that were found the month before. This results in a list of approximately 30,000 potentially new words and expressions that are filtered automatically to form a list of candidates for manual inspection. The outcome is a list of 150-250 genuine new words in the general language, i.e. 1,500-3,000 new words per year. Some of these are new compounds, some are new acronyms and others are loan words or domesticated words. Although this procedure can detect many neologisms more efficiently than the human eye, it cannot completely replace the human inspection, especially when it comes to identifying changes in the use of already existing words, but still it is a great improvement.

European language institutions vary quite a lot with regard to the use of language technology in their core activities. Generally, tools that can facilitate the creation of dictionaries and the use of text corpora are in focus. Lately, we have seen an increasing interest in more sophisticated corpus tools such as, for instance, part of speech taggers and syntactic parsers.

Language institutions are not only potential users of language technology. As central players in the language debate of their countries, language institutions are concerned with the status of the language and with ensuring the access to high quality language technology tools such as word processors with spelling and grammar checkers, translation software, intelligent information retrieval etc. This will be further elaborated in the following sections.

3. Language technology in the Nordic countries

In the language institutions of the Nordic countries language technology has been an important concern for several years. The main language policy document of the Nordic Council of Ministers (Nordisk Ministerråd), *Declaration on a Nordic Language Policy,* which was adopted by the Nordic ministers in 2006, lays out a strategy for the relation between the global lingua franca, English, the Nordic languages essential to the state (Danish, Finnish, Icelandic, Norwegian, and Swedish), the Nordic languages which in addition to the languages of state are essential to other societies (Greenlandic, Faroese and the different varieties of Sami), languages which in some of the Nordic countries are recognized as official minority languages (Meänkieli (Tornedalian language)), the Kven language, different varieties of Romani, Yiddish, German, and the various Nordic sign languages) and, finally, the about 200 immigrant languages.

The declaration states as its main goals:

- *that* all Nordic residents being able to read and write the language or languages that are essential to society in the area where they live
- *that* all Nordic residents being able to communicate with one another, preferably in a Scandinavian language,
- *that* all Nordic residents having a basic knowledge of linguistic rights in the Nordic countries and the language situation in the Nordic countries
- *that* all Nordic residents having very good skills in at least one language of international importance and good skills in another foreign language
- *that* all Nordic residents having a general knowledge of what language is and how it works.

These goals also require that all Nordic residents exhibit tolerance for variety and diversity in language, both between and within languages.

(Declaration on a Nordic Language Policy 2006, official English version, 93)

In order to define the relation between the various languages, the declaration operates with the term *parallel use of languages*, which in practice is used to refer to the parallelism between the Nordic languages on the one hand, and English on the other:

> The parallel use of languages refers to the concurrent use of several languages within one or more areas. None of the languages abolishes or replaces the other; they are used in parallel.
>
> Nordic residents, who internationally speaking have good English skills, have especially favorable conditions for developing skills in the parallel use of English and one or more of the languages of the Nordic countries in certain fields. A consistent policy to promote the parallel use of languages requires:
>
> - *that* it be possible to use both the languages of the Nordic countries essential to society and English as languages of science
> - *that* the presentation of scientific results in the languages of the Nordic countries essential to society be rewarded
> - *that* instruction in scientific technical language, especially in written form, be given in both English and the languages of the Nordic countries essential to society
> - *that* universities, colleges, and other scientific institutions can develop long-range strategies for the choice of language, the parallel use of languages, language instruction, and translation grants within their fields
> - *that* Nordic terminology bodies can continue to coordinate terminology in new fields
> - *that* business and labor-market organizations be urged to develop strategies for the parallel use of language.
>
> (Declaration on a Nordic Language Policy 2006, Goals 2.1, 94)

As one of the means to fulfill its goals, the declaration points at the use of language technology and contains two important recommendations:

> 1. inter-Nordic dictionaries should be compiled in printed and electronic form
> 2. computer translation programs for the languages of the Nordic countries essential to society and programs for multilingual searches in Nordic databases should be developed.
>
> (Declaration on a Nordic Language Policy 2006, Issue 1, 93)

Although the declaration is not legally binding, all Nordic language councils are committed to fulfilling the goals of the declaration. The secretariat of the Council of Nordic Ministers has the task of following up with regular progress reports. In 2009 the Council of Nordic Ministers decided to establish a new body, Nordic Language Coordination, in order to intensify the follow up on the declaration and to strengthen the cooperation between the language councils and numerous other organizations working with researching and teaching Nordic languages.

Since 2005 the Network of the Nordic language councils has entrusted a special language technology group, ASTIN,[1] with the task of developing LT solutions for language institutions, stimulating research and development of language technology for the Nor-

---

[1] ASTIN: Arbejdsgruppen for sprogrøgt og sprogteknologi (Nordic task force for language and language technology) was initiated in 2005 by the Network of the Nordic Language Councils and currently consists of: Torbjørg Breivik (Language Council in Norway), Rickard Domeij (Language Council in Sweden), Per Langgård (Language Council of Greenland), Sjur Nøstlebo Moshagen (Sametinget/Sami Council), Jakob Halskov (Language Council in Denmark).

dic languages, ensuring that important language technology is adapted to the Nordic languages, and monitoring the consequences of the use of language technology for the development of each language. ASTIN has a special focus on facilitating the dialogue between language institutions, LT-researchers, LT-developers and policy makers through conferences, workshop and publications.

In 2008 ASTIN made a survey of the kind of data and tools that are already in use in the Nordic language councils. The survey asked for information on which software modules and language data were available, which LT-tools were most frequently used, and which tools the institutions would like to use in the near future.

All language institutions were asked to indicate whether they made use of software in the following categories:

Software

- Parsers (e.g. automatic morphological analysis, sentence analysis)
- Tools for information extraction
- Tools for automatic mark-up (e.g.part-of-speech, syntax, topics)
- Concordance programs (e.g. frequency counts and keyword in context)
- Tools for annotation (e.g. manual annotation of language data)
- Transcription tools (e.g. transcription of spoken data)
- Statistical tools
- Automatic analysis of document structure
- Spell checkers
- Grammar checkers
- Tools for automatic extraction of new words
- Databases with linguistic questions and answers
- Dictionary databases
- Tools to develop language teaching programs
- Other

Furthermore, institutions were asked to indicate whether they were using or had access to the following types of resources:

Language resources

- Digital lexica
    - Monolingual
    - Bilingual
    - Multilingual
- Corpora
    - Standards
    - Speech corpora
    - Text corpora
    - Multilingual corpora
    - Parallel multilingual corpora

- Terminology databases
- Thesauri/word nets
- Ontologies
- Digitalized records of questions and answers about languages
- Digital word collections
- Digital language training suites
- Other

In all cases, institutions were asked to indicate whether they had developed the indicated software or resources by themselves and/or were holding the copyright, or whether software and resources were bought or licensed from other public institutions or private vendors.

The answers to the questionnaires, which were given by Denmark, Iceland, Norway and Sweden, showed that the following software was most widely used: tools for information extraction, word databases, databases for linguistic questions and answers, spell checkers, statistics programs and concordance programs. Regarding language resources, the Nordic language institutions could report frequent use of the following: monolingual lexica, digitalized questions and answers about language problems, text corpora and terminology databases.

59% of the software was commercial, 41% produced by the language institutions themselves or freeware. 18% of the language resources were commercial products whereas 82% were produced by the language institutions or freeware.

The language councils were also asked what kind of tools and resources they envisage using in the future. The list below only shows the top priorities:

Software
- Automatic analysis of document structure
- Programs for automatic extraction of new words and new word senses
- Tools for automatic/semi-automatic mark-up/tagging
- Tools for language training
- Specialized analyzers and parsers
- Transcription tools for spoken text

Language resources
- Bilingual lexica
- Wordnets and ontologies
- Thesauruses
- Multilingual corpora
- Parallel multilingual corpora
- Common standards for corpora

From the example of the Nordic language councils we can conclude that:

- language institutions can make use of language technology tools
- language institutions expect to be using more language technology in the future
- language institutions have been and still are collecting large repositories of language resources
- language institutions are getting prepared to maneuver in a multilingual context

4. How can language technology developers and language institutions work together?

It has emerged from the previous sections that there are several areas of mutual interest between language technology and languages institutions. Here we shall focus only on four important areas: 1. development of language technology software for language institutions, 2. sharing language resources, and 3. cooperating in policy making for a language technology infrastructure, 4. cooperating on research to improve the adaptation of language technology products to language change.

Better language technology software can help language institutions to do their work more efficiently with text analysis tools to monitor language use, with databases and workbenches to facilitate the development of mono- and multilingual dictionaries, with language teaching programmes, with translation tools for all language pairs including minority languages, etc.

Language institutions can help to improve language technology applications by developing and sharing language resources such as text collections, dictionaries and other linguistic information in a common infrastructure such as CLARIN (www.clarin.eu) and METANET (www.meta-net.eu). In this context it is absolutely imperative that the obstacles that exist due to the current legislation on intellectual property rights can be overcome – not in the sense that intellectual property rights should no longer be granted, but in the sense that an exception should be made for projects that aim at using the text as a collection of words to produce a linguistic tool in which the original text can no longer be reproduced and thus not be misused.

Language technology is also important for the status and the use of a language in every domain of a society (Crystal 2000). Language institutions have an obligation to ensure that language technology products are developed and continuously kept up to date. Cooperation in the area of policy development between language institutions and language technology could thus include

- convincing political decision makers to support the development of language technology,
- convincing political decision makers to make available language data for language technology,
- convincing political decision makers that it is important that there exist experts in language technology for their language.

Last but not least, a joint research effort should be made in order to improve the adaptation of language technology to language change. Computer programs are generally of static nature; once a dictionary or a grammar has been loaded or the system has been trained on available language data, there is hardly any adaptation to changes in the grammar and vocabulary of a given language. The figures from the word-trawler described in section 2 above showed that in general language between 2000 and 3000 words enter the language each year. We have not tried to estimate the growth in the vocabulary of a language if specialized domains were taken into account as well.

National institutions of language are experts on language change and would be able to provide substantial contributions in collaborative research projects with researchers on language technology.

5. Language technology for lesser used languages

Widely used languages such as English, Chinese, Spanish, French, German, Russian etc. constitute attractive markets for the big players of the IT-industry, and language technology based tools for these languages are made readily available and constantly being improved. With the development of social communication platforms and more interactive communication tools, the field for language technology has broadened immensely. In the coming years we will see more:

- Multilingual knowledge sharing using encyclopedia, knowledge bases and terminology databases.
- Automatic or semi-automatic translation on the web.
- Automatic interpretation through combinations of translation systems with speech recognition and speech synthesis.
- Quick access to knowledge through multilingual information retrieval combined with automatic summarization and translation.
- Linguistic services such as mono- and multilingual dictionaries and translation services on mobile platforms.
- Better support for the disabled such as language controlled ambient computing.
- More and more programs with spoken interfaces.
- More intelligently personalized web services and social communication platforms.

However, very little of all this will be available for the less widely spoken languages unless political decision makers contribute substantially through public funded research and development.

It is generally acknowledged that the costs to produce high quality language technology for a given language are the same regardless of the number of speakers, and thus the smaller the number of speakers and potential customers, the less the return on investment. For less widely used languages, the lack of high quality language technology tools and advanced language resources is a disadvantage as the use of the language is no longer supported in all domains. Users of the language will eventually be inclined to use a more widely spoken language in his or her communication or search for information because the tools are better and make it easier and faster to reach a given goal.

Political decision makers who wish to maintain the status of, for instance, the state language and/or preserve and develop the linguistic diversity of the country, should be alert about this development and in due course develop research and development programs that support language technology for the languages of their countries.

Otherwise, if technology does not adapt to people and their language, people will adapt themselves and their language to technology. One striking example: in spite of the remarkable progress that has been made in many areas of IT, a fundamental problem such as the support of different character systems for different languages still has not found a satisfactory solution, and for Danish there are still IT-products, especially on the web, that cannot cope with the 3 national characters *æ, ø, å*. Danes are still forced to use ae, oe, aa for instance in email-addresses, not to mention the fact that basic functions such as alphabetization do not work and that in some applications the Danish characters are simply ignored or replaced by arbitrary symbols making information retrieval a rather arduous task. With explicit reference to the view that it was difficult to market Århus, one of the major Danish cities, in an international digital setting, the city in 2010 changed its name to Aarhus countering the latest major orthographic reform for Danish which took place more than 60 years ago.

Projects such as Euromatrix have already documented the biased situation for the less widely used languages. The matrix shows the available software and language resources for machine translation products for each country and for different language pairs. For English there is almost 8 times as much material (1,320) than there is available for Danish (181). For a language like Estonian the ratio 80 to 1.

	eng	fra	deu	spa	ita	por	nld	swe	ell	pol	dan	ces	fin	rom	hun	bul	slv	lav	lit	slk	est	mlt	gle
eng	**1320**	109	111	107	100	84	50	30	24	35	13	11	15	10	16	10	10	7	5	5	4	3	2
fra	109	**847**	79	66	52	41	36	19	22	14	11	9	9	8	8	7	8	7	5	5	4	3	2
deu	111	79	**720**	42	38	26	20	18	14	18	12	10	10	9	10	7	8	7	5	5	4	3	2
spa	105	65	40	**650**	35	29	19	17	14	11	12	9	9	8	8	7	8	5	5	5	4	3	2
ita	100	52	38	36	**599**	25	19	16	14	11	11	9	9	8	8	7	8	5	5	5	4	3	2
por	85	41	25	29	25	**497**	18	15	13	11	11	9	9	8	8	6	8	5	5	5	4	3	2
nld	49	36	20	19	19	18	**376**	16	14	10	11	9	9	8	8	6	8	5	5	5	4	3	2
swe	30	17	18	17	16	15	16	**272**	13	8	12	9	10	8	8	6	8	5	5	5	4	3	2
ell	23	22	14	14	14	13	14	13	**267**	7	9	7	8	7	6	7	6	5	5	3	3	3	2
pol	35	14	18	11	11	11	10	8	7	**250**	7	9	8	7	7	6	7	7	5	4	3	3	2
dan	13	11	13	12	11	10	11	12	9	7	**181**	7	8	7	7	6	7	5	3	4	4	3	2
ces	10	9	9	9	9	9	9	9	7	9	7	**168**	9	8	8	7	7	6	5	4	3	3	2
fin	16	9	10	9	9	9	9	10	8	8	8	9	**157**	7	7	6	7	5	5	4	3	3	2
rom	10	8	9	9	8	8	8	8	7	7	7	8	7	**144**	7	7	7	4	4	4	3	2	1
hun	15	8	9	8	8	8	8	8	6	7	7	8	7	7	**129**	5	8	5	5	5	4	3	2
bul	9	7	7	7	7	6	6	6	7	6	6	7	6	7	5	**151**	5	4	4	2	2	2	1
slv	10	8	8	8	8	8	8	8	6	7	7	7	7	7	8	5	**112**	5	5	5	4	3	2
lav	7	7	7	5	5	5	5	5	5	7	5	6	5	4	5	4	5	**93**	5	3	3	3	2
lit	5	5	5	5	5	5	5	5	5	5	5	5	5	4	5	4	5	5	**75**	3	3	3	2
slk	5	5	5	5	5	5	5	5	3	4	4	4	4	4	5	2	5	3	3	**5**	4	3	2
est	4	4	4	4	4	4	4	4	3	3	4	3	3	3	4	2	4	3	3	4	**4**	3	2
mlt	3	3	3	3	3	3	3	3	3	3	3	3	3	2	3	2	3	3	3	3	3	**3**	2
gle	2	2	2	2	2	2	2	2	2	2	2	2	2	1	2	1	2	2	2	2	2	2	**2**

Fig. 4: Euromatrix for MT – systems and corpora

6. Conclusions

Language technology and language institutions are becoming more closely linked and for good reasons: both can gain a lot from working together by sharing software and language resources. Language technology is important for keeping languages alive, relevant and useful in all domains of society in our digital and global age. For their own sake and for the sake of their languages, language institutions should continuously promote the development of all aspects of language technology, and engage in sharing their unique knowledge about language and language change.

7. References

Crystal, D. (2000): *Language death.* Cambridge et al.: Cambridge University Press.

Declaration on a Nordic Language Policy (2007). Copenhagen: Nordic Council of Ministers.

Halskov, J./Jarvad, P. (2010): Automated extraction of neologisms for lexicography. In: Granger, S./Paquot, M. (eds.): *eLexicography in the 21st Century: new challenges, new applications. Proceedings of eLex 2009. Cahiers du CENTAL.* Louvain: Presses universitaires de Louvain.

Nordic Council: Internet: www.norden.org/en/nordic-council.

Sproat, R. (2010): *Language, technology, and society.* Oxford: Oxford University Press.

Tamás Váradi

The relevance of language technology infrastructures: national and European initiatives

Abstract

In this short paper I intend to show the increasing importance of language technology as infrastructure that can support research and development and various ICT applications. I will present two large scale European projects (CLARIN and CESAR) and two examples from the Hungarian scene (The Language and Speech Technology Platform and the National Register of Research Infrastructure). Finally, I will discuss the relevance of these initiatives for EFNIL.

E rövid dolgozat célja, hogy bemutassa, hogy a nyelvtechnológia mint infrastuktúra egyre fontosabbá válik a kutatás-fejlesztés és különböző információ-technológiai alkalmazások támogatásában. Mindezt két nagyszabású európai (CLARIN és CESAR) valamint két magyar projekt (Magyar nyelv- és beszéd-technológiai platform valamint a Nemzeti társadalomtudományi hivatkozás adatbázis) ismertetésével illusztrálom. A dolgozat végén röviden utalok ezen munkálatok relevanciájára az EFNIL számára.

1. The mission of language technology

It requires little reflection to realise that in our age communication is increasingly digital. Whether we already live in information societies is a moot point. Almost exclusively, we already use digital technology to talk and write to each other through electronic devices (mobile phones, computers, mobile various communication devices) in our personal lives. They all generate a huge amount of texts (to consider, for simplicity, just the written medium). On a larger scale, we find that in an increasingly globalised world, digital information is generated at a rate that threatens with information explosion. It becomes impossible to keep pace with the amount of information that is created in the media, science, economy, wherever we look, in fact.

Despite the prominent role of multimedia, human communication is and will always be based on language, a facility that is widely held to be an innate characteristic of humans. Language is so intricately involved in thinking and the whole human existence that it is inconceivable that human communication will be conducted in any other medium.

This situation presents an enormous challenge to language technology, a multidisciplinary field comprising of computer science, computational linguistics, artificial intelligence, psychology etc. If we use machines to communicate with each other, we must enable these machines to process language with the same ease and intelligence that humans do. In other words, we must equip them with linguistic knowledge and intelligence that, ideally, approximates the linguistic competence of humans. In a sense, this is a futuristic goal converging with the vision of artificial intelligence. Some people may not even like positing such goals, contemplating with abhorrence the idea of thinking machines. We need not be too much concerned about the philosophical implications as it is doubtful if, in principle, this aim can be realised at all. On the other hand, the pressing global need for facilitating human communication via machines is undeniable and is already an everyday experience. Making machines more adept at processing language helps us to communicate with machines. In other words, it increasingly frees us from the constraints imposed on us by limitations of the hardware and the operations of the machines. But language technology not only serves the purposes of human-machine communication since we use machines nowadays for human to human communication, therefore, a major part of the mission of language technology is to serve human communication in general.

Language technology may not be a familiar field, yet its results are already with us. Spell checkers, scanners that recognise texts (optical character recognition systems), internet search engines and particularly machine translation, these are all examples of what language technology can do to facilitate human communication. None of these technologies is perfect, yet all of them already serve their purpose and, indeed, we'd immediately feel their absence if we did not have recourse to them.

2. Language technology as infrastructure

Language technology should aid us to create, translate and summarize texts. (I am using text as a cover term to refer to language output whether written or spoken.) A very important requirement in this age of information explosion is to find relevant information in free text and organize it into useful knowledge. With respect to speech, it would be extremely useful if machines understood what we say, at least in some basic sense of the word and if they responded to it in an intelligent way and if they were able to speak to us in a natural manner.

It is important to realise that all the above general requirements are domain independent tasks. This leads us to suggest that the provision of all these facilities should be considered part and parcel of the services that digital communication technology should provide. In other words, language technology should be regarded as a part of the *infrastructure* that we use in modern information communication technology (ICT). If this proposal needs justification, let us just consider what good it is to bring broadband internet access to the remotest corners if the language barrier does not make accessible the content of what becomes available down the lines.

This is the concept of language technology as infrastructure at the most basic layer of ICT. It is a long-term vision but, as we saw earlier, elements of this infrastructure are increasingly becoming reality.

There is another sense in which language technology is already recognised as infrastructure and, indeed, is being developed under various European and national initiatives that will be described in the next two sections. This is at one remove from being deployed in front-end applications. One such infrastructure (CLARIN) serves the purposes of scientific research, and within it, scholarly research in the humanities, in particular. Another major on-going project (CESAR) intends to foster multilingual Europe through the provision of language resources and tools in a standard format widely distributed in a dedicated network of exchange facilities.

3. CLARIN

The CLARIN infrastructure was called to life by ESFRI (European Strategic Forum for Research Infrastructure), a European political initiative that was set up in 2002 following a decision by the Council of Ministers "to support a coherent and strategy-led approach to policy-making on research infrastructures in Europe and to facilitate multilateral initiatives leading to a better use and development of research infrastructures".[1] The newly formed body proceeded to compile a roadmap of European Research Infrastructures out of infrastructure proposals submitted in response to a call and which was judged by independent peer review. CLARIN was born as a result of the merger of three language technology proposals and became one of the six proposals selected in the social sciences and humanities category.[2] The initiatives in the ESFRI Roadmap were invited in a closed call to submit project proposals to DG Research and Innovation. As a result, the CLARIN project was launched in 2008 with the coordination of Steven Krauwer of Utrecht University involving 35 partners from 25 countries.

The CLARIN project (www.clarin.eu) has the ambitious long-term mission to develop a distributed infrastructure that would serve ultimately as a virtual research environment in which the users could benefit from language resources and tools as well as advice on how to apply them to the research questions at hand. CLARIN intends to focus primarily on scholars in the humanities and social sciences as they were judged to require special attention for the following reasons: their work typically involves texts, which are increasingly available in vast quantities in electronic format. Research in the humanities is carried out as individual efforts by scholars who are relatively less familiar with the benefits of language technology. In addition to the perceived needs and requirements of the target audience, the CLARIN infrastructure is also motivated by the fragmented nature of the language technology sector. In particular, it was noted that there is a huge number of language resources and tools that were developed as isolated efforts, with little regard to standardised formats and the additional benefits that come from interoperability, the possibility that any particular tool can operate with a variety of resources. The planned infrastructure would locate these isolated centres and would make their tools and language resources available in a unified framework for the benefit of the humanities scholar.

CLARIN as an EU-funded project is only the beginning, the preparatory phase of an open-ended enterprise. The EC provided only the seed money, formally only to work out the legal, organisational and governance structure of the future infrastructure. The preparatory phase is to enter the period of the construction of the infrastructure, designed to last for five years and funded exclusively by the member states. Since the launch of the ESFRI infrastructure projects the EC has created a special European legal entity, called ERIC, European Research Infrastructure Consortium. CLARIN is currently transforming itself into CLARIN ERIC and the construction of the infrastructure is about to begin early 2012.

---

1 Cf. http://ec.europa.eu/research/infrastructures/index_en.cfm?pg=esfri-background.

2 http://ec.europa.eu/research/infrastructures/index_en.cfm?pg=esfri-roadmap&section=roadmap-2006.

While the national support in the form of governmental commitment proved difficult to secure for the majority of the CLARIN consortium members (CLARIN ERIC is likely to begin its operation with at most 14 members), CLARIN itself has attracted enormous community support. The number of research centres that aligned themselves with the aims of CLARIN is now above 200 and still growing. The register of mono and multilingual corpora, lexica as well as processing tools is truly impressive. Their list is available with faceted browsing at http://clarin.eu/vlo.

The activity within CLARIN in the preparatory phase did not confine itself to the formal aims of the original call for proposals. Indeed, the CLARIN project proceeded to develop a prototype of the planned infrastructure. It tackled this complex task in several dimensions. There was the task of building the technical backbone of the infrastructure. When fully completed in the construction phase, the CLARIN infrastructure will allow the individual humanist scholars to access a large range of resources residing at different centres across Europe and process them using tools supplied by other centres, all this achieved in a seamless operation from the comfort of their laptop. A schematic view of the intended CLARIN infrastructure is displayed in Figure 1.

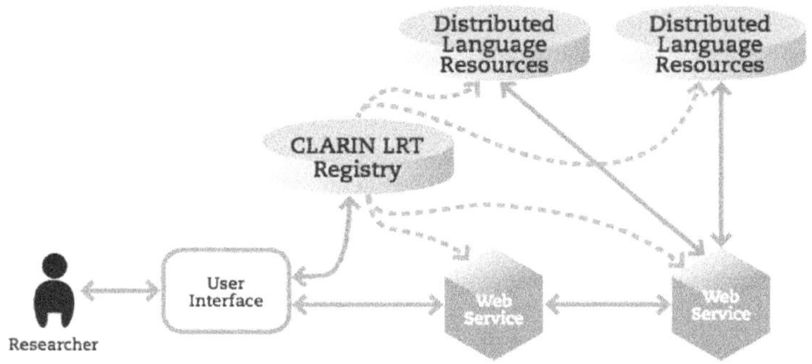

Fig. 1: Overview of the planned CLARIN infrastructure

The second pillar of the infrastructure relates to the content that will be made available down the electronic pipelines. This raises the issue of the language policy that CLARIN has adopted. Being an all-European research infrastructure, CLARIN is committed to supporting all the official national languages small and large, with particular attention to the former. In addition, CLARIN has to extend the linguistic horizon both in space and time if it wants to cater to the needs of humanist scholars. In other words, it has to provide support, on the one hand, for historical stages of modern European languages and, on the other hand, for languages that are not native to Europe but have a great tradition of being studied in leading European centres.

The third pillar can be aptly called the knowledge infrastructure. Right from the start, it was realised that the target audience needs advice and guidance in applying language technology to solve the particular research questions they are concerned with. An important activity, then, was to reach out to the community of scholars, to understand their research concerns, methodology and to find out about potential bottleneck in their uptake of the technology developed within CLARIN. The main instruments CLARIN decided to adopt in pursuit of the above aims was to create a large-scale survey of relevant organisations, projects and conferences, to liaise with professional humanities organisations and to engage in actual collaboration with individual projects. To the latter end, CLARIN selected a handful of projects through an open call and supported them by advising on how to apply language technology to realise their objectives. Making a large-scale impact on the target community proved an extremely difficult task, yet working with selected groups of researchers turned out to be a mutually rewarding task.

4. CESAR and META-NET

The CESAR (Central and South-Eastern European Language Resources) infrastructure (www.meta-net.eu/projects/cesar/) is a two-year ICT-PSP project consisting of nine partners from six countries (Poland, Slovakia, Hungary, Croatia, Serbia and Bulgaria) coordinated by the Research Institute for Linguistics, Hungarian Academy of Sciences that started its work in February 2011. One of the main objectives of the project is to make available language resources and tools that exist within the respective language technology community properly documented, equipped with a rich amount of metadata and cross-linked, where possible, to ensure they are interoperable. The resources and tools will be contributions to an open language resource infrastructure. The CESAR project is part of a larger initiative called META-NET (META standing for Multilingual Europe Technical Alliance) that is now a growing alliance that aims to reach all stakeholders interested in fostering multilingual Europe through modern language technology. META-NET currently includes 47 members from 31 European countries.

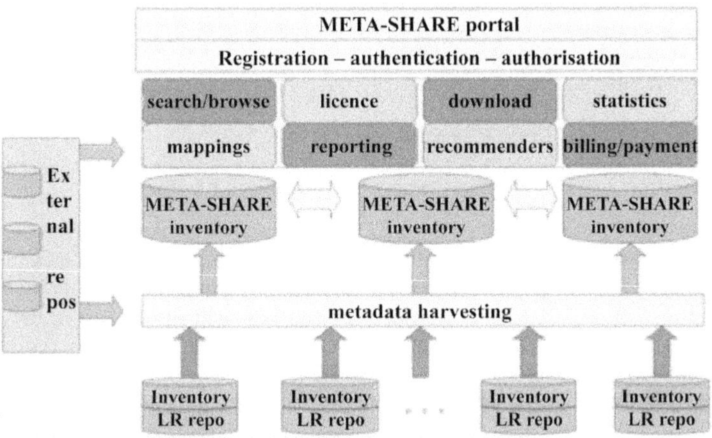

Fig. 2: Schematic view of META-SHARE

META-NET is not a research infrastructure, it rather aspires to build a large-scale alliance of technology partners, industry, policy makers and corporate and individual users. While its overall ambitions are rather general, it tends to foster the cause of multilinguality by providing support for the development of online web services. The paradigm application is widely considered to be statistical machine translation (SMT). Machine translation is the pinnacle of what language technology can offer and requires complex technology as well as an enormous amount of data. The pooling of language resources and tools is one of the central activities in META-NET and they will be made available in a distributed network of repositories organised in the META-SHARE system.

Following the rules of the call for proposal, the CESAR project involves one or two partners per language. However, their mandate is to act as a catalytic force and mobilize all stakeholders of the language technology scene of the respective language including not just research and development centres but industrial partners, potential users and policy makers and the media. Indeed, one of the measures of success of their activities as contributors to META-SHARE will be the extent to which they will be able to increase their portfolio of resources with those that come from partners. In this context, EFNIL institutions as owners and providers of valuable resources of the national languages across all Europe are important strategic partners for META-NET.

Figure 3 shows (at the top) the strategic documents META-NET plans to produce as well as (at the bottom) the process of planned consultation and communication that is leading to and follows the creation of these documents. The presentation given by Hans Uszkoreit, coordinator of META-NET at this conference is part of these efforts.

Fig. 3: Timeline of the META-NET agenda

5. Hungarian Language and Speech Technology Platform

The Europe-wide project META-NET had a close parallel on the national scene in the form of the creation of technology platforms. The technology platform as an industry-led instrument to strengthen the European Research Area was called to life by the European Commission in 2003.[3] The European initiative was followed up in the member states and as a result, the National Office for Research and Technology (currently renamed to National Innovation Office) issued the first call for proposals to form national technology platforms. The objectives of the projects were to be the following:

- Unite and mobilize all major technology partners in a given field;
- Develop a Strategic Research Agenda;
- Work out Implementation Plan based on SRA;
- Raise awareness of the field (public, media, policy makers);
- Reach out to major stakeholders in the sector.

[3] http://cordis.europa.eu/technology-platforms/about_en.html.

The nature or the size of the sector was not defined and the first ten winning projects included platforms of hugely different sizes. The rationale for the national technology platforms was that it should enable stakeholders in particular research and development fields to organize themselves in a bottom-up way and to define their own strategic vision for themselves as well as to compile an implementation plan. These documents would inform policy makers who would base national strategic research and development plans on the SRA's of the national platforms.

The Hungarian Language and Speech Technology Platform (www.hlt-platform.hu) was founded by four academic and four industrial partners. Most of them had been collaborating in various projects in the past few years so it was a tested and tried consortium led by the Research Institute for Linguistics. The technology platform was welcomed as an excellent opportunity to engage in ancillary activities that go beyond the scope of ordinary R&D projects such as strategic planning and large scale PR activities. The project staged three high profile events in the form of public conferences, the first one to introduce the Platform and the achievements of Hungarian language technology, the second conference focused on the Strategic Research Agenda and the third major publicity event introduced the Implementation Plan. Each event included a demo session where the latest language technology developments were showcased.

The two year platform ended with all the goals of the project successfully completed. The visibility of the mission and potential of language technology was greatly enhanced as evidenced by the fact that the hugely popular Hungarian open university television series *Mindentudás Egyeteme* included language technology as one of the first subjects covered in its recently opened second season.[4] The members of the Platform more than doubled and the majority of the new members came from small and medium size enterprises. The major achievements of the project included the Strategic Research Agenda[5] and the Implementation Plan,[6] which were compiled and submitted to public debate on the website and the two conferences.

6. Bibliographic Reference Database for the Humanities

The idea for this project arose when the Initial List of the European Reference Index for the Humanities (ERIH)[7] was published in 2009. The purpose of ERIH is to increase visibility of European Humanities research and introduce some solid measuring criteria of evaluating research output. It was compiled through a Europe-wide community effort coordinated by ESF.

The Bibliographic Reference Database for the Humanities project was inspired by the general objectives of the ERIH. Research results in the Humanities suffered from the same lack of recognised standards of quality and the resultant low prestige with respect to natural sciences, for example. In addition, in the absence of a central reference database,

4 http://mindentudas.hu/elodasok-cikkek/item/2520-sz%C3%B3b%C3%B3l-%C3%A9rt?-%E2%80%93-ember-g%C3%A9p-nyelvtechnol%C3%B3gia.html.

5 http://www.hlt-platform.hu/skt.

6 http://www.hlt-platform.hu/sites/default/files/MT_vegleges.pdf.

7 http://www.esf.org/research-areas/humanities/erih-european-reference-index-for-the-humanities.html.

humanities researchers are forced to compile the list of references to their publications, which they are often ill-equipped to carry out and most of them consider it an unnecessary burden at best. The projected Reference Database aims to cover the comprehensive list of Humanities journals published in Hungary. The scope of the database had to be carefully defined both in terms of geographical and chronological dimensions. For practical constraints, inclusion of references to Hungarian journals published abroad could not be considered. Coverage of journals would start with recent numbers and proceed in reverse chronological order. As the Reference Database is expected to serve the very practical scientometrical requirements of the present-day generation of Humanities research, we do not expect to go back in time longer than the stretch covering living authors.

The Reference Database would serve as a metric not only for authors but at the same time for journals themselves and is widely welcomed by librarians, publishers, administrators and officials at universities as well as the Hungarian Academy of Sciences. The Research Institute for Linguistics has decided to launch this project because, although the work is complex and involves the deployment of robust hardware and software technologies, it crucially depends on language technology. The challenge is to parse the citations that appear either appended to the articles or at the bottom of the page and convert them into structured information. While the citations may have originated a bibliographical database, they are published in more or less free form as text. Although journals typically publish style sheets containing instructions for the format of bibliographical entries and indeed there are a great number of standard citation formats widely published and used in a number of journals, our initial findings indicate that, unfortunately, Hungarian journals in the humanities are very slack in enforcing a standard form even within the same journal.

Bibliographic references seemingly represent a fairly closed format and humans are very good at understanding them at a glance. Nevertheless, processing them with computers presents technological challenges. Even if some standard format is followed (which, unfortunately, cannot be taken for granted) the title field of the citation can hardly be processed adequately without a measure of understanding it. This, however, typically goes beyond current technology, therefore lack of deep processing of the title must be compensated for with some heuristics. It must be accepted, nevertheless, that automatic processing will have to be complemented with manual effort, the crucial question is rather the extent to which the work will have to rely on manual work.

7. Conclusions

In the above sections we described four language technology projects that vary in scope and domain but all provide valuable infrastructure. In this concluding section, we consider the relevance and implications of these projects for EFNIL.

First of all, the relevance of EFNIL can be twofold, depending on the two kinds of members that make up EFNIL's strength. EFNIL is unique in that it unites national language institutes as well as representatives of organisations dealing language policy and language planning.

National language institutes are typically the centres where the major language resources such as dictionaries, corpora and other collection of valuable linguistic datasets are produced. In fact, often their fundamental mission centres on the creation and publication of these resources. Therefore, they should be inherently interested in seeing that their resources are actively used among the widest possible audience. In this increasingly digital age, this goal can only be ensured by dissemination methods using modern technology. On the other hand, the technological know-how and facilities are often not available at EFNIL institutions – rightly so, we might add, as such activities fall outside their core agenda. It is all the more important and opportune that EFNIL members as providers of invaluable and often unique language resources of the respective language should join infrastructures such as CLARIN and META-NET in order to use their distribution and data curation services. Fortunately, quite a number of EFNIL institutions are already participating in one or both of these infrastructure projects.

Policy makers responsible for language policy within particular EFNIL member states can be most efficient partners to EFNIL institutes in their effort to join these infrastructures. CLARIN is no longer a project but will resume its operations as CLARIN ERIC, which entirely depends on national support at governmental level. Clearly, EFNIL members representing relevant governmental organisations having a clear understanding of the goals and importance of language technology infrastructure can further the dissemination objectives of partner EFNIL institutions.

The two national projects also bear some relevance to EFNIL members in that they can be implemented in other member states. The work on the Reference Database is also eminently suitable to scaling up, preferably in a coordinated way as a pan-European effort culminating in a European Reference Database for the Humanities.

In conclusion, it is hoped that this brief overview has shown how language technology infrastructure can be useful in furthering the general objectives of EFNIL and why it is therefore important for individual EFNIL institutes and organisations on the one hand and EFNIL as an organisation on the other to cooperate with current infrastructure initiatives on the national and European level.

Dimitrios Koutsogiannis

ICTs and language teaching: the missing third circle

Περίληψη (abstract)

Συμπληρώνονται ήδη περισσότερο από σαράντα χρόνια από τις πρώτες απόπειρες για αξιοποίηση των υπολογιστών στη γλωσσική διδασκαλία. Τα χρόνια αυτά είναι τόσο πλούσια σε επιστημονικό προβληματισμό και ποικιλία απόψεων, ώστε δικαίως να δημιουργείται σύγχυση ως προς το τι πράγματι νέο έχει εντωμεταξύ προκύψει και να υπάρχει ιδιαίτερη δυσκολία στην ομαδοποίηση των απόψεων αυτών και, κυρίως, εντοπισμού των κενών που προκύπτουν. Στόχος του παρόντος κειμένου είναι να επιχειρήσει μια ταξινόμηση των ως τώρα αναζητήσεων και κυρίως να εστιάσει σε τομείς που έχουν διερευνηθεί ελάχιστα ή καθόλου. Προκειμένου να γίνει αυτό σαφές χρησιμοποιείται η μεταφορά των τριών ομόκεντρων και συγκοινωνούντων μεταξύ τους κύκλων.

Στον εσωτερικό πρώτο κύκλο τοποθετούνται οι αναζητήσεις που στρέφουν το ενδιαφέρον τους στον υπολογιστή ως ένα μέσο που θα συνεισφέρει στην καλύτερη διδασκαλία των γλωσσών. Πρόκειται για τις παλιότερες χρονικά συζητήσεις με ιδιαίτερη διάδοση και στις μέρες μας. Στο δεύτερο κύκλο τοποθετούνται οι αναζητήσεις που αντιμετωπίζουν τις Τεχνολογίες της Πληροφορίας και Επικοινωνίας (ΤΠΕ) ως μέσα πρακτικής γραμματισμού και αναζητούν το νέο που προκύπτει στην επικοινωνία, και επομένως στο περιεχόμενο της γλωσσικής διδασκαλίας, μετά από την ευρεία διάδοση των ψηφιακών μέσων. Ο προβληματισμός αυτός εστιάζει κυρίως το ενδιαφέρον του στις μεταβολές που έχουν προκύψει στο τρίγωνο συγγραφέας – κείμενο – αναγνώστης και τις συνέπειες που έχουν στη διδασκαλία των γλωσσών. Πρότασή μου είναι το περιεχόμενο των δύο κύκλων να συνεξετάζεται, να αντιμετωπίζονται δηλαδή τα νέα μέσα παράλληλα, τόσο ως μέσα πρακτικής γραμματισμού όσο και ως μέσα διδασκαλίας, αξιοποιώντας δημιουργικά και τις δύο παραδόσεις.

Μετά από σύντομη συζήτηση του περιεχομένου των δύο αυτών κύκλων, η εστίαση μεταφέρεται στην ανάδειξη ενός τρίτου κύκλου –ο οποίος αποτελεί το πλαίσιο για την καλύτερη ανάγνωση των άλλων δύο– για τον προσδιορισμό του περιεχομένου του οποίου έχει επιδειχθεί πολύ μικρό ενδιαφέρον. Οι τομείς που συζητούνται είναι ενδεικτικοί, προκειμένου να αναδειχθεί η λογική και όχι να εξαντληθεί ένα τόσο σύνθετο ζήτημα. Υποστηρίζεται ότι οι περισσότερες από τις επιστημονικές συζητήσεις σήμερα, κινούμενες στο πλαίσιο των δύο εσωτερικών κύκλων, υπερτονίζουν το ρόλο, τη δύναμη και τις ιδιαιτερότητες του μέσου, υποβαθμίζοντας ποικίλες διαστάσεις που έχουν σχέση με την ιδιαιτερότητα των γλωσσών και την τοπική πολιτισμική παράδοση. Παράλληλα, εστιάζοντας στο «εδώ και τώρα» της διδασκαλίας, «θαμπώνονται» από τη λάμψη της εκάστοτε νέας τεχνολογικής δυνατότητας και αδυνατούν να εντάξουν τις εξελίξεις σε ένα σαφές ιστορικό πλαίσιο.

Η έμφαση στην ιδιαιτερότητα της κάθε γλώσσας και κυρίως στο ιστορικό όλο είναι ο εξωτερικός τρίτος κύκλος που προτείνεται ως πλαίσιο, προκειμένου να διαβάζεται με μεγαλύτερη επιστημονική ψυχραιμία το περιεχόμενο των άλλων δύο. Είναι η κατεύθυνση που ταιριάζει περισσότερο στην ακαδημαϊκή ευρωπαϊκή παράδοση και μπορεί να αποτελέσει το πλαίσιο για χάραξη ευρωπαϊκής πολιτικής σε ένα τόσο σημαντικό ζήτημα, όπως αυτό της αξιοποίησης των ΤΠΕ στη διδασκαλία των γλωσσών.

1. Introduction

More than forty years have now passed since the first attempts to use computers in language teaching.[1] These years have been so rich in scientific thinking and wealth of views that confusion has rightly arisen about what actually new has emerged in the meantime,

[1] I make no distinction in the present text between L1 and L2 teaching, in an attempt to express thinking common to both scientific fields. The undersigned has been more engaged in the utilization of New Technologies in the teaching of L1, a fact which is probably reflected in the text.

and about how to group these views under discrete categories. This text attempts to classify the research to date and to focus on fields that have been little if at all explored. In order to make this clear, I employ the metaphor of three concentric and overlapping[2] circles (see diagram 1).

In the first (inner) circle is the research that regarded ICTs as a means that contributed significantly to better language teaching. This includes earlier discussions which are, however, widespread today. In the second circle is the research that regarded ICTs as literacy practice environments, which is in search of whatever new emerges in communication and, accordingly, in the content and context of language teaching, in the wake of the wide dissemination of digital literacy practice environments. This research focuses primarily on the changes that have resulted in the well known triangle of author – text – reader, and the consequences these changes have for language teaching. Discussion starts with a brief presentation of the contents of these two circles. Then the focus shifts to the emergence of a third circle, which is proposed as a necessary framework for a better reading of the other two, in which very little interest has been shown so far. This text gives particular weight to highlighting and discussing indicative facets of this third circle.

This paper draws on data related to the Greek language, which are consequently of greater concern to the lesser-spoken languages. However, a conscious effort is made to ensure that the discussion is of more general interest and that it is not exhausted by linguistic and local particularities.

2. The first circle: Computer Assisted Language Learning (CALL)

Initial attempts to use computers in language teaching date back to the 1960s, when the first efforts were made to seek out in computers[3] the ideal intelligent means that could significantly contribute to an improvement in the quality of language teaching as it was then understood. Emphasis was placed on the teaching of grammatical "micro-structures", and especial weight was given to the surface characteristics of the text, e.g. spelling, grammar and assessment (Hawisher et al. 1996). Within this framework, the computer was a patient teacher who offered learners language materials in small sections; it strengthened success with praise, and in the case of failure offered the learners feedback to guide them to an understanding of the problem and choice of the correct response.[4] This view is clearly reflected in the first title attributed to this newly-created field whose subject was language teaching with computers: *Computer Assisted Language Learning* (*CALL*). Within this context, the computer was considered a medium that could significantly aid in the better teaching of both L1 and L2 (Hawisher et al. 1996).

This version of CALL was dramatically enriched during the decades that followed, given also the post-structuralist research in language teaching. Within this framework, computers gradually ceased to be seen as "teaching machines", but as *tools* to facilitate lan-

---

2 This is indicated in diagram 1, with the broken lines of the two inside circles.

3 At the time, computers were enormous "calculating machines" that few research institutions made use of; personal computers began circulating widely only in the early 1980s.

4 A well known system of this type, widespread in the U.S. during the sixties and seventies, was PLATO (Programmed Logic for Automatic Teaching Operations), which was used for everything from the teaching of English and Chinese to Mathematics and Biology (Hawisher et al. 1996, 35).

guage teaching. For example, the weight given in the 1980s to the utilization of word processing and Local Area Networks (LANs) is well known (Selfe/Hilligoss 1994), as are the efforts after 1990 to utilize the array of possibilities offered by the internet for synchronous and asynchronous communication, for drawing upon authentic linguistic material, for communicating with native speakers, for distance/e-learning and for making use of multimedia and text corpora.[5] Recently, there has been a great deal of discussion about the possibilities afforded by the various social networking environments (e.g. blogs, Facebook), known as Web 2.0 environments, in language teaching (e.g. Kárpáti 2009; Purdy 2010).

Today we could say that we are in a phase that has been dubbed the "vertical spread of CALL", in the sense that the utilization of digital means and the internet both for learning material as well as teaching is taken for granted (Chapelle 2010). Textbooks, for instance, are accompanied by CD-ROMs that refer to specific pages which support both teacher and learner with further material; in the course of teaching, both the use of the internet for obtaining authentic language material and the use of synchronous and asynchronous web communication are considered a matter of course. As Chapelle (2010, 67) characteristically points out, "In a sense, today almost anyone who is working on materials for classroom language learning is working in CALL".

3. The 2nd circle: new technologies – new literacies

In the previous section our interest was focused on the utilization of ICTs as pedagogical means in language teaching. However, rapid developments over the course of the last three decades have created many new givens that compel a careful review of the relationship between ICTs and language teaching. One important new given is the wide utilization of ICTs, in parallel with older tools (print, pencil and paper) in every facet of daily life as tools for writing, reading, communicating, and entertainment, i.e. as literacy practice environments. Thus, the computer, from having once been a specialist tool initially employed more in the natural and physical sciences, gradually came to occupy a central place as a communication tool at all levels of daily life (work, entertainment, information, scientific/scholarly work, education, the arts etc.). This has led to the emergence of a "new communicative order" (Street 2000). Defining the features of this "new communicative order" today has become the main concern in the scholarly field under discussion here, since these changes redefine and re-determine the content and the context of language teaching. It would be difficult to discuss all this research in the present text, and for this reason we shall merely touch upon some indicative facets of the issue.

An issue of major interest is the new givens created with the use of ICTs as communication tools on all sides of the well known triangle: author – text – reader. An author can more easily become "authors" from the minute that the co-production of written discourse is much easier, without the spatial/temporal restrictions imposed by traditional communication technology. Also different is the process of writing in digital environments, from the moment that the text becomes fluid and easily-mutable (Hawisher et al. 1996). However, even more innovative is the fact that for the first time we can have texts with a collective (and simultaneously anonymous) origin, e.g. those of Wikipedia.

[5] For a general overview of the variety of research within the framework of CALL see Hubbard (2009).

There have also been important changes in the concept of the text as we once knew it only a few decades ago. The distinctive features of ICTs (Kress uses the term "affordances") make it very easy to mingle semiotic modes and simultaneously make achievable the wide dissemination of multimodal texts (combinations of text, image, video, sound, etc.) (e.g. Kress 2003, 2010). The hypertextuality that characterizes (primarily) web texts may also be considered an important special feature (Snyder 1996). Finally, much discussion is also taking place regarding the new language varieties employed in digital environments for synchronous and asynchronous communication (Crystal 2001, 2008).

Within such an environment of wider changes, the reading processes and consequently the type of reader who needs to be cultivated in language teaching cannot remain intact. The multimodality of texts, hypertextuality and the possibility for information retrieval from enormous (language and multimodal) databases demand other types of knowledge and reading skills. We should not underestimate the wide dissemination of e-books, as well as new generation mobile phones through which it is now possible for someone to be "always on" line (Baron 2008). The wide dissemination of onscreen reading is not simply a different practice; it forms a significant new given that today's curricula for language teaching cannot ignore (see also 4.3.1).

At the same time, but also in connection with the changes in the triangle "author – text – reader", we should also point out the significant changes that we have in children's socialization. There is intense scholarly concern growing today in relation to the fact that the internet and the various Web 2.0 environments structure alternative spaces for social and, consequently, discourse participation. The lively participation by young people in these environments is connected with the various and often different identities they have the opportunity to realize.[6] Everybody (especially marginalized groups, e.g. immigrants) has the opportunity to find a "place at the table", express themselves and engage in a dialogue with a global audience (Koutsogiannis/Mitsikopoulou 2004). Within this framework, the strict limits on the use of languages that were defined by national borders are removed, creating new givens in linguistic socialization and trans-regional communication (e.g. Lam 2009).

Clearly, this new reality could not but be expressed in new theories about language teaching. Terms such as *multiliteracies*, *multimodality*, and *design* belong to this new strand of research; they are widely-employed and express the new orientations language teaching acquires in the light of the widespread use of ICTs as literacy practice environments (see Cope/Kalantzis 2000).

This brief review actually reveals that CALL's classical focus on the utilization of ICTs as pedagogical tools in language teaching (see the first circle, diagram 1) is insufficient, and that what we consider to be the content and context of language teaching needs to be dramatically redefined. Some of the new attempts to utilize every new environment (e.g. Web 2.0 environments) in the teaching of languages (see section 2) are of considerable interest, but in my opinion they remain insufficient. Efforts to create digital language infrastructures (dictionaries, text corpora, speech technology etc.) are also very necessary, since they significantly facilitate modern communication, but they are not enough,

[6] For a critical discussion of the related literature see Koutsogiannis (2007, 2011).

either. A more comprehensive redefinition of the goals, content, and teaching practices in language teaching is necessary, rather than the simple utilization of ICTs as teaching environments and the development of digital linguistic infrastructures. But for that to happen, we need a broader discussion of issues involving communication and literacy from a new communicative perspective.

We know from our experience to date with other literacy practice environments like that of print that when literacy's content and context change, this is connected with broader changes of a historical nature and not simply with the invention of some new technology. For example, changes in how literacy began to be approached in schools during the 19th and 20th centuries were not merely connected with the fact that print technology was being employed, but also with the fact that wider economic and political changes were taking place at the time (Collins/Blot 2003; Anderson 1991). I shall consider indicative directions for such a more comprehensive redefinition below.

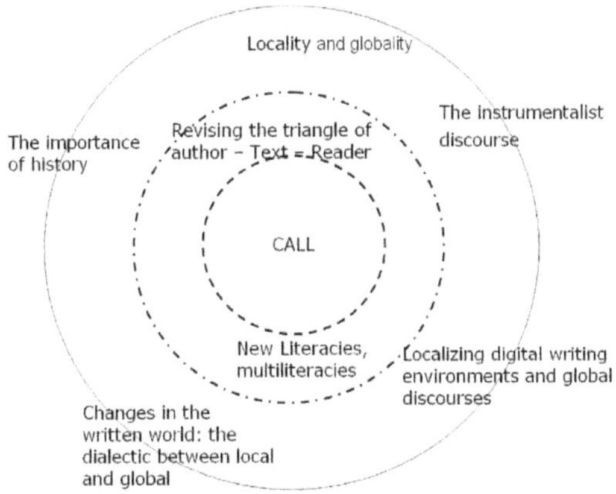

Diagram 1: The "three circles" metaphor

4. The third circle

The issues briefly discussed above as the contents of the second circle, which as we saw significantly redefined the contents of the first circle, are an important aspect of current scholarly investigation. However, since most discussion focuses on the English language, it is important that thinking about this topic be enriched by contributions from other linguistic and cultural viewpoints. Accordingly, one important priority that should be highlighted is *locality*. With this as a starting-point, in what follows I will place emphasis on the emergence of questions connected with the lesser-used languages such as Greek, because in this way we can better comprehend the complexity of everything touched upon in the previous two sections. However, discussion about communication and language teaching on purely local or cultural terms does not entirely illuminate all their dimensions; for this reason, I shall also attempt to highlight a number of common variables of a historical nature with different local versions. It is obvious that such complex issues cannot be exhausted within the confines of the present text. Here I will simply indicate a direction through the use of suggestive examples.

4.1 Locality and globality

4.1.1 Instrumentalist discourse

Focusing on the history of the scholarly field under discussion here, we notice that (almost) every five years there has been a shift to a new digital environment which was attributed unique qualities to improve language teaching. Shortly afterwards it was abandoned for a new digital environment and was hardly discussed thereafter.

It is indicative that in 1989, in the midst of the scholarly community's enthusiasm for the possibilities of *hypertext* in language teaching, Meyrowitz, to deride the exaggerated claims that were being spoken and written, gave the following title to a lecture he delivered at a conference:[7] "Hypertext – Does it Reduce Cholesterol, Too?" (see Meyrowitz 1991). The same ironic question could be posed multiple times in the history of the field under study, altering nothing other than the subject in this question. In the beginning there were *drills and practice* which could deservedly assume this position; then came *Local Area Networks*, followed by *Multimedia* and, during recent years, the internet's turn has arrived, with all its famous individual applications (World Wide Web, E-mail, synchronous and asynchronous communication, Web 2.0, etc.).

Exclusive focus on the possibilities afforded by technology (= the instrument), and its isolation from other important variables (financial, cultural, social, historical, human identities) form the core of what I have termed *instrumentalist discourse* (Koutsogiannis 2009, 2011). I believe that such discourse has negative consequences for the utilization of ICTs in language teaching, because it assigns exclusive emphasis to technology, underestimating the fact that a change in teaching practices is an exceedingly difficult matter (Lewis/Fabos 2008) and one dependent on many other variables (Snyder/Bulfin 2008).

Excessive emphasis on the power of technology and the devaluation of other complex social parameters has deep roots in the U.S., according to Selfe/Hawisher (2004), but spread very quickly to Europe too, at least in relation to ICTs in teaching and education. A common facet in instrumentalist discourse is its particular emphasis on recording progress on the basis of statistics: ratio of children to computers in schools, percentage of computers online, number of educators using ICTs, number of software programs used in language teaching, etc. This was a fairly widespread practice in the European Union. All these led to hasty and makeshift actions, which at heart leave intact the root of the problems, which for the most part are not resolved by an improvement in superficial statistics.

The negative consequences of instrumentalist discourse have been pointed out in the international scholarship (Cuban 2000; Selwyn 2010). However, it appears that these are more pronounced for the lesser-used languages and less-developed countries, because they oversimplify complex issues, leading to the waste of financial resources that are in any case limited (Koutsogiannis 2011).

---

[7] Pittsburgh, PA, 5-8 November 1989.

4.1.2 Localizing digital writing environments and global discourses

Something important that has not been discussed to date is the fact that modern electronic environments for discourse production are not blank white pages on which we are invited to compose our text on the basis of each (specific) communicative event. They are accompanied by libraries of semiotic resources and guides for text composition (viz. word processing), which may influence to a greater or lesser degree the direction taken by the written discourse produced.

Careful study of the best known word processing environments like *Word* and *PowerPoint* (Microsoft), both of which are Hellenized, shows that this Hellenization is superficial and accomplished – to the degree it is accomplished at all – only at the level of user interface. Below we discuss indicatively the most-used environment for digital writing, the word processing program *Microsoft Word for Windows*. The first possibility provided, through the choice of *Δημιουργία* (Create) (in the section *Αρχείο* (File) in the older versions) is that of selecting a "model" text type to support the process of writing that will follow. In every edition of the Greek version of Microsoft *Word*, many templates are provided (e.g. letters, calendars, greeting cards, invitations, job descriptions/announcements, reminders, references, CVs), all of which form a faithful word-for-word transfer from the corresponding English "templates", drawing nothing from Greek textual reality. The "templates", however, are not confined to the specific ones that accompany *Word*; by selecting *επιπλέον πρότυπα* ("additional templates"), the Greek user is redirected to Microsoft's own page, which offers a great wealth and variety of English text "templates", leaving almost no field of literacy practice uncovered. For the most part, the same holds true for Microsoft *PowerPoint*, whose available semiotic resources are likewise a literal translation from English.

On the basis of these remarks, we could say that we find ourselves in the presence of significant new givens. Until now, we have known that texts – all forms of texts – are available social semiotic resources (Cope/Kalantzis 2000), created in close conjunction with the particular social and cultural characteristics of every society. As has been aptly pointed out, "genres are not just forms. Genres are forms of life, ways of being. They are frames of social action. They are environments of learning" (Bazerman 1997, 19). If we understand genres within such a framework as "ways of being", then this means that the new environments for the production of written discourse are proposing via templates "forms of life" and "frames for social action" that have no connection with Greek reality. Thus, the digital environments for the production of written discourse that are advertised in the bibliography as the *par excellence* means, favouring experimentation and creativity during writing (Hawisher et al. 1996), are also shown in the light of more careful investigation to be promoting "guided imitation" for lesser-used languages like Greek.

The fact is that as literacy practice environments, ICTs are not neutral; rather, they embody beliefs connected with the socio-cultural environment in which they were created, clearly creating new challenges and givens for the lesser-used languages and their teaching. These new givens lead us to see everything that has been claimed within the framework of the first and second circles from a different perspective (see Koutsogiannis 2004).

Up until this point, I have attempted to approach digital literacy practice environments from a culturally and linguistically local starting-point. Something of this sort is necessary, but not sufficient. It is preferable to approach this given within the framework of wider – global – changes, which also employ language as a vehicle urging people to new, global "ways of being". I will mention two suggestive examples in this direction. Machin/van Leeuwen (2003) studied 44 local editions of *Cosmopolitan* magazine and identified that the close relation between language and culture appears to be fracturing, for the first time in history. The local (often ethnic) language is a superficial phenomenon which plays no role in the formation of identity, but acts as a vehicle for the transfer of values for the 'global' model of femininity, promoted by the magazine as the 'fun, fearless female'. The article demonstrates that conceptualisations of local and hybrid practices are often extremely superficial and that it is now more essential than ever to seek to understand the key discourses and practices that shape the world of the media.

But it is not only in the world of fashion and lifestyle that something of this sort occurs; it also happens in the very logic that permeate scholarly research in the teaching of languages. Taking into consideration the 'communication skills' adopted in language teaching, Cameron points out that "it is not a new language which is imposed (this is not the danger) but 'unity through difference', the definition of what is acceptable and desirable, through the shaping of norms for global communication. Thus "language becomes a global product available in different local flavours", as she characteristically notes (Cameron 2003, 70).

We may agree that many modern communicative environments like the word processing programs, briefly discussed here, belong to this category of "global products" promoted through theories about language teaching and international magazines such as *Cosmopolitan*, all of which seem entirely natural to us. But if we agree with this finding, this means that we need to review with greater attention all that has been discussed within the context of the first and second circles.

From the discussion in this section, it emerges that digital environments for reading, writing, and communication are not 'neutral' and that a critical approach is required in the course of their utilization for teaching. It also emerges that the focus on locality and cultural difference is necessary but not sufficient. The specific remarks are at heart no different from those made in the foregoing sub-section. There we pointed out the phenomenon of instrumentalist discourse, its wide dissemination as global discourse, and the consequences that are entailed in the utilization of ICTs in the teaching of (primarily) lesser-spoken languages. In this section, the focus was transferred to the non-neutral nature of digital environments for discourse production and the possible consequences for languages other than English. In the one case, we have a global discourse that is considered 'neutral' and adopted indiscriminately, while in the other we have global digital writing environments that are considered neutral when in fact they are not.

In both cases – especially the second – there was an effort to read the examples in the light of not only local but also wider variables. With the second variable, we began to turn our interest towards a broader approach in which the focus on locality, national languages, and cultural difference would enter into a dialogue with broader changes in our times of a global nature.

4.2 Changes in the written world: the dialectic between local and global

4.2.1 The Greek keyboard

There has been much discussion in the field of language teaching as regards the positive consequences of the use of computers in writing (Hawisher et al. 1996). Particular emphasis has also been given to the analysis of new forms of written discourse related to writing in environments featuring synchronous (chat rooms, Instant Messaging) and asynchronous (e-mail, forums) environments (see section 2). Much less weight has been given to the consequences of the wide adoption of computers for the production of written discourse in the lesser-used languages. We have already approached one facet of this topic in the previous section (4.1.2). In what follows, I will mention some indicative examples of the new givens introduced by the use of computers as tools for writing in Greek. The first thing we realize when we take careful note of a Greek keyboard is the fact that there is no key for the Greek semicolon (*ano telia*).[8] Inserting this punctuation mark into a text is therefore not easy for the average user. A variety of techniques are proposed on the internet for inserting it, including the following key combination: Alt + 729 or Alt + 0183 or 0387 + Alt + X.

On my computer (Windows Vista, Microsoft Office 2003), none of those combinations works and for this reason the complicated course of: Menu, insert, symbol, Greek semicolon is followed. The interesting thing is that this issue has not even been discussed, and there is no research concerning the consequences this omission has had on the system of punctuation marks in Greek. An initial estimate by the undersigned from an unpublished study of text corpora of journalistic and school discourse shows that there is a clearly declining trend in the use of the Greek semicolon, primarily in texts that have not been subjected to editing by specialists.

However, the question that has been discussed *in extenso*, and on which we will focus below, is that of the wide use of the Latin alphabet in the production of written discourse in Greek.

4.2.2 Greeklish

The choice of the American Standard Code for Information Interchange (ASCII) as the character set for the first PCs created, as is widely known, less serious problems for languages whose writing system is based on the Latin alphabet (e.g. German, French, Spanish) but greater problems for other languages (Danet/Herring 2007). Since the writing system of Greek falls within the latter category, it was confronted by this initial 'technical' constraint.

To avoid communication problems, people began to make extensive use of the English alphabet in their writing of Greek, producing the hybrid commonly known as Greeklish (Greek + English). Despite technical advances in this area, and despite the fact that Unicode is designed to support the Greek writing system, Greeklish is now identified with

---

8 The English-language symbol for this punctuation mark (the semi-colon, viz. [;]) is used in Greek for the question mark, while the Greek equivalent of the semi-colon is rendered in the Greek alphabet by [·].

the use of the technology by a large part of the population, especially those referred to by Lankshear/Knobel (2003) as 'insiders', i.e. the generation which grew up with the new technologies. Greeklish is used primarily in e-mail and among chat-groups, but also occurs in more formal electronic communication (by government departments and universities, for example) where both writing systems – Greek and Greeklish – are used to avoid communication problems.

This is a subject which has generated keen interest not only in the academic community, but also in the country's press, where opinions are divided (see Koutsogiannis/Mitsikopoulou 2003). There are those who view the spread of this phenomenon as a grave threat to the Greek language, a by-product of the process of globalisation and homogenization. On the other hand, there are those who see the issue as one of negligible significance, an inevitable result of Greece's involvement in global developments, a transitory phenomenon which will disappear as technology advances.

Most of the data at our disposal on this subject come from relatively old research (see Spilioti 2009; Tseliga 2007), and for this reason we provide some data from a more recent investigation. On a questionnaire completed by 4,174 teenagers (14-16 years old) from all over Greece,[9] there was a question about whether they use the Greek script or Greeklish when they are writing in Chat Rooms. Table 1 below shows that the largest percentage employs Greeklish (43.3%), versus 27.9% who use the Greek alphabet and 28.8% who use both, depending on the case. This finding is of particular interest if we take into consideration the fact that these children became familiarized with ICTs after 2000, i.e. when the problems with the Greek script should logically have been overcome due to Unicode's support of the Greek writing system.

		If you visit chat rooms you use:			
		Greek letters	Latin letters	Both, it depends	Total
State schools	%	31.5%	38.6%	29.9%	100.0%
Private school	%	12.1%	63.9%	23.9%	100.0%
Total	%	**27.9%**	**43.3%**	**28.8%**	100.0%

Table 1: Writing in chat rooms

The second result is that the use of the Latin alphabet is not simply a graphemic register employed by young people for specific electronic uses. It appears to be more related with specific social classes of children and specific practices. From the Table above we see that children belonging to the more privileged social classes, and who study at expensive private schools[10] where both computers and English are more widely employed, use Greeklish to a far greater extent (63.9%) than those at state schools (38.6%). To which we may reasonably ask: why do these children use the Latin alphabet to a greater degree than the Greek one?

In fact, the answer cannot be provided unless we examine the totality of English literacy practices by specific social groups. It seems that the use of the Latin alphabet is a con-

[9] This research was conducted in 2006. For a detailed description see Koutsogiannis (2007, 2011).

[10] In our sample there were 759 students, studying at expensive private schools where English is extensively taught; in quite a few of these schools, some other courses (e.g. ICT) were taught in English.

sequence of the extensive use and familiarity with English of children from privileged social classes (private schools in our case), since it has been found that children with precisely the same characteristics participate more in English-language Chat Rooms (Koutsogiannis 2009). In addition, this familiarity (with the functional use of English and ICTs) is a basic strategic objective of most parents belonging to the privileged social classes, a strategy that is *inter alia* implemented by sending their children to particular private schools.

It goes without saying that we do not consider the Greeklish phenomenon the result of this strategy, but of other givens (largely technical) that gave rise to it in the 1980s. Nor do we claim that this phenomenon is to be exclusively interpreted from this perspective. However, the data from this particular research project afford us powerful arguments for maintaining that the phenomenon of the use of Latin writing is fueled in part by a tendency for the wide use of English by some social classes. That is, we could say that it is further supported by the effort of some social classes to strengthen the extroversion of their children (Koutsogiannis 2009; Mitsikopoulou 2007). Within the framework of this logic, we could claim that the more English (obviously, in combination with the wide use of ICTs) permeates the daily lives of children, the more writing with Greeklish will be considered something natural, and the more it will increase.

Until now, we have considered new givens connected with the wide use of ICTs as environments for written expression in the Greek language. Comparable phenomena have been noted for other languages and countries (Paolillo 2007). Thus, we are dealing with givens that are related above all with languages that do not use the Latin alphabet. We also pointed out that heated discussions are being conducted about this phenomenon in the Greek press. But this is only one aspect of the topic. If we look at it from a somewhat broader perspective, we will find that similar discussions are also being conducted regarding English, and they are every bit as heated as the Greek ones. A large part of the press and media generally are noting with intense concern that written English is changing, and there is no dearth of publications suggesting that Computer Mediated Communication signals the slow death of the English language (Thurlow 2006).

We could thus say that we do not have changes related only to some languages. Rather, these are broader changes that are supported or acquire a specific content with the wide use of the new media, but they are not due to these new environments. A careful reading of the scholarly literature shows that wider changes are being observed in written language generally. These are due to larger changes (economic, social, cultural) and not related exclusively to the new media (e.g. Crystal 2008; Baron 2008). Research on text corpora highlight that in fact there is an observable tendency towards "colloquialisation" in written discourse, above all journalistic ones (Hundt/Mair 1999). These global trends towards alterations in written discourse have their local versions, and new technologies certainly play some role in the type and extent of these changes, but they are not solely responsible.

4.3 The importance of history

In the analyses undertaken in the foregoing section, we focused our interest on highlighting local phenomena, since most of the examples come from the Greek language and Greek reality. Keeping in mind the danger lurking in an approach using local terms (Christidis 2009), at the same time we undertook to stress in each case discussed the fact that the local version is of interest, but it is worth recalling the wider, possibly global framework within which it is necessary to understand local particularities. From the discussion of these examples it emerged that focusing on the wider changes also affords us the chance to understand and better interpret the local particularities.

If, however, we have broader changes of the type of examples discussed above, this means that there is particular interest in our directly illuminating some of these. Following this logic, in the present section we will place special emphasis on highlighting the important role played by the historical framework in the understanding of developments. Thus, I will consciously diverge from the discussion of data of a local nature, and endeavour to focus on wider changes during our era, in order to provide further support to my argument that a historically-informed reading better illuminates research on individual local particularities. The discussion will be conducted with two examples chosen by the author, one related to what was discussed for the first circle and the second in connection with an exceptionally talked-about subject in language teaching, viz. e-learning.

4.3.1 Reading the ICT and language education discourse in an historical context

An important problem in the discussion about the utilization of ICTs in language teaching is related to the fact that these become consumed by the 'here and now' of teaching and only rarely is emphasis given to the search for possible developments of an historical nature that often go beyond scientific research.

In the case of the field under discussion, for example, we could consider that there were three key historical givens that marked some of the main perspectives on the utilization of ICTs in language teaching. The first is connected with the historical and political context of the years from 1950 to 1970, more specifically with the educational consequences of the *Cold War*. Following the end of WWII, the foundations began to be laid for the creation of a post-industrial America as global power. Its investments in technology, especially military technology, formed one of the priorities selected to contribute to this dominance, and above all to the elimination of its great rival at the time, the Soviet Union. Parallel to the emphasis on the physical and natural sciences, the investment of much state – and private – capital in technology towards the political-technological dominance of the U.S. offered the opportunity to strengthen research in the field of language teaching, especially foreign languages, for understandable political reasons (Hawisher et al. 1996).

These efforts could only be based on the leading scientific paradigms of the era, viz. behaviourism as regards learning, and structuralism as regards the study of language. These views, which were predominant in the U.S. down to the 1960s, although they had begun to be doubted scientifically, comprised the foundation on which the first computer programs were also based, as we say in section 2.

The second historical given is connected with the gradual transition after WWII, especially during the last three-four decades, to an economy and society of a post-industrial type in quite a few countries of the West and the U.S., where the learner cannot be considered 'passive'; rather, (s)he is 'active'. An emphasis on what we call today 'traditional literacy', known as the 'basics' in the Anglo-Saxon world, was not sufficient from the moment that the U.S. and the rest of the Western world gradually began entering the post-industrial stage of production and economic development. This means that the skills of reading and writing were not enough for the type of citizens the new economy and society demanded. The new-style economy, which gradually began to demand more thoughtful individuals and fewer simple followers of orders, obviously had a need of new theories as well. It is easier for us to comprehend the intense scientific and technological research of the critical decades after 1970 within such an interpretative framework.

If one carefully analyzes the research during the same period in regard to the utilization of computers in language teaching, one finds that this change is easily traced to the sort of digital environments and pedagogical theories being proposed. Basically, we do not have just one "Copernican Revolution" due to the fact that until then the computer was viewed as teacher (= Tutor), while afterwards it was considered a means for facilitating language teaching (= Tool) (Hawisher et al. 1996, 46). We have also a significant revolution as regards how the learners, and by extension teachers, were understood. To put it simply: we have an important turn in the 'technology' of teaching itself,[11] consequently in the sort of learner identities proposed to be created, and not merely in the means employed (to accomplish this).

The third given was discussed above in section 3 and is connected with the second circle, where emphasis was given to the emergence of particularities that the reconstruction of meaning on the screen has in relation to those in print. At heart, however, this is not merely related to the fact that ICTs are literacy practice environments, or with the fact that multimodal expression is made easier. Here too, the change is a deeper one, and is connected with the type of reader created by wide employment of the screen in communication. In many of his texts, Kress (2003, 2010) has aptly remarked that the transition from print to screen and multimodal text both entails and presupposes a different identity for readers: from the discipline imposed on the reader by the strict syntactic arrangement of written discourse in print, to reading as relaxation and pleasure favoured by the multimodal recreation of meaning on the screen; from the concentration demanded by the reading of traditional written discourse to the laxity of browsing favoured by the multimodal web text. This is a development corresponding to other, similar developments in many facets of a largely consumerist everyday life.

However, if we approach matters from an historical perspective, then the question is not only precisely which technology we will employ, which environments we will develop for our language, how many computers we need in our schools, etc. The issue becomes deeply political and we are required to respond to vital questions regarding the sort of teaching practices we want to support and why, the mix of older (e.g. print) and newer (digital media) technologically-mediated communication we will employ and, most profoundly, the sort of literate identities we are interested in cultivating through language teaching. And finally, we are required to provide an answer to the question of what type of society we are interested in creating.

[11] With the content given the term 'technology' by Foucault (see Ball 1990).

4.3.2 E-learning and the new global economic order

In the previous section we attempted to show that the emphasis on history forms the requisite framework for understanding the rapid development in the realms of communication and teaching. In this section we become more specific, aiming to highlight through an example from e-learning the close relationship between technological research and wider changes.

Below I cite two indicative examples from the proceedings of the international conference Online Educa Berlin.[12] Reading these examples, it is difficult to gather that they come from an academic text that endeavours to show other attendees that this particular university is exploiting e-learning in order to adjust to the new givens of European and global competition it is being asked to respond to.

> (1)
> In regards to **competition** to be an early adopter can **pay off**. As Clarc Aldrich (2000), **a senior market analyst** with Gartner Group, states "**Educate your customers before your competitors do**" (Online Educa Berlin 2003, 145).
>
> (2)
> Universities have the choice **to be leaders or followers** in innovation. Advantages for **innovation leaders** are the chance to **capture large market shares**, and **establish a brand name** while disadvantages are the **higher cost** of deployment for early adopters, the **increased risk of failure**, the **limited availability of support services**, and the risk that the E-learning system may have to be replaced after a short time by a new generation of E-learning systems. (Online Educa Berlin 2003, 141)

No particular analysis is needed to ascertain that academic discourse is being completely 'colonized' by market discourse (Fairclough 2003) in these particular examples. We merely highlight the words and expressions that make this obvious.

Below we will offer some material to make the context within which these particular texts were produced more understandable. It is the year 2003, the year when some of the changes in European universities in the direction of the Bologna Process were starting to be implemented. E-learning was beginning to be regarded as not simply a means ('tool') to better serve university teaching, but as an additional means ('tool') for helping universities 'capture large market shares', bring more 'customers', and contribute significantly to 'establishing a brand name'.

The rhetoric normally accompanying e-learning in the case of language teaching is well known. From the above discussion it is obvious that we cannot approach any technology independent of the context in which it is being exploited. The views that permeate the two excerpts above about e-learning are not accidental; rather, they are closely related to wider changes taking place from 2000 onward in the European academic realm.

---

[12] This is a yearly international conference held in Berlin. I provide indicative examples and findings from Mitsikopoulou/Koutsogiannis (2005).

From the discussion about e-learning and that of the sub-section that preceded it concerning the important changes we have in the "identification" process (Fairclough 2003) of modern readers, there emerges the necessity to recontextualize whatever discussions are conducted within the context of the first and second circles into a broader framework, complete with historical awareness.

5. Conclusions

This text attempted to classify discussions about the didactic use of ICTs in language teaching in three circles. In the first circle falls the discussion that treats ICTs as pedagogical tools that contribute significantly to the improvement of teaching. In the second circle falls another category of scholarly discussions that treat ICTs as literacy practice environments with specific features and which goes in search of the consequences of the 'new communicative order' in the content and context of language teaching itself. I propose to re-examine the content of both these circles, i.e. to treat these new means both as literacy practice environments and as teaching tools, making creative employment of both traditions.

However, in order to highlight facets that are only rarely allowed to emerge and be discussed, I gave the greatest weight to those placed in the third circle. The fields discussed were indicative, in order to bring out the logic rather than to exhaust so complex an issue. For this circle, however, the focus on specific cases and examples was not as important as the logic itself. I maintain that most of the scholarly discussions ongoing today and being conducted within the framework of the two inner circles overemphasize the role, power, and particular characteristics of the medium, while minimizing the various dimensions related to the distinctiveness of languages and local cultural traditions. At the same time, focusing on the 'here and now' of teaching, they are 'blinded' by the brilliance of each successive new technological opportunity, and incapable of incorporating developments into a clear historical context.

My emphasis on the overall historic context is the third (outer) circle I propose as the framework for understanding the contents of the other two circles with greater scientific suspicion. I believe that this is the circle that suits the European academic tradition perfectly, and which may form the framework for mapping out a European policy on such an important issue as that of the utilization of ICTs in language teaching.

6. References

Anderson, B. (1991): *Imagined communities: Reflections on the origin and spread of nationalism*. Revised and extended edition. London: Verso.

Ball, S. (1990): *Foucault and education. Disciplines and knowledge*. New York: Routledge.

Baron, N. (2008): *Always on: Language in an online and mobile world*. Oxford: Oxford University Press.

Bezerman, C. (1997): The life of genre, the life in the classroom. In: Bishop, W./Ostrum, H. (eds.): *Genre and writing*. Portsmouth: Boynton/Cook, 19-26.

Cameron, D. (2003): Globalisation and the teaching of 'communication skills'. In: Block, D./Cameron, D. (eds.): *Globalisation and language teaching*. New York: Routledge, 67-82.

Chapelle, C. (2010): The spread of computer-assisted language learning. In: *Language Teaching*, 43 (1), 66-74.

Christidis, A.-F. (2009): The "local" and the "global" and their social content. In: Koutsogiannis, D./Arapopoulou, M. (eds.): *Literacy, new technologies and education: Aspects of the local and global*. Thessaloniki: Zitis, 19-21.

Collins, J./Blot, R. (2003): *Literacy and literacies: Texts, power, and identity*. Cambridge: Cambridge University Press.

Cope, B./Kalantzis, M. (eds.) (2000): *Multiliteracies. Literacy learning and the design of social futures*. London: Routledge.

Crystal, D. (2001): *Language and the Internet*. Cambridge: Cambridge University Press.

Crystal, D. (2008): *Txtng. The gr8 db8*. Oxford: Oxford University Press.

Cuban, L. (2001): *Oversold and underused: Computers in the classroom*. Cambridge, MA: Harvard University Press.

Danet, B./Herring, S. (eds.) (2007): *The multilingual Internet*. Oxford: Oxford University Press.

Fairclough, N. (2003): *Critical discourse analysis*. London: Routledge.

Hawisher, G./LeBlanc, P./Moran, C./Selfe, C. (1996): *Computers and the teaching of writing in American higher education, 1979-1994: A history*. Norwood, NJ: Ablex.

Hubbard, P. (ed.) (2009): *Computer Assisted Language Learning: Critical concepts in linguistics*. London/New York: Routledge.

Hund, M./Mair, C. (1999): "Agile" and "uptight" genres: The corpus-based approach to language change in progress. In: *International Journal of Corpus Linguistics* 4 (2), 221-242.

Kárpáti, A. (2009): Web 2 technologies for net native language learners: A "social CALL". In: *ReCALL*, 21 (2), 139-156.

Koutsogiannis, D. (2004): Critical technoliteracy and "weak" languages. In: Snyder, I./Beavis, C. (eds.): *Doing literacy online: Teaching, learning and playing in an electronic world.* Cresskill, NJ: Hampton Press, 163-184.

Koutsogiannis, D. (2007): A political multi-layered approach to researching children's digital literacy practices. In: *Language and Education* 21 (3), 216-231.

Koutsogiannis, D. (2009): Discourses in researching children's digital literacy practices: Reviewing the "home/school mismatch hypothesis". In: Koutsogiannis, D./Arapopoulou, M. (eds.): *Literacy, new technologies and education: Aspects of the local and global*. Thessaloniki: Zitis, 207-230.

Koutsogiannis, D. (2011): *Adolescents' digital literacy practices and identities*. Thessaloniki: Centre for the Greek Language. [In Greek].

Koutsogiannis, D./Mitsikopoulou, B. (2003): Greeklish and Greekness: Trends and discourses of "glocalness". In: *Journal of Mediated Communication Discourse* 9 (1). Internet: http://jcmc.indiana.edu/vol9/issue1/kouts_mits.html (accessed 15.01.2011).

Koutsogiannis, D./Mitsikopoulou, B. (2004). The Internet as a glocal discourse environment. In: *Language Learning & Technology* 8 (3), 83-89. Internet: http://llt.msu.edu/vol8num3/koutsogiannis/default.html (accessed 05.01.2011).

Kress, G. (2003): *Literacy in the New Media Age*. London/New York: Routledge.

Kress, G. (2010): *Multimodality. A social semiotic approach to contemporary communication.* London/New York: Routledge.

Lam, W.S.E. (2009): Multiliteracies on Instant Messaging in negotiating local, translocal, and transnational affiliations: A case of an adolescent immigrant. In: *Reading Research Quarterly* 44 (4), 377-397.

Lankshear, C./Knobel, M. (2003): *New Literacies*. Buckingham: Open University Press.

Lewis, C./Fabos, B. (2008): Instant Messanging, literacies, and social identities. In: Coiro, J./ Knobel, M./Lankshear, C./Leu, D. (eds.): *Handbook of research on new literacies*. New York: Lawrence Erlbaum, 1109-1159.

Machin, D./Van Leeuwen, T. (2003): Global schemas and local discourses in Cosmopolitan. In: *Journal of Sociolinguistics* 7 (4), 493-512.

Meyrowitz, N. (1991): Hypertext – does it reduce Cholesterol, too? In: Nyce, J./Kahn, P. (eds.): *From Memex to Hypertext*. San Diego: Academic Press, 287-318.

Mitsikopoulou, B./Koutsogiannis, D. (2005): *Changing European university discourses of e-learning*. Paper presented at the Annual Critical Discourse Analysis Meeting, Athens, May 20-21 2005.

Mitsikopoulou, B. (2007): The interplay of the global and the local in English language learning and electronic communication discourses and practices in Greece. In: *Language and Education* 21 (3), 232-246.

Paolillo, J. (2007): How much multilingualism? Language diversity on the Internet. In: Danet, B./Herring, S. (eds.): *The Multilingual Internet*. Oxford: Oxford University Press, 408-430.

Purdy, J. (2010): The changing space of research: Web 2.0 and the integration of research and writing environments. In: *Computers and Composition* 27, 48-58.

Selfe, C./Hawisher, G. (2004): *Literate lives in the Information Age: Narratives of literacy from the United States*. Mahwah, NJ: Lawrence Erlbaum.

Selfe, C./Hilligoss, S. (eds.) (1994): *Literacy and computers*. New York: Modern Language Association of America (MLA).

Selwyn, N. (2010): *Schools and schooling in the Digital Age: A critical analysis*. London/New York: Routledge.

Snyder, I. (1996): *Hypertext: The electronic labyrinth*. New York: New York University Press.

Snyder, I./Bulfin, S. (2008): Using new media in the secondary English classroom. In: Coiro J./ Knobel, M./Lankshear, C./Leu, D. (eds.): *Handbook of research on new literacies*. New York: Lawrence Erlbaum, 805-837.

Spilioti, T. (2009): Graphemic representation of text-messaging: Alphabet-choice and code-switches in Greek SMS. In: *Pragmatics* 19 (3), 393-412.

Street, B. (2000): New literacies in theory and practice: What are the implication for language in education? In: *Linguistics and Education* 10 (1), 1-24.

Thurlow, C. (2006): From statistical panic to moral panic: The metadiscursive construction and popular exaggeration of new media language in the print media. In: *Journal of Computer-Mediated Communication* 11 (3). Internet: http://jcmc.indiana.edu/vol11/issue3/thurlow.html (accessed 15.05.2007).

Tseliga, T. (2007): "It's all Greeklish to me!": Linguistic and sociocultural perspectives on Roman-alphabeted Greek in asynchronous computer-mediated communication. In: Danet, B./ Herring, S. (eds.): *The multilingual Internet*. Oxford: Oxford University Press, 116-141.

John C. Paolillo

Language, the Internet and access: do we recognize all the issues?

1. Introduction

The Internet is so ubiquitous and global that it is now widely regarded as a significant site of contact among people of all linguistic and cultural backgrounds. Representatives of language groups from the smallest to the largest see Internet access as a major policy objective, as do governments and policy makers worldwide. Policy discussions and academic research tend to focus questions of representation and dominance at either the global or local level, systematically neglecting a range of related social and technical issues such as the central role of written language, the linguistically non-neutral implementation of technical protocols, programming and markup languages and the social infrastructure governing the technical aspects of the Internet. When these are taken into account, it becomes clear that the current Internet promotes an emerging global diglossia, in which exclusively English is used for technical purposes, and all other languages are merely "content", without full range of use. Recognition of this issue points toward a need to emphasize truly language-neutral technologies for the Internet.

Public awareness of Internet language issues has focused on the "use of languages on the Internet". This notion is often not fully explicated, but three principal concerns are discussed more frequently than others: (1) the ability to produce web pages in whatever language is at issue (typically for language preservation), (2) the ability to use different languages to name Internet hosts and (3) the various adaptations of users to technical systems that were not designed for their own languages. The first of these is addressed through the Unicode effort and the World Wide Web recommendations process. The second of these dominated the agenda of the United Nations World Summit on the Information Society (held in Geneva 2003 and in Tunis 2005), resulting in the establishment of the Internet Governance Forum (IGF), and the modification of the Domain Name System, regulated by the US non-profit corporation ICANN, to allow International Domain names. The third is the subject of intense research among academics around the world, resulting in collections such as Danet/Herring (2007), Androutsopoulos (2006) and Wright (2004), among many other individual publications. However, the technical situation behind the first two issues remains disconnected from the academic research on Internet language use, and does not get the full examination it deserves, given its importance to the status of languages on the Internet.

In this plenary, I argue that the technical issues of language use on the Internet require a closer look. We examine three core Internet technologies: the representation of text in Unicode, the naming of Internet hosts in the Domain Name System, and the programming and markup of websites using HTML and web scripting languages. All three are shown to have a bias toward English, with other languages experiencing greater costs that could otherwise be technically unnecessary. This situation is interpreted in terms of the ethics of computer system design, and the sociolinguistic phenomenon of diglossia, to illuminate the ways in which technical design choices reflect extrinsic social values. We conclude with a discussion of principles for the remediation of technical language bias.

2. Use of text

The Internet is primarily a text-based environment, so the use of the Internet for communication presupposes and the ability to represent written language text is a basic requirement. In fact, information technology is heavily dependent on text in general, and so it follows that languages without written representations, or in particular, languages without "machine readable" written form, are at a disadvantage in their ability to use IT.

The principal effort to address this issue is the Unicode project, led by a consortium of technology companies (eight full members), government agencies (four, primarily South Asian), supporting and associate members (24) and individual members (102). The Unicode project began in the late 1980s as an effort to reconcile what were then vendor-specific, incompatible ways of representing non-English text (Becker 1988). The consortium officially incorporated in 1991, and by 1993 the Unicode standard was formally merged with ISO-10646 (a formerly competing encoding for text); it is currently in version 6 (Unicode 2011).

Unicode recognizes three problems relating to the representation of multilingual text: the problem of *encoding* and processing written language in machine-readable form, the problem of *rendering* machine-readable text in human-readable form, and the problem of *inputting* text into a computer by people. Unicode only addresses the encoding issue, and does not specify the rendering or input methods that should be used, permitting vendors (e.g. Unicode's commercial software company members) to compete to fill these needs. This delimitation of scope has delayed full Unicode implementation for many languages, especially those using non-Latin orthographies.

Unicode's solution to the encoding problem was to develop a universal encoding (hence "Unicode") for all written languages by assigning each distinct textual *character* in each writing system a unique binary number, or *code-point*. The notion of character in Unicode is an abstraction lacking a universally fixed definition.[1] It is implemented differently for different writing systems, e.g. Latin letters with diacritics are typically different characters, as are circle-enclosed Latin letters, but Han (Chinese) characters in Chinese, Japanese and Korean are expected to be unified across all three languages, even where these characters have divergent written shapes (and no circle-enclosed versions are recognized). Code points are fixed and finite in number. Unicode is limited to 1,114,112 unique code-points, so no more than this number of characters can ultimately be recognized without significant revision; 109,499 code points are actually defined at present.

Unicode code points are broken up by numerical range into *planes* (of which there are 17) and blocks (units of up to 256 characters). Each plane has a maximum of 65,536 code points. The lowest-numbered plane (zero) is known as the *Basic Multilingual Plane* (BMP).

---

1 "*Abstract character*: A unit of information used for the organization, control, or representation of textual data. When representing data, the nature of that data is generally symbolic as opposed to some other kind of data (for example, aural or visual). Examples of such symbolic data include letters, ideographs, digits, punctuation, technical symbols, and dingbats. An abstract character has no concrete form and should not be confused with a glyph. An abstract character does not necessarily correspond to what a user thinks of as a 'character' and should not be confused with a grapheme [...]." (Unicode 2011, 66).

Outside of the BMP, the currently defined planes are the *Supplementary Multilingual Plane* (for historical scripts and musical and mathematical symbols), the *Supplementary Ideographic Plane* (for additional Chinese, Japanese and Korean ideographic symbols), the *Tertiary Ideographic Plane* (reserved for additional ideographs) and the *Special Use Plane* (for application-specific purposes). The remaining 13 planes are not presently assigned, but reserved for future use.

The allocation of the BMP, by script and block, is illustrated in Figure 1. The largest share of the BMP is taken up by East Asian Languages: there are 111 blocks used for "unified CJK", which is the Chinese character set common to Chinese, Japanese and Korean. Identifying this set was a major preoccupation of Unicode in the 1990s. In addition to this, there are 55 blocks for Southeast Asian languages, 11 for South Asian scripts, 10 for Latin, 4 for Cyrillic, and one for Greek and Coptic. Other assignments are made for African, American, Middle Eastern and linguistic scripts.

The lowest block of the BMP contains the most commonly used Latin characters; this single block is generally sufficient for Western European languages, being the same as the 1989 specification ISO-8859-1 (Latin-1). The map of the character assignments in this block is given in Table 1. This block consists of assignments for upper and lower case Latin characters, including vowels with diacritical marks, special symbols common in Euro-American print usage, and 52 "control codes", most of which are presently unused, but are retained for compatibility with older encodings. The lower half of Block 0 is identical to a 1963 standard known as US-ASCII or simply ASCII, the most commonly used character set prior to Unicode; ASCII is only adequate for representing US English.

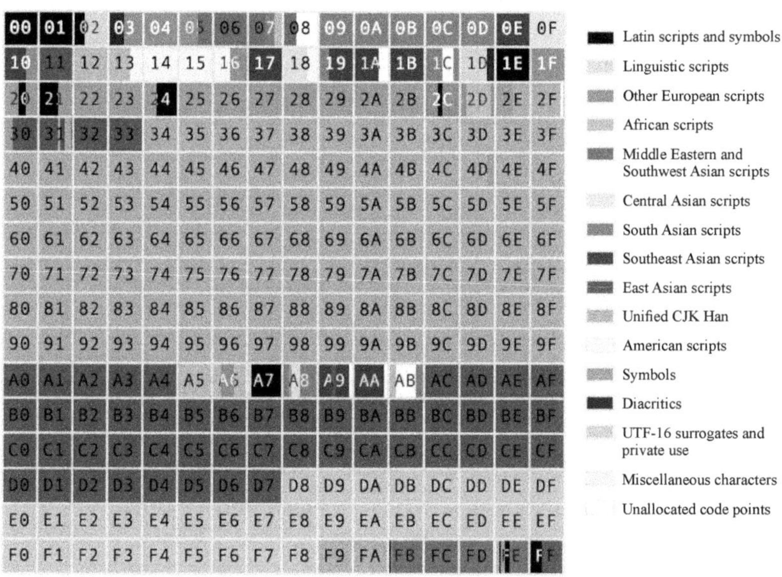

Figure 1: The Basic Multilingual Plane of Unicode
(public domain image: http://en.wikipedia.org/wiki/File:Roadmap_to_Unicode_BMP.svg)

One might be tempted to argue from the existing Unicode character assignments that most of the existing Unicode standard is devoted to the needs of Chinese, Japanese and Korean, and it therefore exhibits a bias toward those languages. This would be a superficial view, however, because the actual bias depends on other technical aspects of Unicode's use. Unicode has been designed to preserve a continuity of standards from ASCII to ISO-8859 to the present Unicode, thereby privileging the encoding of US English. In terms of code-point assignments, this advantage is small, but has broader ramifications.

Unicode offers three options for representing text: UTF-32, a 32-bit fixed-width encoding, UTF-16, a 16 bit variable-width encoding, and UTF-8, an eight-bit variable-width encoding. Fixed width encodings require the same amount of space for each character, regardless of its location in the Unicode system. Variable-width encodings allow some characters to be encoded in less space, while others take up more. In UTF-8, the most common Unicode text encoding, characters of 7-bit ASCII are encoded using the value of the code-point in a single eight-bit byte, whereas other Unicode characters (including Latin with diacritical markings) are encoded using 2, 3 or 4 bytes. For efficiency, variable-width encodings should encode more frequently used characters in shorter sequences; for UTF-8 it appears that the design assumption was that Unicode would be most commonly used for US-English. The advantage cited, however, is that any pre-existing ASCII text remains valid in Unicode, without modification.

	ISO-8859-1 (Basic Latin)															
	US-ASCII															
	0	16	32	48	64	80	96	112	128	144	160	176	192	208	224	240
0	NUL	DLE	SPC	0	@	P	`	p	XXX	DCS	NBSP	°	À	Ð	à	ð
1	SOH	DC1	!	1	A	Q	a	q	XXX	PU1	¡	±	Á	Ñ	á	ñ
2	STX	DC2	"	2	B	R	b	r	BPH	PU2	¢	²	Â	Ò	â	ò
3	ETX	DC3	#	3	C	S	c	s	NBH	STS	£	³	Ã	Ó	ã	ó
4	EOT	DC4	$	4	D	T	d	t	IND	CCH	¤	´	Ä	Ô	ä	ô
5	ENQ	NAK	%	5	E	U	e	u	NEL	MW	¥	µ	Å	Õ	å	õ
6	ACK	SYN	&	6	F	V	f	v	SSA	SPA	¦	¶	Æ	Ö	æ	ö
7	BEL	ETB	'	7	G	W	g	w	ESA	EPA	§	·	Ç	×	ç	÷
8	BS	CAN	(	8	H	X	h	x	HTS	SOS	¨	¸	È	Ø	è	ø
9	HT	EM	)	9	I	Y	i	y	HTJ	XXX	©	¹	É	Ù	é	ù
10	LF	SUB	*	:	J	Z	j	z	VTS	SCI	ª	º	Ê	Ú	ê	ú
11	VT	ESC	+	;	K	[	k	{	PLD	CSI	«	»	Ë	Û	ë	û
12	FF	FS	,	<	L	\	l	|	PLU	ST	¬	¼	Ì	Ü	ì	ü
13	CR	GS	-	=	M	]	m	}	RI	OSC	SHY	½	Í	Ý	í	ý
14	SO	RS	.	>	N	^	n	~	SS2	PM	®	¾	Î	Þ	î	þ
15	SI	US	/	?	O	_	o	DEL	SS3	APC	¯	¿	Ï	ß	ï	ÿ

Table 1: Character Assignments in Block 00 of Unicode

The significance of this design choice, while greater than that of numeric code-point assignments, might still appear small. For most European languages using Latin characters, the extra difficulty of encoding diacritics is small, and it does not affect the core fifty-two Latin characters shared with English. The encoding would be no more complex if diacritics were encoded as separate characters. For scripts such as Arabic script, Cyrillic or Greek, the situation is different, affecting each and every character in a text. Texts in such scripts require approximately twice as much space to store and incur twice as much transmission cost as comparable texts in Latin.

An even greater cost to international text is the same one that Unicode sought to preserve for English: any previously encoded text for something other than US-ASCII is simply not valid Unicode. This includes ISO-8859-1, and the many (non-standard) eight-bit encodings of Arabic and Cyrillic, alongside others (e.g. East Asian and South Asian encodings). This, alongside the many years' lag in support for input and rendering of the same scripts, imposes significant legacy-text conversion costs on non-English and non-Latin script use (Hardie 2007; McEnery/Xiao 2005).

3. ASCII and the Internet: domain names

Another major area of contention over the use of languages online has been in the naming of Internet hosts. Internet host names are maintained by the Domain Name Service (DNS), a system conceptualized in 1981 to replace the original file-based directory scheme known as HOSTS.TXT (Rader 2001). The DNS was conceived as a way to maintain a global, distributed directory system within a delegated model of hierarchical control. As a global system, it was intended to index every host on the Internet; as a distributed system, it was intended to permit the index to be updated in a responsive and timely fashion, to avoid the cumbersome centralized management that had been a problem with HOSTS.TXT.

The DNS was established in 1985 under a US Department of Defense contract for the ARPANET, the precursor to the Internet. DNS authority was essentially delegated by sub-contracts under the Department of Defense and the National Science Foundation from 1985 to 1997; in 1995, Network Solutions Inc. (NSI) operated the DNS and began charging fees for host registration. Because of this commercialization and the monopoly control of whoever was to run the DNS, DNS authority was heavily contested until 1998, when a new legal structure was forged, and the US Department of Commerce forced the transfer of DNS authority from NSI to a new body, the Internet Corporation for Assigned Names and Numbers (ICANN), which runs the DNS and other aspects of the Internet to this day (Rader 2005).

On a technical level, the DNS is a set of protocols for the resolution of host names, which serve as human-readable mnemonics for computers on the Internet. Nothing in the Internet protocols requires that a host be named this way; an Internet host need only have an Internet Protocol number (or IP number, a 32 bit number that serves as a computer's address, also administered by ICANN). The sole technical role of the DNS is to translate conveniently remembered mnemonics into IP numbers, which can be done (arbitrarily) by any Internet host designed to use the DNS protocols. On a political level, the designers of the DNS intended that there be only one such service, centrally managed and controlled.[2] Because of this, the DNS and the naming of Internet hosts have enormous commercial and political significance, involving the legal use of commercial trademarks, freedom of political speech and minority rights.

Under the DNS protocols established in 1985, hostnames are limited to a strict subset of seven-bit ASCII characters: the 26 lower case Latin letters a to z (with no diacritics), the digits 0 through 9, and hyphen. Clearly, this technical limitation favours US English at the expense of all other languages; the lack of Latin characters with diacritics being a long-standing rub (Pargman/Palme 2009). From the time that ICANN assumed control over the DNS, international pressure over this issue from governments and community groups intensified, leading to the key concession at the UN World Summit on the Information Society (WSIS) 2003 and 2005, where ICANN agreed to establish the Internet Governance Forum (IGF). An outcome of the WSIS and IGF processes was the implementation of Punycode, a seven-bit encoding of Unicode suitable for use on the DNS. The intent of Punycode was to permit the use of Unicode for the naming of Internet hosts, to respond to the need for "internationalized domain names" (IDNs); in 2009, a process for registration of top-level internationalized domain names was initiated by ICANN.

As it relies on Unicode, the Punycode implementation of IDNs has all of the same problems as text encoding in Unicode, but actually in an even more severe form, as Punycode is limited to bytes corresponding to the subset of ASCII already used by the DNS. Thus, Punycode is a variable width encoding in which the lower case characters of ASCII are unchanged, and other characters require two more bytes to encode. For example, the Greek word παράδειγμα becomes hxajbheg2az3al in Punycode, and the domain name παράδειγμα.gr becomes xn--hxajbheg2az3al.gr. The result of a Punycode encoding is thus, not in general human-readable without considerable application support.

Figure 2 is an attempt to indicate how this might affect different languages for which information is available; the pages for "What is Unicode" in each of the available script encodings as of November 2007 were converted to Punycode word-by word, and heatmap histograms were plotted. Each column in Figure 2 represents a distinct language/script, with brighter areas indicating higher frequency. Hence we can see that English has fairly short typical word lengths (under ten ASCII characters), whereas Albanian, Finnish, French, Slovenian and Turkish all have words of more than 20 ASCII characters in length (indicated by the horizontal white line). Hence the number of characters required to encode a typical hostname in these languages can be expected to be greater.

These requirements do more than make hostnames longer in non-English scripts; they also impose upper limits on what a valid hostname can be that are sharply lower for non-English languages than for English. The DNS requires that hostnames consist of dot-separated fields, that the fields not be longer than 63 ASCII characters, and the total length of the name not be longer than 255 ASCII characters, including all field-delimiting dots and

[2] Users, institutions and ISPs can configure their computers to use an alternative "DNS root" from that overseen by ICANN. Many alternate roots do exist, and some were instrumental in increasing pressure on ICANN for internationalizing domain names. ICANN, however, has considerable financial incentive to downplay the significance of alternate roots, to avoid what it calls "fragmenting the Internet" (Kahn 2006).

top-level domain (e.g. .com, .net, country code domain such as .fr, or internationalized top-level domain, such as .рф [Russian Federation]). As a consequence, some desired domain names are likely to be impossible to register. A three-word name in a language where typical words encode as 20 or more ASCII characters would raise this problem, whereas English does not encounter it until six-word combinations are used for fields. Once a large number of single-word names are registered, as happened quite quickly with English, longer names are required; IDNs are likely to experience this as well, and the ICANN will eventually have to face an IDN issue from these field and hostname length limits. Since these limits come from obsolete data types,[3] it is not clear why ICANN has worked so hard to keep them in place.

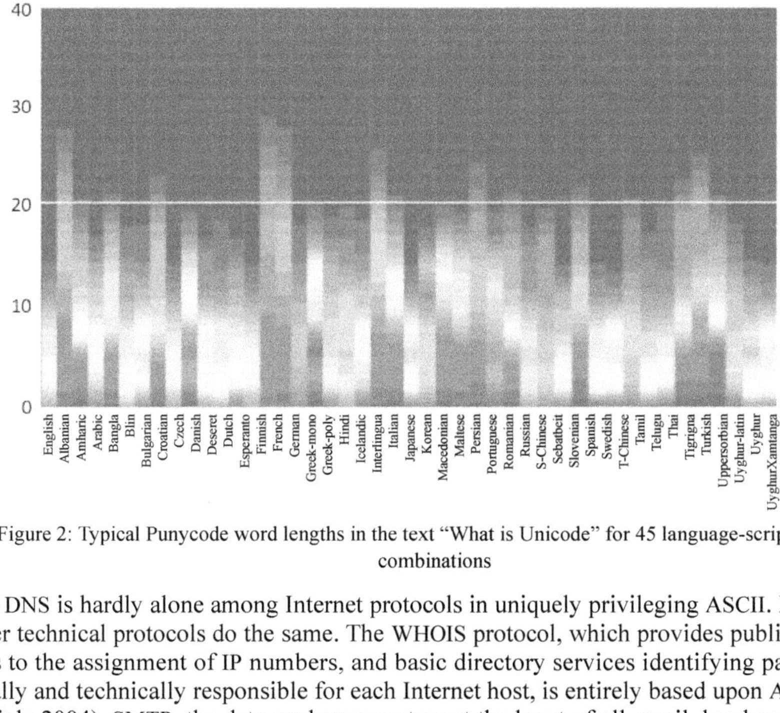

Figure 2: Typical Punycode word lengths in the text "What is Unicode" for 45 language-script combinations

The DNS is hardly alone among Internet protocols in uniquely privileging ASCII. Most other technical protocols do the same. The WHOIS protocol, which provides public access to the assignment of IP numbers, and basic directory services identifying parties legally and technically responsible for each Internet host, is entirely based upon ASCII (Daigle 2004). SMTP, the data-exchange system at the heart of all email, has been extended to permit messages to have content from any character set, but headers and other information used directly by SMTP remain in ASCII (Klensin 2001). Even the HTTP protocol underlying the World-Wide Web requires command, error and header information to be transmitted in ASCII or ISO-8859-1 (Berners-Lee et al. 1996). Others could be mentioned as well. What is remarkable about ICANN's management of the DNS is the slow pace of its adaptation in the face of intense public demand and mounting international pressure (Mayer-Schönberger/Ziewitz 2006). Should the remaining protocols ever become internationalized, we can expect similar difficulties with them as well.

[3] The 255-character limit suggests a Pascal data type originally defined in 1971.

4. Web markup and programming

Another major role of language is found in the markup and programming of web sites, as contrasted with the development of content; markup refers to the HTML, XML, RDF and other markup vocabularies that are used to format web page content, and to indicate something about its semantics for whatever applications use it. While the content may be in whatever language is desired for the target audience, markup must be in the formally specified vocabularies used for markup. Similarly, web programming is the writing of processing algorithms to be used either by the server, before data is delivered to the client, or by the client program, to dynamically control the presentation of data to the user. Web programming is accomplished in formally specified scripting languages.

Purpose	*Name*	*Data*	*Identifiers*	*Keywords*
General data definition	XML	Unicode	Unicode	Unicode
Formatting text	HTML	Unicode	Unicode	ASCII
Markup definition for XML	XML-DTD	Unicode	ASCII	ASCII
	XML Schema	Unicode	Unicode	ASCII
Transformation of XML to other formats	XSLT	Unicode	Unicode	ASCII
Server-side programming	Python	Unicode	Unicode	ASCII
	Ruby	Mainly ASCII	ASCII	ASCII
	Perl	Mainly ASCII	ASCII	ASCII
	PHP	Mainly ASCII	ASCII	ASCII
Client-side (browser) programming	JavaScript	Unicode	ASCII	ASCII
	ECMAScript	Unicode	ASCII	ASCII
Database query language	SQL	Mainly ASCII	ASCII	ASCII

Table 2: Support for Unicode in web markup and programming languages

Because of the Unicode effort, the international spread of the Internet and the development of web standards under the Worldwide Web Consortium (W3C), Unicode support is now seen as a requirement for most programming languages. Currently, the web markup languages HTML and XML support Unicode. All of the major web scripting languages, whether on the server side like Perl, PHP, Python, Ruby, and others, or on the client side, like JavaScript and ECMAScript, now support Unicode, although this means different things for different markup or programming languages.

Table 2 lists some common markup and programming languages, describes their functionality, and indicates the level of their support for Unicode. The "Data" column indicates the encoding permitted as data for each language; "Identifiers" indicates the encoding permitted for function, variable or other identifier names; "Keywords" indicated the encodings permitted (required) for special keywords defined in the language. From Table 2 we can see that only XML is defined to permit Unicode in all three. However, this appearance is a little deceptive, because XML is used to represent data; the XML data formats themselves are defined in either XML-DTD or XML Schema, using ASCII keywords. Among the server programming languages, full support for Unicode data is rare; when it exists it is generally enabled by extensions, and secondary to ASCII or other 8-bit encodings. All the languages use ASCII keywords; it is worth examining these in more detail.

The Appendix lists keywords for several markup and programming languages: the data-formatting languages HTML and XML-DTD, the server scripting languages Python, Ruby and PHP, and the compiled languages Fortran, C and C++. These keywords represent computational features in each language; i.e. they are that part of the code, apart from mathematical operators etc., which is actually interpreted in terms of computer instructions, and has computational semantics. While the keywords vary by language, what is remarkable is that all of these keywords come from English words, phrases or abbreviations.

```
#!/usr/local/bin/cpython
# answer = raw_input('Do you think the Chinese language has value? (Yes / no)')
回答 = 读入('你认为中文程式语言有存在价值吗？(有/没有)')
# if answer == 'yes':
如 回答 == '有':
        # print 'Well, let's work together!'
        写 '好吧, 让我们一起努力!'
# elif answer == 'no':
不然 回答 == '没有':
        # print 'Well, not as a programming language'
        写 '好吧, 中文并没有作为程式语言的价值.'
# else:
否则:
        # print 'Please give serious consideration before answering.'
        写 '请认真考虑后再回答.'
```

Figure 3: A Chinese Python program. The comment lines in English gloss the function of the Chinese-language code (www.chinesepython.org)

The English-lexified nature of computer programming is so entirely deep-seated that it is often treated by computer scientists and professionals as unremarkable. The number of computer programming languages is thought to exceed the number of human languages,[4] but it is English which is the overwhelmingly the parent language of the codes actually used to program computers. Yukihiro Matsumoto, the Japanese author of Ruby, chose to use English keywords for his creation. A few projects exist to "translate" programming languages into Chinese and other languages, but the remark most often made about them, including by their authors, is that they are strange, as can be seen from Figure 3. Such projects seldom gain traction; the Chinese Python project, for example, appears to have been abandoned. Native-language programming is a cause sometimes taken up for educational purposes, but it is generally assumed to have no other practical significance.

[4] The HOPL website (http://hopl.murdoch.edu.au/) currently catalogs 8,512 programming languages, whereas the Ethnologue (http://www.ethnologue.com/) lists 6,909 living human languages.

```
<!DOCTYPE html PUBLIC "-//W3C//DTD XHTML 1.0 Transitional//EN" "http://www.w3.org/TR/xhtml1/DTD/xhtml1-transitional.dtd">
<html xmlns="http://www.w3.org/1999/xhtml" xml:lang="en"
      lang="en">
  <head>
    <meta http-equiv="Content-Type"
          content="text/html;charset=utf-8" />
      <base href="http://www.efnil.org/mission-1" /><!--[if lt IE 7]></base><![endif]-->
    <meta name="generator" content="Plone - http://plone.org" />
    <link rel="kss-base-url" href="http://www.efnil.org/mission-1" />
      <script type="text/javascript"
              src="http://www.efnil.org/portal_javascripts/SubSkins/event-registration-cachekey3888.js">
      </script>
      <script type="text/javascript"
              src="http://www.efnil.org/portal_javascripts/SubSkins/fckeditor-cachekey6635.js">
      </script>
      <style type="text/css"><!-- @import url(http://www.efnil.org/portal_css/SubSkins/base-cachekey5313.css); --></style>
      <style type="text/css" media="screen"><!-- @import url(http://www.efnil.org/portal_css/SubSkins/projectprogressstyle-cachekey0528.css); -
-></style>
   <link rel="kinetic-stylesheet" type="text/css"
        href="http://www.efnil.org/portal_kss/SubSkins/at-cachekey0389.kss" />
  <link rel="kinetic-stylesheet" type="text/css"
        href="http://www.efnil.org/portal_kss/SubSkins/resourcecmfnotification-cachekey9316.kss" />
<title>Mission &mdash; European Federation of National Institutions for Language</title>
    <!-- Internet Explorer CSS Fixes -->
    <!--[if IE]>
        <style type="text/css" media="all">@import url(http://www.efnil.org/IEFixes.css);</style>
    <![endif]-->
    <link rel="author"
          href="http://www.efnil.org/author/varadi"
          title="Author information" />
    <link rel="shortcut icon" type="image/x-icon"
          href="http://www.efnil.org/favicon.ico" />
    <link rel="home" href="http://www.efnil.org"
          title="Front page" />
    <link rel="contents" href="http://www.efnil.org/sitemap"
          title="Site Map" />
    <link rel="search"
          href="http://www.efnil.org/search_form"
          title="Search this site" />
    <!-- Disable IE6 image toolbar -->
    <meta http-equiv="imagetoolbar" content="no" />
  </head>
  <body class="section-mission-1 template-document_view"
        dir="ltr">
    <div id="visual-portal-wrapper">
      <div id="portal-top">
        <div id="portal-header">
```

Figure 4: A fragment of the HTML in the home page of the EFNIL website (www.efnil.org)

Whatever its presumed status, the net effect of the English lexis is that the majority of the human-readable information associated with a web page tends to be English-based, requiring a technical English education to use, modify and otherwise appreciate. This is evident in EFNIL's own website: each page of the site, whatever the content language, is bracketed by about eight pages of HTML code like that in Figure 4 (alongside another five pages of JavaScript). This is true in spite of the fact that the Python-based Plone content management software system used by the EFNIL website was probably chosen for its superior Unicode support.

5. Diglossia in computer systems

In sociolinguistic terms, the situation with programming and markup on the web is a diglossia (Ferguson 1959): a situation in which two or more language varieties are used side-by-side for different functions. On the Internet, the "High" variety (English, in this case) is the exclusive code of all technical functions, while the "Low" varieties (all other languages) are used only as content, i.e., for everyday communication. This diglossia is global in scope, but concerns a specific set of technical functions in which English alone is used.

This situation is not a necessary part of computer programming. Keywords for programming and markup are actually stand-ins for abstract operations implemented by the computer, and any other replacements would work just as well. The abstract operations are no more naturally expressed in English than in any language: English programming keywords are often used in meanings only remotely related to their English meanings (e.g., "for" and "while" do not function as temporal prepositions, but indicate a computation performed some number of times). The Unicode project maintains the Common Locale Data Repository (CLDR), which consists of lists of internationalized keywords for other domains: dates, language names, currencies, measurement systems, territories, time zones, etc.; a unified list of programming and markup terms would not be very long, compared to the number of language names, for example (the longest keyword list in the Appendix is HTML, with 211 terms). Moreover, many programming languages, such as C++, already use preprocessors that perform replacements similar to what is required for language localization. Technical extensions of this nature may not be trivial, but they are also not onerously difficult.

Nor is this situation a simple consequence of voluminous literature – e.g., technical documentation – in English. Such technical documentation can readily be found in many other languages; technical documentation is often localized when technologies are adopted (e.g., projects for localizing Linux, which mostly means translating documentation), but computer code almost never is. Moreover, English is not just the preferred language for programming; it is also the favoured language of scientific research and many international functions. Other linguists have noted the same English diglossia in other domains (Crystal 1997; Graddol 1999; Phillipson 2003), further connecting it to linguistic bias (Phillipson 1992, 27, 104).

This situation is, rather, an outcome of the historical development of computer and Internet technology in the post World War II era. The shift of the centre of scientific and engineering innovation from Europe to the US occurred at a time when computing technology was still largely nascent. Many innovations in computing were led by US-based industrial, military and academic research efforts; meanwhile the developing telecommunications infrastructure, on which computing has long depended, became cantered in the US. The rapid adoption of computing and Internet technology in the 1980s and 1990s took place in a context in which US-English was already favoured by a number of other factors. In spite of the significant contributions of many European scientists to computing (Bauer 2002; Tomayko 2002) and even Internet protocols, the commoditization of computers and their coupling to the telecommunications network largely benefitted US English.

Friedman/Nissenbaum (1996) examined bias in computer systems, and developed a set of categories for describing biases and identifying appropriate remedies. They recognize three kinds of bias: Pre-existing, technical and emergent bias. Pre-existing bias arises from circumstances outside the technical system, via attitudes toward, conflict with or oppression of groups of people; such circumstances tend to be institutionalized in the social system or culture. Technical biases exist when the technical systems themselves have some built-in bias. Emergent biases arise through the interaction of a technical system with the people using it in some particular context. Many times, emergent biases are the consequence of taking a technical system out of its original context and deploying it elsewhere. Evaluations that were not intended in the design of the technical system become part of its use in the new context, resulting in bias.

Different types of bias require different types of remedies. Pre-existing biases can only be addressed through social changes and are usually not the direct responsibility of computer system designers. Technical biases are part of the technologies themselves, and therefore require technical changes, and addressing them is the responsibility of designers. Emergent biases involve properties of both the technology and the society in which it is used; they are sometimes the responsibility of designers, but they often involve interactions that can be difficult to anticipate.

As we have seen, there is a clear technical bias toward English in the core Internet technologies. Yet Internet technologies, such as the DNS and ASCII text encoding, were adopted from an US-English context (the ARPANET) by countries where English is not generally spoken; this suggests that an emergent bias. The development of Unicode and other technologies are technical efforts to address this emergent bias. At the same time, pre-existing bias is present in the attitudes of members of the technical professions, whether they be those emphasize backward-compatibility with ASCII at the expense of other encodings, or those that treat English as the only suitable medium for technical aspects of computing.

The English bias of the Internet is thus deeply inscribed in the Internet technologies themselves, but more than a mere technical bias; it has complex causes, and simple remedies are unlikely to successfully address it. At the same time, it should be clear that an important locus of these biases is in the community of engineers developing computing and Internet technologies. The organization operating the DNS (delaying the implementation of IDNs for fifteen years) and the technology consortia creating Unicode (deciding that only ASCII would be a directly supported legacy encoding) and HTML (originally from CERN in Geneva, Switzerland) all belong to the same international community of researchers, academics and technologists; they hold meetings to discuss these technologies in North America, Europe, Asia and elsewhere, and citizens of EU member countries are prominently represented among the participants. For both technical and social reasons, a program to address linguistic bias in Internet technologies should begin with these people.

6. Designing a program for change

The need to address the issue of English bias and diglossia in the Internet technologies should be evident. Diglossias are rarely stable, and tend to develop toward one of two outcomes: inter-generational language shift to the High code (English) or replacement of the High code by the Low code in High functions (i.e., the use of non-English languages for programming computers). The first outcome is favoured when individuals perceive greater rewards, economic or otherwise, in using the High variety. But to the extent that the European Union values its language diversity, the second outcome is the more desirable one. Since the technologies of the Internet impose high costs for non-English languages, maintaining Internet infrastructure, web sites, and language-localized information resources costs more in countries where English proficiency is less prevalent.

A program to address the US-English bias needs to recognize certain principles. First, it must acknowledge the importance of written language on the Internet. Much has been made of the prospect for voice, video and translation applications to assist Internet users in connecting across language barriers. However, any assessment of these technologies must be guarded. The dream of machine translation is as old as the origins of modern computing in World War II military code breaking, but despite many rosy predictions and heavy research expenditures over the years, its promises remain unfulfilled. Video cannot be expected to do much better than television and film have already done in crossing language barriers; these technologies are much better at delivering powerful cultures to large audiences than they are at promoting the interests of minorities. As for voice, as long as the gateway technologies are programmed and configured via written text, voice telephony will only be an application.

Second, as suggested immediately above, the accessory role of specific enabling technologies needs to be recognized. The text-encoding problem targeted by Unicode is such a technology, as is the DNS, WHOIS and many others. These technologies should have high priority for internationalization, as that is the only real guarantee of access to the technologies. In some cases, as Unicode, and the IDNs of the DNS, internationalization is well underway, although its exact form may not be all that is desired. Others, like computer programming, need urgent attention. It will not be possible for international citizens to innovate Internet technologies in their own languages without learning computer programming. Since the web programming and markup languages are an important entry-point for computer programming, including among primary school age children, internationalization of these technologies should be a high priority.

Third, internationalization of the Internet requires social change in large social institutions, and that change needs to be coupled with other interests to be successful. Many of the core Internet technologies like the DNS, WHOIS, mail, etc., were designed very poorly from the perspective of security considerations. The DNS, for example, is susceptible to various kinds of attacks that direct users to incorrect hosts, and ICANN faces increasing public pressure to update the DNS for security. Coupling internationalization concerns with security is actually a necessity for both: many of the DNS security concerns come from the combined, sometimes conflicting assumptions of Unicode and ICANN when applied to IDNs.

Fourth, changes in the core technologies of the Internet will require significant institutional support. EFNIL is one such institution, but many others need to be engaged as well, from the many organizations overseeing different aspects of the Internet (ICANN, the IP registries ARIN, RIPE, APNIC, the Internet Engineering Task Force, etc.), to the national telecommunications regulators of member states, to technical consortia such as the Unicode Consortium and the W3C, to commercial entities manufacturing and marketing computers and Internet software; the list is long. Engagement of these institutions can happen in different times and places and by different means: via workshops sponsored at technology conferences for the WWW, Unicode, Internet networking, etc., via international for a such as the Internet Governance Forum and via institutional membership for EFNIL or member organizations in technology consortia. Corporations and other organizations tend to move in directions where there are clear rewards (e.g. access to markets), so there is an important role for regulation and market incentives as well.

Finally, the changes described here are likely to take some time to implement. The Internet itself was created with significant institutional support, but that support was more like a trickle over a long period of time than a sudden flood: packet-switching, the basis for all Internet communications, was first envisioned in the early 1960s; it took nearly ten years to have an operating network, and another twenty to bring that same network to academia. Internationalizing the Internet probably will not take as long; for the sake of the future of the languages of Europe and the rest of the world, it also *needs* to be more rapid. Significant groundwork has been laid, which can continue to be improved as long there are people and institutions who persist in demanding its improvement, and who apply their efforts strategically.

7. References

Androutsopoulos, J. (ed.) (2006): Sociolinguistics and computer-mediated communication. Themed issue, *Journal of Sociolinguistics* 10.4, 419-438.

Bauer, F. (2002): Pioneering work on software during the 50s in Central Europe. In: Hashagen, U./Keil-Slawik, R./Norberg, A.(eds.): *History of computing: software issues*. Berlin: Springer Verlag, 11-24.

Becker, J.D. (1988): *Unicode 88*. Palo Alto, CA: Xerox Corporation. Reprinted 1998 by the Unicode Consortium. Internet: http://unicode.org/history/unicode88.pdf.

Berners-Lee, T./Fielding, R./Frystyk, H. (1996): *Hypertext Transfer Protocol – HTTP 1.0*. Internet: www.ietf.org/rfc/rfc1945.txt.

Costello, A. (2003): *Punycode: A bootstring encoding of Unicode for Internationalized Domain Names in Applications (IDNA)*. RFC-3492. IETF Network Working Group. Internet: http://tools.ietf.org/html/rfc3492.

Crystal, D. (1997): *English as a global language*. Cambridge: Cambridge University Press.

Daigle, L. (2004): *WHOIS Protocol Specification*. RFC-3912. IETF Network Working Group. Internet: http://tools.ietf.org/html/rfc3912.

Danet, B./Herring, S.C. (2007): *The multilingual Internet*. Oxford: Oxford University Press.

Faltstrom, P./Hoffman, P./Costello, A. (2003): *Internationalizing Domain Names in Applications (IDNA)*. RFC-3490. Internet: http://tools.ietf.org/html/rfc3912.

Ferguson, C.A. (1959): Diglossia. In: *Word* 15, 325-340. Reprinted in: Ferguson, C.A. (1996): *Sociolinguistic perspectives: Papers on language in society, 1959-1994*. Ed. by Thom Huebner. Oxford: Oxford University Press, 25-39.

Friedman, B./Nissenbaum, H. (1996): Bias in computer systems. In: *ACM Transactions on Information Systems* 14 (3), 330-347.

Gillam, R. (2002): *Unicode demystified*. New York: Addison-Wesley.

Graddol, D. (1999): The decline of the native speaker. In: Graddol, D./Meinhof, U. (eds.): English in a changing world. In: *AILA Review* 13, 57-68.

Hardie, A. (2007): From legacy encodings to Unicode: the graphical and logical principles in the scripts of South Asia. In: *Language Resources and Evaluation* 41, 1-25.

Kahn, R. (2006): *Remarks from the opening session of the first Internet Governance Forum*. Athens, Greece. Internet: www.intgovforum.org/cms/IGF-OpeningSession-301006.txt.

Klensin, J. (2001): *Simple Mail Transfer Protocol*. RFC-2821. Internet: www.ietf.org/rfc/rfc2821.txt.

Loewis, M. van. (1997): *Internationalization and nationalization. Proceedings of the Sixth International Python Conference, San Jose, CA, October 1997*. Internet: www.python.org/workshops/1997-10/proceedings/loewis.html.

Mayer-Schönberger, V./Ziewitz, M. (2006): *Jefferson rebuffed: The United States and the future of Internet governance*. (= Kennedy School of Government Faculty Research Working Paper Series, RWP06-018). Cambridge, MA: Harvard Kennedy School of Government. Internet: http://ksgnotes1.harvard.edu/Research/wpaper.nsf/rwp/RWP06-018.

McEnery, A.M./Xiao, R.Z. (2005): Character encoding in corpus construction. In: Wynne, M. (ed.): *Developing Linguistic Corpora: A Guide to Good Practice*. Oxford: AHDS, 47-58.

Pargman, D./Palme, J. (2009): ASCII imperialism. In: Lampland, M./Star, S.L. (eds.): *Standards and their stories: How quantifying, classifying, and formalizing practices shape everyday life*. Ithaca, NY : Cornell University Press, 177-199.

Phillipson, R. (1992): *Linguistic imperialism*. Oxford: Oxford University Press.

Phillipson, R. (2003): *English-only Europe? Challenging language policy*. Oxford: Routledge.

Rader, R.W. (2001): *One history of DNS*. Internet: www.byte.org/one-history-of-dns.pdf.

Tomayko, J.E. (2002): Software as engineering. In: Hashagen, U./Keil-Slawik, R./Norberg, A. (eds.): *History of computing: software issues*. Berlin: Springer Verlag, 65-76.

Unicode (2011): *The Unicode Standard, Version 6.0.0*. Mountain View, CA: The Unicode Consortium. Internet: www.unicode.org/versions/Unicode6.0.0/.

Wright, S. (ed.) (2004): Multilingualism on the Internet. Themed Issue, *International Journal on Multicultural Societies* 6.1. Internet: www.unesco.org/shs/ijms.

8. Appendix: Keywords sets of several common markup and programming languages

HTML (91)	A, ABBR, ACRONYM, ADDRESS, APPLET, AREA, B, BASE, BASEFONT, BDO, BIG, BLOCKQUOTE, BODY, BR, BUTTON, CAPTION, CENTER, CITE, CODE, COL, COLGROUP, DD, DEL, DFN, DIR, DIV, DL, DT, EM, FIELDSET, FONT, FORM, FRAME, FRAMESET, H1, H2, H3, H4, H5, H6, HEAD, HR, HTML, I, IFRAME, IMG, INPUT, INS, ISINDEX, KBD, LABEL, LEGEND, LI, LINK, MAP, MENU, META, NOFRAMES, NOSCRIPT, OBJECT, OL, OPTGROUP, OPTION, P, PARAM, PRE, Q, S, SAMP, SCRIPT, SELECT, SMALL, SPAN, STRIKE, STRONG, STYLE, SUB, SUP, TABLE, TBODY, TD, TEXTAREA, TFOOT, TH, THEAD, TITLE, TR, TT, U, UL, VAR
(120)	abbr, accept-charset, accept, accesskey, action, align, alink, alt, archive, axis, background, bgcolor, border, cellpadding, cellspacing, char, charoff, charset, checked, cite, class, classid, clear, code, codebase, codetype, color, cols, colspan, compact, content, coords, data, datetime, declare, defer, dir, disabled, enctype, face, for, frame, frameborder, headers, height, href, hreflang, hspace, http-equiv, id, ismap, label, lang, language, link, longdesc, marginheight, marginwidth, maxlength, media, method, multiple, name, nohref, noresize, noshade, nowrap, object, onblur, onchange, onclick, ondblclick, onfocus, onkeydown, onkeypress, onkeyup, onload, onload, onmousedown, onmousemove, onmouseout, onmouseover, onmouseup, onreset, onselect, onsubmit, onunload, profile, prompt, readonly, rel, rev, rows, rowspan, rules, scheme, scope, scrolling, selected, shape, size, span, src, standby, start, style, summary, tabindex, target, text, title, type, usemap, valign

XML-DTD (22)	ELEMENT, DOCTYPE, IGNORE, INCLUDE, SYSTEM, PUBLIC, #PCDATA, ANY, EMPTY, CDATA, NMTOKEN, NMTOKENS, ID, IDREFS, ENTITY, ENTITIES, NOTATION, #REQUIRED, #IMPLIED, #FIXED, xml:space, xml:lang
Python (31)	and, as, assert, break, class, continue, def, del, elif, else, except, exec, finally, for, from, global, if, import, in, is, lambda, not, or, pass, print, raise, return, try, while, with, yield
Ruby (38)	alias, and, BEGIN, begin, break, case, class, def, defined, do, else, elsif, END, end, ensure, false, for, if, in, module, next, nil, not, or, redo, rescue, retry, return, self, super, then, true, undef, unless, until, when, while, yield
PHP (71)	Abstract, and, array(), as, break, case, catch, cfunction, class, clone, const, continue, declare, default , do, else, elseif, enddeclare, endfor, endforeach, endif, endswitch, endwhile, extends, final, for, foreach, function, global, goto, if, implements, interface, instanceof, namespace, old_function, or, private, protected, public, static, switch, throw, try, use, var, while, xor, __CLASS__, __DIR__, __FILE__, __LINE__, __FUNCTION__, __METHOD__, __NAMESPACE__, Language, constructs, die(), echo(), empty(), exit(), eval(), include(), include_once(), isset(), list(), require(), require_once(), return(), print(), unset()
Fortran (41)	assign, backspace, block data, call, close, common, continue, data, dimension, do, else, else if, end, endfile, endif, entry, equivalence, external, format, function, goto, if, implicit, inquire, intrinsic, open, parameter, pause, print, program, read, return, rewind, rewrite, save, stop, subroutine, then, write
C (31)	auto, break, case, char, const, continue, default, do, double, else, enum, extern, float, for, goto, if, int, long, register, return, short, signed, static, struct, switch, typedef, union, unsigned, void, volatile, while
C++ (16)	bool, catch, class, delete, friend, inline, new, namespace, operator, private, protected, public, tempate, this, throw, try, template

Guy Berg

Babel life
Informations- und Kommunikationstechnologien im Dienste der Mehrsprachigkeit bei den Organen und Einrichtungen der Europäischen Union

Abstracts

Babel life – Multilingualism and language technologies within the European Institutions

The main political institutions of the European Union – European Parliament, Council and European Commission – follow different approaches in internal language policy matters. While Council and European Commission use a reduced set of so called working languages, European Parliament commits itself to an extensive multilingualism which implies virtually and practically equal rights to all 23 official languages of the European Union.

Full and simultaneous working in these languages is only possible with the intense use of ICT language technologies. Multilingual parliamentary work in commission and plenary sessions is managed with the help of a great number of interpreters and translators who have at their disposal a wide range of ICT tools like machine translation, translation support applications, electronic dictionaries, data banks and other specific applications like language recognition programmes, full document search etc.

In the light of the accession of new candidates like Island, the Balkans and Turkey, who will bring in additional official languages, maintaining this unique and basically democratic, pluralistic and non discriminatory multilingualism policy will only be possible if high skilled and sophisticated ICT applications are implemented. ICT thus turns out to be a prominent tool of European language policy.

Babel life – Méisproochegkeet a Sproochentechnologië bei den Institutioune vun der Europäescher Unioun

Déi grouss politesch Institutioune vun der Europäescher Unioun – Europäescht Parlament, Conseil an Europäesch Kommissioun – hu bei hirer respektiver interner Sproochepolitik ënnerschiddlech Approchen.

Wann de Conseil an d'Europäesch Kommissioun wéi all déi aner Institutiounen vun der Unioun fir gewéineklech mat enger reduzéierter Zuel vu sougenannten Aarbechtssprooche schaffen, da bekennt sech d'Europäescht Parlament zu enger extensiver Méisproochegkeet, wat theoretesch a praktesch bedeit, datt a senger Enceinte all 23 offiziell Sprooche vun der Europäescher Unioun déiselwecht Rechter hunn.

Permanent a simultan an all dëse Sproochen ze schaffen ass fir d'Parlament dobäi nëmme méiglech mat der intensiver Hëllef vun IKT-Sproochentechnologien. Déi méisproocheg parlamentaresch Aarbecht an de Commissiounen an an der Plénière geschitt mat der Ënnerstëtzung vun honnerte vun Dolmetscher an Iwwersetzer, déi hirersäits op e breeden Eventail vun IKT-Instrumenter zeréck gräife kënnen, wéi maschinell Iwwersetzung, Applicatiounen als Ënnerstëtzung beim Iwwersetzen, elektronesch Dictionnairen, Datebanken a spezifesch Applicatioune wéi Sproocherkennungsprogrammer, Dokumentevergläichsprogrammer asw.

Mat Bléck op de Bäitrëtt vun neie Kandidatelänner wéi Island, de Länner vum Balkan an der Tiirkei, mat deenen d'Zuel vun den offizielle Sprooche vun der Unioun weider wuesse wäert, kann dës eemoleg a fundamental demokratesch, pluralistesch an diskriminéierungsfräi Sproochepolitik nëmme mat der Hëllef vun héich sophistikéierten a spezialiséierten IKT-Applicatioune bäibehale ginn. D'Informatiouns- a Kommunikatiounstechnologië ginn domadder zu engem eminent wichtegen Instrument vun der europäescher Sproochepolitik.

Seit ihren Anfängen im Jahre 1952 und erst recht mit den Römischen Verträgen 1957 hat sich die Europäische Union, die damalige Europäische Wirtschaftsgemeinschaft, zur politisch wie wirtschaftlich bedeutendsten Leistung des europäischen Aufbauwerks nach dem Ende des Zweiten Weltkriegs entwickelt. Zunächst war es diesem Staatenbund gelungen, in den Jahren des Kalten Krieges ein neuartiges Kerneuropa aus der Taufe zu heben, dieses wirtschaftspolitisch zusammenzuschweißen und in den folgenden Jahrzehnten um neue Mitgliedstaaten zu erweitern. Sodann nutzte die Gemeinschaft den Zusammenbruch der kommunistischen Systeme in Osteuropa, um den teilweise neu- oder umgebildeten mittel- und osteuropäischen Staaten zu einer neuen politischen Perspektive als Mitglieder der Europäischen Union zu verhelfen.

Dieser in mehreren Etappen erfolgte Erweiterungsprozess führte im Laufe der Zeit zu einem Anstieg nicht nur der Anzahl der Mitgliedstaaten, sondern auch der Amtssprachen der Union. Begnügte sich die Sechser-Gemeinschaft der 1950er und 1960er Jahre noch mit den vier Amtssprachen Deutsch, Französisch, Italienisch und Niederländisch, so zählt die heutige Union mit ihren 27 Mitgliedstaaten nicht weniger als 23 Amtssprachen, die – zumindest theoretisch – ausnahmslos auch Arbeitssprachen sind. In der Verordnung Nr. 1 des Rates der Europäischen Wirtschaftsgemeinschaft vom 15. April 1958 zur Regelung der Sprachenfrage für die Europäische Wirtschaftsgemeinschaft[1] werden nämlich in Artikel 1 die Begriffe *Amtssprache* und *Arbeitssprache* gleichgestellt. Die vier genannten Sprachen werden sowohl zu Amtssprachen als auch zu Arbeitssprachen der Gemeinschaft erklärt.

Als sprachpolitische Grundlage und somit als Rechtfertigung für diesen Ansatz wird in der Verordnung der Umstand angeführt, „dass jede der vier Sprachen, in denen der Vertrag abgefasst ist, in einem oder in mehreren Mitgliedstaaten der Gemeinschaft Amtssprache ist“. Im Laufe ihrer Erweiterung hat die Gemeinschaft diese Auffassung *mutatis mutandis* stets fortgeschrieben, so dass grundsätzlich alle Amtssprachen der Union gleichzeitig auch ihre Arbeitssprachen sind. Dieser Ansatz beruht offensichtlich auf dem Grundgedanken der Gleichwertigkeit und Gleichberechtigung aller nationalen Amtssprachen der Mitgliedstaaten. Demnach gibt es keine Bevorzugung der einen Sprache etwa aufgrund ihrer größeren kommunikativen Reichweite und keine Benachteiligung der anderen etwa wegen der relativ geringen Anzahl ihrer Sprecher.

Dass dieser demokratische Ansatz in der Alltagspraxis jedoch nur schwer gelebt werden kann, liegt angesichts der mittlerweile hohen Anzahl von Amtssprachen auf der Hand.

So zeigt schon ein Blick auf die Webseiten der einzelnen Organe und Einrichtungen der Union, wie unterschiedlich die sprachpolitischen Vorgaben aus der Gründerzeit der Gemeinschaft von den einzelnen Institutionen konkret umgesetzt werden. Das Internetportal europa.eu bietet in allen Amtssprachen einen Zugang zum institutionellen Europa. In allen Amtssprachen präsentieren sich auch die großen politischen Organe: das Europäische Parlament, der Rat, die Europäische Kommission, der Gerichtshof der Europäischen Gemeinschaften und der Europäische Rechnungshof sowie andere zentrale Einrichtungen wie der Ausschuss der Regionen oder der Europäische Bürgerbeauftragte. Dagegen ist der Internetauftritt der Europäischen Zentralbank grundsätzlich englischsprachig, ein-

[1] Amtsblatt der Europäischen Gemeinschaften Nr. 17 vom 6.10.1958, S. 385-386.

zelne Inhalte sind aber auch in anderen Amtssprachen abrufbar. Nur zweisprachig (Englisch/Französisch) sind die Seiten des Europäischen Wirtschafts- und Sozialausschusses EWSA und dreisprachig (Deutsch/Englisch/Französisch) diejenigen der Europäischen Investitionsbank EIB.

Aber selbst denjenigen Organen und Einrichtungen, die sich um eine Internetpräsenz in allen Amtssprachen bemühen, scheint es vielfach nicht möglich zu sein, die umfassende Mehrsprachigkeit auf allen Internetseiten zu gewährleisten, teils wegen der Menge an Inhalten, deren Verfügbarkeit in allen Amtssprachen aus organisatorischen, personellen und finanziellen Gründen nicht möglich ist, teils auch deswegen, weil etwa viele Referenztexte wie Studien, Berichte oder Gutachten nur in einer Sprache abgefasst sind und somit auch nur in dieser Sprache abgerufen werden können. So bleibt denn die umfassende Mehrsprachigkeit bei einigen Institutionen faktisch auf das jeweilige Internetportal und einige Informationsseiten beschränkt, während die meisten Links zu englisch- und/oder französischsprachigen Seiten weiterleiten.

Als Musterschüler der institutionalisierten Mehrsprachigkeit, wenigstens im Internet, erweisen sich die besonders öffentlichkeitsorientierten politischen Organe Europäisches Parlament, Europäische Kommission und Rat, die sich mit ihrer konsequenten Außendarstellung und Öffentlichkeitsarbeit in allen Amtssprachen um konkrete Bürgernähe bemühen.

Wie dieser Grundsatz der Mehrsprachigkeit im institutionellen Gefüge der Europäischen Union seine konkrete Umsetzung erfährt, soll im Folgenden etwas genauer am Beispiel derjenigen Institution beleuchtet werden, die wie keine andere dem demokratischen Ansatz verpflichtet ist, nämlich am Beispiel des Europäischen Parlaments.

Von der sogenannten *Versammlung* der ersten Jahre, in der lediglich die Delegationen der nationalen Parlamente tagten, wurde das Europäische Parlament mit den ersten allgemeinen unmittelbaren Wahlen im Jahre 1979 zur demokratisch gewählten Volksvertretung aller Bürgerinnen und Bürger der Europäischen Union und damit zu derjenigen europäischen Institution, die über die größte demokratische Legitimation verfügt.

Dem Grundsatz der Gleichberechtigung aller Amtssprachen und damit der auch praktisch umgesetzten umfassenden Mehrsprachigkeit wird beim Europäischen Parlament große Bedeutung beigemessen. Die Institution beschreibt ihre Sprachenpolitik u.a. mit folgenden Worten:[2]

> Die in den europäischen Verträgen verankerte Mehrsprachigkeit ist das Spiegelbild der kulturellen und sprachlichen Vielfalt in der Europäischen Union. [...] Beim Europäischen Parlament sind alle Amtssprachen der Gemeinschaft gleich wichtig. Alle parlamentarischen Unterlagen werden in allen Amtssprachen der Europäischen Union veröffentlicht und jeder Abgeordnete hat das Recht, sich in der Amtssprache seiner Wahl zu äußern. Damit gewährleistet das Parlament auf einzigartige Weise, dass seine Tätigkeiten für alle Bürger transparent und zugänglich sind.
>
> Das Europäische Parlament unterscheidet sich von den übrigen Organen der EU durch seine Verpflichtung, ein Höchstmaß an Mehrsprachigkeit zu gewährleisten. Alle Bürger der Union müssen die Möglichkeit haben, in der Sprache ihres Landes auf die Rechtsvorschriften zuzugreifen, die sie unmittelbar betreffen. Da außerdem jeder Bürger der Union das Recht hat, sich zum europä-

---

[2] Siehe Internet-Portal des Europäischen Parlaments europarl.europa.eu.

> ischen Abgeordneten wählen zu lassen, könnte von den Mitgliedern des Europäischen Parlaments nicht verlangt werden, dass sie eine Verkehrssprache perfekt beherrschen. Das Recht eines jeden Abgeordneten, die parlamentarischen Unterlagen in seiner eigenen Sprache zu lesen, die Debatten in seiner Sprache zu verfolgen und sich in seiner eigenen Sprache zu äußern, wird ausdrücklich von der Geschäftsordnung des Europäischen Parlaments anerkannt.

Die derzeit 754 Abgeordneten im Europäischen Parlament sind in 7 Fraktionen organisiert und üben ihre poltitische Arbeit in insgesamt 22 parlamentarischen Fachausschüssen sowie einer Vielzahl von Delegationen und weiteren Gremien aus, die alle regelmäßig zu Sitzungen zusammenkommen. In den monatlich stattfindenden Plenartagungen treten die Abgeordneten im Plenum zusammen, hier wird der gesamte Gesetzgebungsprozess der Europäischen Union bewältigt. Bei diesen Plenartagungen, bei denen simultan aus allen Amtssprachen der Union und in diese Sprachen gedolmetscht wird, werden durchschnittlich zwischen 800 und 1000 Dolmetscher eingesetzt.

Die parlamentarische Tätigkeit des Europäischen Parlaments erfolgt räumlich disloziert: während sein Generalsekretariat in Luxemburg angesiedelt ist, halten sich die Abgeordneten monatlich jeweils für die einwöchige Plenartagung in Straßburg, für die Ausschusssitzungen in Brüssel und in den sogenannten Wahlkreiswochen in ihrem jeweiligen Wahlkreis des Mitgliedstaates, in dem sie gewählt wurden, auf. Jeder Abgeordnete verfügt deshalb über Büros in Brüssel, in Straßburg und in seinem Wahlkreis. Darüber hinaus nehmen viele Abgeordnete periodisch an Auslandsmissionen der Europäischen Union und an Delegationsreisen des Parlaments in Länder außerhalb der Union teil.

Unter diesen Voraussetzungen erweist sich ein auf Informations- und Kommunikationstechnologien gestütztes Arbeitsumfeld als unverzichtbar für eine effiziente Ausübung des Abgeordnetenmandats. So sollen neben der bestehenden Vernetzung der drei Arbeitsorte Straßburg, Brüssel und Luxemburg die Abgeordneten in absehbarer Zeit mit Tablet-PCs ausgestattet werden, die es ihnen ermöglichen, an jedem beliebigen Ort laufend und in Echtzeit über sämtliche Dokumente zu verfügen, die sie für die Wahrnehmung ihrer parlamentarischen Tätigkeiten benötigen.

IKT-Anwendungen werden vom Europäischen Parlament selbstverständlich auch eingesetzt, um das Organ und seine Arbeit den Bürgern in Europa näher zu bringen. So werden etwa die Ausschusssitzungen in Brüssel und die Plenartagungen in Straßburg life über Webstream im Internet übertragen, so dass jeder Bürger mit Internet-Zugang die parlamentarischen Debatten und Abstimmungen in Echtzeit mitverfolgen kann. Dabei hat er die Wahl zwischen der Originalsprache oder Muttersprache des jeweiligen Redners und seiner eigenen Muttersprache, sofern sie Amtssprache der Union ist, und zwar über die jeweilige Verdolmetschung in die gewünschte Sprache.

Das Ausführliche Sitzungsprotokoll der monatlichen Plenartagung in Straßburg mit den originalen Redebeiträgen der Abgeordneten wird in allen verwendeten Sprachen mitgeschrieben und in diesen Sprachen veröffentlicht.

Die Textmengen, die im Rahmen der legislativen Tätigkeit des Europäischen Parlaments anfallen, belaufen sich jährlich auf insgesamt annähernd zwei Millionen Seiten. Die Textsorten umfassen sowohl die Sitzungsunterlagen für das Plenum und die parlamentarischen Ausschüsse (Tagesordnungen, Berichtsentwürfe, Änderungsanträge, angenommene Berichte, Stellungnahmen, Entschließungen, Anfragen, Protokolle usw.) als auch die Dokumente anderer politischer Organe wie die Unterlagen der Gemischten Parlamentarischen Versammlungen, die Entscheidungen des Europäischen Bürgerbeauftragten, den Schriftverkehr mit den Bürgern, den Mitgliedstaaten und den nationalen Parlamenten sowie die Beschlüsse der internen Organe des Europäischen Parlaments. Insbesondere die Sitzungsunterlagen und alle legislativen Texte werden grundsätzlich in die 23 Amtssprachen übersetzt.

Um die einzelnen Sprachfassungen zu gewährleisten und den Schriftverkehr mit den Bürgern in allen Amtssprachen zu bewältigen, verfügt das Europäische Parlament über einen Übersetzungsdienst, der rund 700 Übersetzer und 200 Assistentinnen umfasst und seinen Anforderungen nach Qualität und Wahrung der vorgegebenen Fristen gerecht wird. Bei nicht prioritären Texten wird auch auf externe Übersetzer zurückgegriffen.

In aller Regel übersetzen die Übersetzer die Texte aus der Originalfassung in ihre Muttersprache. Mit den jüngsten Erweiterungen auf 27 Mitgliedstaaten und dem damit einhergehenden Anstieg der Anzahl der möglichen Sprachkombinationen auf 506 (d.h. 23 Amtssprachen, von denen jede in jeweils 22 andere Amtssprachen übersetzt werden kann) ist es mitunter schwierig geworden, Übersetzer zu finden, die sowohl eine bestimmte Ausgangssprache als auch eine bestimmte Zielsprache beherrschen, vor allem, wenn es sich dabei um weniger verbreitete Sprachen handelt.

Um Übersetzungsengpässen vorzubeugen, wurde deshalb das System der sogenannten *Pivot-Sprachen* eingeführt. Bei diesem System wird der in einer weniger verbreiteten Sprache verfasste Text bei Bedarf zunächst in eine der Pivot-Sprachen Englisch, Französisch oder Deutsch übersetzt und anschließend auf der Grundlage dieser Pivot-Fassung in die übrigen Amtssprachen. Das gleiche System gibt es entsprechend auch beim Simultandolmetschen, wo es als Relais-Dolmetschen bezeichnet wird.

Das Volumen der zu übersetzenden Texte, die hohe Anzahl der Amtssprachen und damit der möglichen Sprachkombinationen, das Gebot der Gleichberechtigung aller Amtssprachen und die Maßgabe der zeitgleichen Vorlage der Texte in diesen Sprachen machen den Übersetzungsdienst des Europäischen Parlaments zum komplexesten und kompliziertesten Sprachendienst der Welt. Dass dieses multilinguale Gefüge nur dank eines konsequenten und umfassenden Einsatzes modernster Anwendungen der Informations- und Kommunikationstechnologien reibungslos funktionieren kann, liegt auf der Hand.

Schlüsselbegriffe der IKT beim Europäischen Parlament sind, wie andernorts auch, die Interoperabilität, also die Vereinbarkeit von Hard- und Software sowie von Programmen und Anwendungen, und die Interkonnektivität, d.h. die optimale Vernetzung und Verknüpfung unterschiedlicher IKT-Systeme.

Mit seiner Generaldirektion Innovation und technologische Unterstützung (ITEC) verfügt das Europäische Parlament über eine hauseigene IKT-Kompetenz, die überwiegend in der Direktion Informationstechnologien (DIT) gebündelt wird.

Diese Dienststellen haben u.a. den Auftrag, für den Sprachendienst geeignete IKT-Anwendungen zu identifizieren, an die internen Bedürfnisse anzupassen, zu implementieren und ihre Anwendung zu begleiten. Darüber hinaus entwickeln sie eigene, auf den

Übersetzungsdienst zugeschnittene Anwendungen. Auf diese Weise lassen sich viele Übersetzungsvorgänge vereinfachen, beschleunigen, zuverlässiger gestalten und damit rationalisieren.

Im Bereich der Übersetzung reichen die IKT-gestützten Anwendungen von reinen Übersetzungsmaschinen und elektronischen Wörterbüchern über übersetzungsunterstützende Anwendungen bis hin zu speziellen Suchmaschinen und der Abfrage vernetzter Datenbanken.

Entscheidend für die zügige und fehlerfreie Übersetzung eines Textes ist die schnelle Informationsgewinnung, die am ehesten durch eine hohe Interkonnektivität gewährleistet wird. So besteht über das System *EUR-Lex* ein direkter Zugang zu sämtlichen Ausgaben des Amtsblatts der Europäischen Union in allen Amtssprachen sowie zu sämtlichen Rechtstexten der Union, bei Bedarf einschließlich einer beliebigen zweisprachigen Anzeige des angesteuerten Textes. Somit kann jede Verordnung oder Richtlinie und jeder Erlass in zwei beliebig wählbaren Amtssprachen aufgerufen werden. Gleiches gilt für weitere umfassende Datensammlungen, etwa den Haushaltsplan der Union, die Mitteilungen der Kommission, die Berichte und Sonderberichte des Europäischen Rechnungshofs oder die Urteile des Europäischen Gerichtshofs, die beispielsweise mit der Interinstitutionellen Dokumentensuche *RDI* mit wenigen Suchschritten abrufbar sind. Intern steht darüber hinaus das hauseigene Intranet zur Verfügung.

Spezielle Suchmaschinen ergänzen die Palette der Möglichkeiten zum Auffinden von Dokumenten und Referenzen, etwa Google.eu, eine speziell auf die Bedürfnisse der europäischen Institutionen zugeschnittene Web-Suchmaschine, oder die parlamentseigene Anwendung *Fuse*, die ein schnelles Auffinden von parlamentarischen Referenzdokumenten nach Textsorte, nach Verfahrens- oder Dokumentennummer und nach weiteren einschlägigen Kriterien in allen verfügbaren Sprachfassungen ermöglicht.

Das bei der Kommission angesiedelte Dokumentensuchsystem *Euramis*, das auch anderen europäischen Institutionen offensteht, bewährt sich im Zusammenspiel mit dem übersetzungsunterstützenden Programm *Translator's Workbench* (*TWB*), das nach dem Prinzip der Abfrage zuvor eingegebener und gespeicherter mehrsprachiger Textsegmente funktioniert.

Dieses Programm zeichnet sich dadurch aus, dass es nicht wie ein elektronisches Wörterbuch funktioniert und somit keine Übersetzungsvorschläge für den eingegebenen Text auf der Grundlage einzelner Begriffe, sondern dank evolutiver Textsegmentspeicher ganze Textstellen, also Satzteile, Sätze oder ganze Absätze, anbietet – unter der Voraussetzung allerdings, dass diese Segmente zu einem früheren Zeitpunkt ganz oder teilweise, identisch oder mit teilweise anderem Wortlaut, in die Speicher eingegeben wurden.

Dazu wird ein Großteil der anfallenden Dokumente auf leistungsstarke Server hochgeladen, entweder durch direkte Einspeisung oder durch ein Alignment oder im Rahmen des Übersetzungsvorgangs mit der *Translator's Workbench*, und kann von dort in vielfältiger Form abgefragt werden, sei es durch eine direkte Dokumentensuche, eine Konkordanzabfrage oder in Form eines *Translation Memory*, das die Grundlage für die Erstellung späterer Übersetzungen bildet. Daneben bietet die Anwendung *Volltextsuche* die Möglichkeit, durch einfachen Mausklick einzelne Begriffe, Stichwörter, Satzteile, ganze Sätze oder Absätze sprachenpaarweise (Ausgangssprache und Zielsprache) zielgenau in sämtlichen gespeicherten Dokumenten nachzusuchen und aufzurufen.

Auch die in den 23 Übersetzungsreferaten des Europäischen Parlaments erstellten Übersetzungen sind in allen Spachen jederzeit elektronisch einsehbar, so dass die einzelnen Sprachfassungen eines Textes bei Bedarf problemlos miteinander verglichen werden können.

Als sehr ergiebig erweist sich seit vielen Jahren die interinstitutionelle elektronische Terminologie-Datenbank *IATE*, die nahezu das gesamte Fachvokabular aller Organe und Einrichtungen der Europäischen Union sowie anderer internationaler Organisationen nach Möglichkeit in allen Amtssprachen zusammenfasst und dank zahlreicher Vorab-Einstellungsvariablen eine personalisierte und gezielte, u.a. nach Institutionen und Fachgebieten sortierte Abfrage von Fachbegriffen erlaubt.

Regelrechte Übersetzungsmaschinen wie *SYSTRAN*, *ECMT*, *Google Translator* oder die entsprechende Funktion in *Euramis*, die nach dem System der ausgangs- und zielsprachlichen Wort-für-Wort-Entsprechung konzipiert sind und Übersetzungsvorschläge in der Zielsprache anbieten, runden die Vielfalt der übersetzungsrelevanten IKT-Anwendungen ab. Den spezifischen Bedürfnissen der Übersetzungsdienste des Europäischen Parlaments werden sie indes nur bedingt gerecht.

Als überaus hilfreich erweisen sich dagegen die von den einzelnen Institutionen erstellten terminologischen Datenbanken, deren umfangreicher und gesicherter Bestand in Form von internen oder interinstitutionell zugänglichen elektronischen Wörterbüchern in allen Amtssprachen und vielfach auch weiteren Sprachen abgefragt werden kann.

Vor dem Hintergrund der politisch gewünschten und angestrebten Förderung der Mehrsprachigkeit auch im institutionellen Europa und der damit einhergehenden Sachzwänge bieten die Informations- und Kommunikationstechnologien somit jene Vorteile, die für eine konkrete Umsetzung dieser Mehrsprachigkeit unverzichtbar sind:

- Schnelligkeit der Informationsgewinnung, etwa beim Auffinden von Referenzdokumenten und Textquellen sowie bei der terminologischen Bearbeitung eines Textes;
- Zuverlässigkeit der gewonnenen Informationen;
- Verlässlichkeit und Verifizierbarkeit der terminologischen Angaben;
- uneingeschränkter Zugriff auf alle einschlägigen Informationen und deren dauerhafte Verfügbarkeit;
- Vermeidung von Doppelarbeit im Bereich des Übersetzungsdienstes etwa dadurch, dass ein übersetzter Text als solcher identifiert und damit eine erneute Übersetzung vermieden werden kann.

Die Europäische Union bereitet sich zur Zeit auf neue Erweiterungsrunden vor, Länder wie Island und Kroatien dürften in absehbarer Zeit als neue Mitgliedstaaten dazustoßen. Serbien und Montenegro haben ihr Interesse an einer Mitgliedschaft angemeldet. Die im

Herbst 2005 eingeleiteten Beitrittsverhandlungen mit der Türkei sind zwischenzeitlich zwar etwas ins Stocken geraten, werden aber dennoch fortgesetzt. Mit weiteren Mitgliedstaaten wird auch die Zahl der Amtssprachen der Union und damit die Zahl der möglichen Sprachkombinationen weiter zunehmen.

Mit dem Inkrafttreten des Vertrags von Lissabon zum 1. Dezember 2009 sind andererseits aber auch die Aufgaben und Zuständigkeiten des Europäischen Parlaments in den Gesetzgebungsverfahren der Europäischen Union ausgeweitet und gestärkt worden.

Dieser Machtzuwachs des demokratischen Arms des europäischen Gesetzgebers bedingt in Verbindung mit der steigenden Anzahl der Amtssprachen und dem Anstieg der Zahl der Sprachkominationen eine weitere Steigerung des Übersetzungsaufwands, der zweifellos nur mit noch leistungsfähigeren Instrumenten der Informations- und Kommunikationstechnologien wird gemeistert werden können.

Die IKT erweisen sich damit als ein wichtiger, ja entscheidender Faktor für eine erfolgreiche Umsetzung des Postulats der Mehrsprachigkeit innerhalb der Organe und Einrichtungen der Europäischen Union und bei deren Interaktion mit den Bürgern in Europa, als ein wichtiger Faktor auch für eine lebendige multilinguale Demokratie, in der die einzelnen Amtssprachen der Mitgliedstaaten auf der Ebene der Union *de jure* und nach Möglichkeit auch *de facto* gleichberechtigt und einander ebenbürtig sind.

Auf diese Weise erfährt das Bekenntnis der Europäischen Union zum Grundprinzip des sprachlichen und kulturellen Pluralismus, wie es in Artikel 22 der Charta der Grundrechte der Union[3] mit dem Satz verankert ist: „Die Union achtet die Vielfalt der Kulturen, Religionen und Sprachen", seine konkrete Umsetzung. Gleichzeitig wird damit auch der besondere Stellenwert der Mehrsprachigkeit in Europa hervorgehoben und gewürdigt, und zwar ganz im Sinne der Entschließung des Europäischen Parlaments vom 15. November 2006 zu einer neuen Rahmenstrategie zur Mehrsprachigkeit,[4] in der es in Erwägung B feststellt, „dass Mehrsprachigkeit eine Besonderheit der Europäischen Union ist, die sie zu einem klaren Vorbild und einem Grundelement der europäischen Kultur macht".

[3] Amtsblatt der Europäischen Gemeinschaften Nr. C 364 vom 18.12.2000, S. 13.

[4] Angenommene Texte P6_TA(2006)0488, Verfahrens-Nr. INI/2006/2083 – A6-0372/2006.

c) Reports on various countries

Manuel Casado Velarde[1] / Fernando Sánchez León[2]

Notes on Real Academia Española's tools and resources

Resumen / Abstract

Este documento esboza las herramientas y recursos más sobresalientes que está desarrollando la Real Academia Española para su inclusión en el nuevo portal web de la Institución. El proyecto del nuevo portal web, que verá la luz en 2011, pretende ser el eje vertebrador que permita dar a conocer la profunda renovación tecnológica que se ha realizado en el seno de la Academia. Por tanto, con alguna excepción, no se mencionan, de forma intencionada, las versiones actuales de estos recursos que se encuentran accesibles en las páginas de la Academia (www.rae.es), por considerar que son suficientemente conocidos para la comunidad hispanohablante.

1. Introduction

This document outlines the main tools and resources that the Spanish Royal Academy (Real Academia Española, RAE) is developing to include on its new web site, which is scheduled for publication in 2011. This webpage will demonstrate the profound technological renovation undertaken at the heart of the Academy. Therefore, with occasional exceptions, we deliberately do not mention here the present version of the resources now available on the Academy site (www.rae.es), since they are well known, at least to Spanish speaking scholars.

2. Basic aspects

Some years ago the RAE engaged itself in the creation of new linguistic resources that may supplement those which were historically developed in order to prepare its linguistic works. In this sense, the Academy owns at the moment a Spanish Data Bank constituted by three reference corpora: CORDE (*Corpus Diacrónico del Español*, 'Spanish Diachronic Corpus'), CREA (*Corpus de Referencia del Español Actual*, 'Present Day Spanish Reference Corpus'), and CORPES (*Corpus del Español del Siglo XXI*, '21st Century Spanish Corpus'), supplemented by several specialized corpora: CDH (*Corpus del Diccionario Histórico*, 'Historical Dictionary Corpus'), *Corpus Escolar* ('School Corpus') and CCT (*Corpus Científico-Técnico*, 'Scientific-Technical Corpus'), among others.

The RAE has taken care to develop its own linguistic technology which allows for both Spanish Data Bank linguistic tagging and for easier consultation of the rest of its linguistic resources, such as dictionaries of several kinds, the academic grammar, lexical lists index cards, or bibliographical data bases on Spanish vocabulary. Investment in linguistic technology began modestly some ten years ago, with the use of programs and tools already available in the public domain as a result of European projects like MULTEXT or CRATER. At the moment, the Technology Department of the Academy itself draws up text segmentation and morphological analysis and disambiguation programs, as well as the associated lexicons to these automatic tasks. Similarly, the RAE has other resources

[1] Correspondent Member, Spanish Royal Academy (RAE).
[2] Head of Technology Research, Center of Studies, Spanish Royal Academy (RAE).

linked to the diachronic analysis of Spanish that therefore allow the tagging of Spanish corpora throughout time. Finally, there are lexical resources taken from dictionaries of Latin American Spanish. They will enable the tagging of texts belonging to the different American varieties of Spanish.

The digitalization of the RAE's most valuable repositories is a priority for this institution. In fact, the Academy has already started to lay the foundations of a digital library containing the most important works from its archives; it has begun the digitalization of its lexical and lexicographical files. At present, there already exists a digital version of the Academy's *General File*, which includes all quotes appearing in the first edition of the Academic Dictionary, as well as the references accumulated by RAE's members and occasional collaborators in order to elaborate successive editions of the *Spanish Language Dictionary*. The total amount of index cards now approaches 12 million.

The interoperability between different resources is a short to medium term aim. The RAE is working on the idea of a "unified window" (*ventana única*) access to all those resources.

3. Applications

3.1 Lexicographic applications

Only two interfaces have been designed to consult the academic dictionaries: one for the synchronic dictionaries, and the other for the American Spanish lexicons. Along with these two interfaces, the application to consult the *Nuevo Tesoro Lexicográfico de la Lengua Española* (NTLLE, *New Lexicographic Thesaurus of Spanish Language*) is also preserved, until the future integration of all the academic dictionaries in a search only window.

The following three pictures provide some examples of these two interfaces. Figure 1 exhibits a unified search within the latest academic dictionaries. Consultable dictionaries in this application are, besides the DRAE, a preview of the 23rd edition of the aforementioned dictionary, the *Essential Dictionary* (*Diccionario esencial*), the *Student's Dictionary* (*Diccionario del estudiante*), the *Panhispanic doubts dictionary* (*Diccionario panhispánico de dudas*), and the *American Spanish Dictionary* (*Diccionario de americanismos*). Results appear on the left in a word list (all the headings beginning with *bab-*). By clicking on a word (in this case, *baba*, 'dribble') the window shows each article in the RAE's Spanish Dictionary (DRAE) in its current edition (the 22nd) . At the same time, a series of tabs to other dictionaries can also be seen, which are active only if the word is included in any of those particular dictionaries. Finally, in this case, this word has two homographs (*baba*^{1} and *baba*^{2}), which are displayed on the same screen.

Figure 2 reveals the same word (*baba*) with its American meanings, as they have been listed in the *American Spanish Dictionary*. Access to this information is as simple as clicking on the appropriate tab on the application screen, provided that it is not dimmed (in grey), which would mean that the word is not included in that dictionary. This application greatly simplifies the consultation of dictionaries thanks to its ergonomics, which save users much search time.

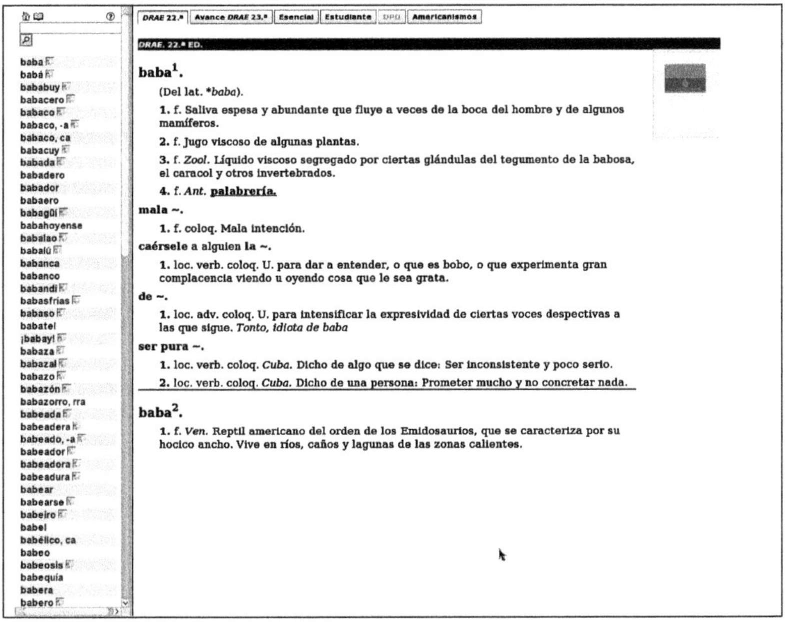

Figure 1: Unified search within the latest academic dictionaries

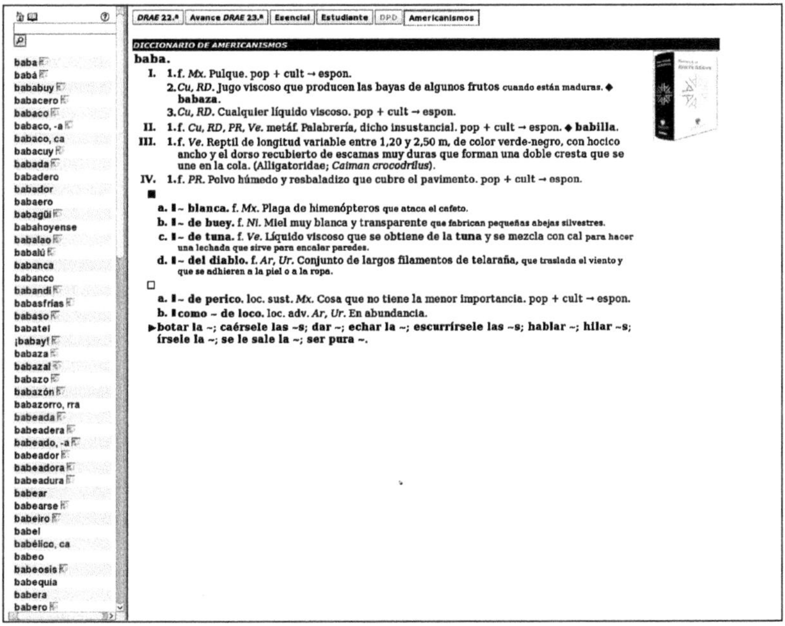

Figure 2: Meanings of *baba* in the *American Spanish Dictionary*

During the preparation of the *American Spanish Dictionary*, an application has been designed, with the same philosophy in mind, allowing the running of a unified query of over 120 American lexical repertoires. This application, called ARU (meaning 'word' and 'dictionary' in Aymara) shows the contents of these dictionaries in text format (see Figure 3). In this regard, all dictionaries that do not come from digital sources have been digitalized and have gone through an optical character recognition (OCR) reader. Only the nomenclature of this process outcome has been revised manually, using the double cross-validation method. At all times, users will be able to access the original image (the scanned page) by clicking on the icon that appears next to each lemma. A table displays the distribution of each word (in this case, *baba*, once again) in every dictionary depending on the language area in which each word is located. Finally, the wordlist (the query is conducted again on the word *bab**) exhibits, next to each heading, an icon indicating its presence or absence in the *American Spanish Dictionary*. Next to each heading there is a list of diatopic markings reflecting the overlap between the *American Spanish Dictionary* and the different sources available: black listed countries reflect matches between these two sets; blue diatopic markings indicate that, although that word is included in the *American Spanish Dictionary*, it does not appear in any of the ARU dictionaries; and the red ones represent the reverse situation. The mark *Am*, from general American Spanish dictionaries, it is not used in the *American Spanish Dictionary* of the Association of Academies; for this reason, it appears in a different colour, orange (in this case).

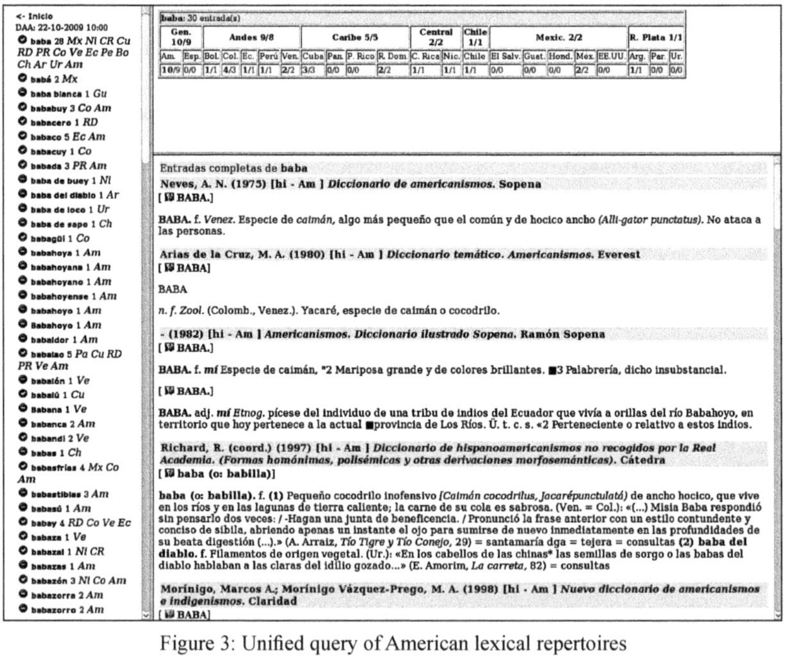

Figure 3: Unified query of American lexical repertoires

Finally, ARU contains about 40,000 digital images (from which the aforementioned textual conversion has been made) and is composed of over 550,000 items.

3.2 Lexical and lexicographic applications

The Royal Academy has begun digitalizing its lexical files, starting with the so-called *General file* (*Fichero general*). This file consists of just over 10 million records on index cards that directly reflect the uses of a word – in its various diachronic and dialectal variants – or they have attached an article taken from a dictionary. The oldest index cards contain the examples, or 'authorities', that were used in the first dictionary published by the Royal Academy between 1726 and 1739.

Due to the technical difficulty in obtaining reasonable results in optical character reading – since many of these index cards were handwritten or have low contrast or archaic fonts –, the index cards are stored as images, linked to the heading contained therein. For now, we have developed a query interface on this material, with different viewing modes. The following images provide some examples:

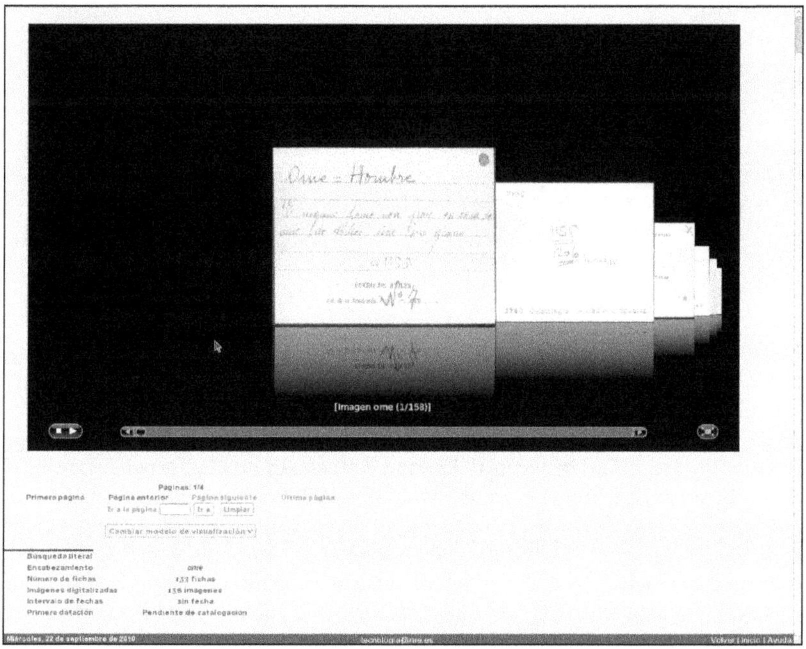

Figure 4: Pictures of index cards of *ome* 'man'

Figure 4 shows some examples of *ome* (one of the historical variations of the word *hombre*, 'man') as a slideshow. Both the horizontal scroll bar and the mouse wheel can be used to see the images, which are organized in batches, or lots, of 50. They can also be displayed in this format as a slide carousel, where users can stop at any point. On the other hand, the following image (figure 5) presents the same information (the first index card) as a mosaic, barely noticeable because it has been maximized. This card, which has a red circle mark, is the first dating of that word found by this institution: as can be seen, *ome* dates from around 1155, and is documented in the *Fuero de Avilés*.

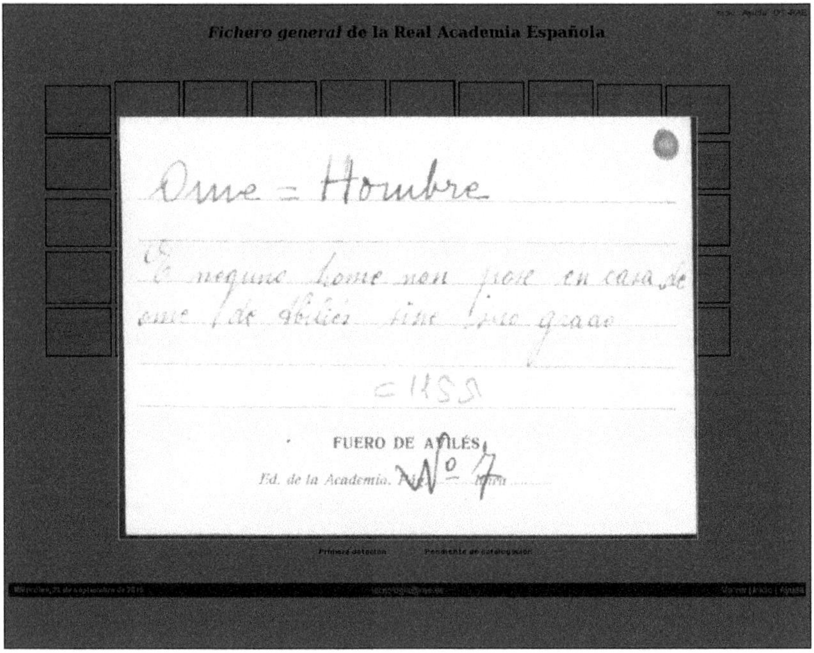

Figure 5

3.3 Lexical applications

Fifteen years ago the Royal Academy began the construction of two corpora that would include the synchronic and diachronic linguistic usage: CREA (*Corpus de Referencia del Español Actual*, 'Present Day Spanish Reference Corpus', with some 170 million words covering the period between 1975 and 1999) and CORDE (*Corpus Diacrónico del Español*, 'Spanish Diachronic Corpus', with almost 300 million covering from the origins of Spanish until 1974). We have to add to these two corpora the CORPES (*Corpus del Español del Siglo XXI*, '21st Century Spanish Corpus', currently with 70 million words but expected to reach 300) and a series of satellite corpora: one organised in terms of specific types of language (CCT, *Corpus Científico-Técnico*, 'Scientific-Technical Corpus'), another in terms of the linguistic level of the target language of the texts that comprise it (*Corpus Escolar*, 'School Corpus', consisting of textbooks from different levels of secondary education), and another in terms of the purpose of the corpus itself (*Corpus del Diccionario Histórico*, 'Historical Dictionary Corpus', CDH). All these corpora, but especially the first three and the last one, are integrated into the so-called Spanish Data Bank.

During the construction of the latter, the usual design criteria for developing these resources have been taken into account, usually at the national level, but without detriment to the transnational dimension of the Spanish language (*Pan-Hispanic*, as it is called in this case). Thus, the proportions awarded to American texts change over time, which indicates the recognition of the growing importance of American Spanish. Consequently, the initial proportions of CORDE, which give a rate of 70% to European Spanish texts (compared to a 30% for American Spanish), become equivalent in CREA, which provides 50% of each variety in this dichotomy; and that rate 70%/30% returns, though in reverse, in the distribution of CORPES (70% of texts from America, 30% from Spain).

The coding of the texts that form each corpus follows the recommendations of the *Text Encoding Initiative* (TEI), both with respect to the encoding format (XML), and in relation to the bibliographic and textual elements to be registered.

Finally, the corpora have been part of speech (POS)-tagged and each word has been assigned a lemma that connects it to an article in the dictionary (when the voice is included in it). The lematization is, in fact, a consequence of disambiguation.

Once analyzed, the texts are indexed to facilitate quick consultation. As in the rest of the applications described in this paper, all the indexing software was also developed by the Spanish Royal Academy. This indexer competes favourably with other corpus indexers, both in efficiency and versatility, as well as in the size of the corpus that can be managed. The query interface on the Spanish Data Bank allows observation of the absolute and relative frequency and the use and dispersion that the search terms offer. It is possible to consult the lemma and the lexical category (along with its morphological features) on the textual form, even combining several of these criteria, including distance bounded operators on a radio that may be directional or not; this way users can run queries on textual elements which are not necessarily contiguous. The application shown here is not the one that will ultimately be integrated into the new website of the Academy, as this is still under construction.

4. Conclusion

This document offers an illustrated summary of some of the technological developments undertaken in recent years by the Spanish Royal Academy to improve working conditions for the teams of collaborators attending academics in their language tasks (which may or may not be lexicographic). Again as part of its mission to serve the Hispanic speaking community, the Royal Academy is making an effort to make available these tools that allow speakers to have a better knowledge of their language. Due to the limitations of such a summary, this paper leaves out some developments already underway, such as the Neologism Observatory and, of course, does not dwell on the great technological effort (both in software engineering and language technology) on which applications presented here are supported. The immediate future will allow any user to view these resources through any browser in the world, which in turn will be supplemented with new interfaces and a more profound treatment of those already available.[3]

[3] We would like to thank Dámaso Izquierdo Alegría for his thorough revision and editing of this text.

Seán Ó Cearnaigh*

A brief report to Information Computer Technologies in Ireland

1. Background / overview

1.1 ICT and status

The Information Computer Technologies (ICT) industry is universally associated with modernity and economic progress and the forces of globalization while lesser-used languages are often associated with the geographic and economic margins. The paradigm of a perceived incongruity or incompatibility between ICT and lesser-used languages is one which is often discussed.

Lesser-used languages are often associated with the geographic and economic margins, so in terms of intergenerational transmission within the Gaeltacht (the Irish-speaking areas which compromise a very small minority of the population) and in terms of motivation to learn the language outside the Gaeltacht areas, the perceived status and utility of the language are important factors.

In the case of the Irish language, the issue of status is particularly important as a factor in motivating learners of the language for a number of reasons. In the first instance the majority of the speakers of the language are 'produced' by the education system rather than 'reproduced' by intergenerational transmission (Ó Riagáin 1997). Strategies to strengthen positive attitudes towards the language and working to lessen negative attitudes are vital to support motivation to learn the language. The associations which technology has for the young in particular are those of modernity, creativity and innovation.

1.2 Localization

The fact that a localization project is undertaken in a language by one of the bigger multi-national technology companies illustrates both an appreciation that the majority of emerging technologies reach the market in the first instance through the medium of a single language – usually English – and an aspiration that for primarily practical reasons a degree of localization is required to optimise the market reach of new technologies. While the motivation behind localization is primarily that of increasing market share, other factors undoubtedly influence localization decisions. In the case of Irish, there are no monoglot Irish speakers, so the impetus for localization does not derive from a simple analysis of core market requirments, but from additional factors such as public sector requirements, or perceived goodwill towards a project which offer a local language choice, for example.

* I am grateful to my colleagues Deirdre Davitt, Breandán Mac Craith and Seosamh Ó Coinne for their assistance.

1.3 20-Year Strategy for Irish: 2010-2030

The Irish Government's *20-Year Strategy for the Irish Language 2010-2030* lists nine 'areas for action', one of which is one of which is 'Media and Technology'.

The Strategy recognizes that education, community, arts and media are no longer separate language domains which can be governed by discrete policies and that this is due to the prevalence of information and communication technology. In areas outside the Gaeltacht, Irish language speakers have traditionally been at a disadvanage by being dispersed among the general populace – effectively networks of speakers rather than communites delineated by geographical location. The Strategy recognizes the possibilities which virtual networks afford such speakers and states of "these developments have immense potential for resource building in the arts and education and open up new channels for individuals and communities to increase their knowledge and regular use of Irish".

The section specifically dealing with Information and Communication Technology is worth quoting in full:

> The Government will request the inclusion of Irish in all EU-developed ICT programmes. It will also actively engage with major IT suppliers to license and distribute Irish-medium IT programmes. An IT strategy will be developed, to include IT terminology and lexicographical resources; localisation and open source applications; switchability of interface and language attributes; additional content creation aids to supplement spellcheckers and computerised dictionaries; diacritic markers; multilingual web pages; terminology for computer-aided translation; multilingual content/document management systems; language technology issues and corpora; speech technology, speech synthesis, speech recognition, adaptive technology and embedding issues; capacity building for end users and technology specialists; e-learning and the Irish language; call centre software; back end databases and bi/multilingualism; metadata; mobile devices; optical character recognition; and handwriting recognition.
>
> Such IT developments need also to be embedded in educational, social and work-related practices to become effective means of enhanced communication.

1.4 The Official Languages Act, 2003

The Strategy and such legislation as may come into being on foot of it are likely to have a major impact, just as a previous piece of legislation, the *Official Languages Act, 2003*, did. This sought to set out minimum standards of service provision for those who choose to use Irish in their dealings with the public sector. A direct consequence of the act was the professionalisation and standarisation of the translation sector by means of a 'seal' of accreditation which is overseen by Foras na Gaeilge. Other ICT-based initiatives which support the translation sector either began or were further developed as a result of the Act. The development of translation memories based on a corpus of parallel texts is perhaps the most obvious example.

2. Resources, tools, projects and other initiatives

2.1 NEID – the New English-Irish Dictionary Project

This is a flagship project of Foras na Gaeilge which has statutory responsibility for lexicography. The aim is to produce a modern bilingual dictionary containing c. 40,000 headwords to be published in both printed and electronic format. An on-line version of the dictionary will be made available in late 2012. Part of the preparatory work involved the creation of a corpus of English as it is used in Ireland (25 million words) and a corpus of Irish texts (30 million words). More information and examples of the work can be accessed on the project's website cited below:
www.focloir.ie

2.2 The National Terminology Database

The national database of Irish-language terminology was developed by FIONTAR in Dublin City University (DCU) in collaboration with An Coiste Téarmaíochta/The Terminology Committee of Foras na Gaeilge. The Terminology Committee has statutory responsibility for the development of new terminology. The database contains over 325,000 terms and more than 880,000 unique visitors have used the website between 2006 and 2011. Further information about the project is available on the project's website:
www.focal.ie

2.3 WinGléacht

An electronic version of the Ó Dónaill *Irish-English Dictionary*. This is a commercial product for purchase from
www.litriocht.com

2.4 Acmhainn

A website with dictionaries, word-lists, and resources for translators including texts about the art of translation, samples of best practice translations and a forum.
www.acmhainn.ie.

2.5 Microsoft Office

Foras na Gaeilge works on an ongoing basis with Microsoft to produce LIPs (Language Interface Packs) for operating systems and various other resources such as proofing tools. Current information is available at:
www.irish.ie/UsingLearning/default.asp?catid=510

2.6 OpenOffice

This open source, open standards suite is available in Irish and a support sub-project of 'native-lang' exists for Irish.

Native Language homepage: openoffice.org/projects/native-lang
Irish language project: ga.openoffice.org/foireann.html

2.7 Other localisations

ICT staples such as *Google*, *Firefox*, *Opera* and *Facebook* are all available in Irish and Irish is an option among the languages in *Google Translate* is available for Irish.

2.8 Gaelspell and Ceart

Gaelspell is an Irish-language spellchecker for Microsoft Word which is available for MS platforms and for Mac and Unix. Ceart is a powerful free-standing software package which corrects spelling and grammar and is available commercially.
www.cruinneog.com

2.9 Scriobh

This is a useful website which lists many of the ICT resources related to writing in the Irish language (dictionaries, spellcheckers etc) but also resources such as information on accent marks, on older Gaelic fonts and suchlike, and provides links to them.
www.scriobh.ie

2.10 Getthefocal

A mobile phone application (iPhone/Java) which offers a dictionary function, sentence translation and pronunciations. A less powerful version is available free via iPhone and Android app stores.
www.getthefocal.com

2.11 Freagra

A free translation service for short translations – accessible by phone, text, email or web.
http://ling.ie/freagra/

2.12 Predictive Text and other mobile technologies

The availability of predictive text in Irish is important for practical usage and for reasons related to status, particularly as perceived among the young who constitute the majority of learners. To positively influence attitudes, Foras na Gaeilge has worked in conjunction with various partners to ensure the availability of predictive text in various technologies as these have evolved. A brief history runs as follows: in conjunction with Vodafone in Ireland, a jav applet was developed for predictive text in the Irish language. T9 and XT9 options followed after this. Foras na Gaeilge worked in conjunction with Samsung on the "Gael Fón" which featured Irish language user interface as an option. This localized feature, since offered on all Samsung phones in the Irish market, has been a unique selling point. Foras na Gaeilge is currently in discussion with another major mobile phone manufacturer about Irish language features.

2.13 Abair.ie

This is an on-going text-to-speech voice synthesis project, based in Trinity College, Dublin which has received funding from Foras na Gaeilge.
www.abair.ie

2.14 Taisce Téacsanna

Taisce Téacsanna is a web-based project which aims to provide a comprehensive choice of standard documents in Irish (government forms, local government forms, policy documents, information leaflets etc.) which Public Sector bodies can download and use. This system allows State bodies to share common documents (English and Irish), saving money on production and translation costs, and it also helps organizations to fulfil their obligations under the Official Languages Act, 2003.

www.gaeilge.ie/Terms_and_Translations/Taisce_Teacsanna_Text_Bank_.asp

2.15 Database of Public Sector Terminology

www.gaeilge.ie/TermsTranslations/Terms.asp

2.16 Translation Memories

A Translation Memories project for Irish funded by Foras na Gaeilge is nearing completion and beta versions have been provided to accredited translators for testing before a wider release is planned.

2.17 Internet Strategy

As a result of research which it commenced in 2009, Foras na Gaeilge has just developed an Internet Strategy for Young People aimed at ensuring the provision of the best possible range of services and technologies for young people.

3. Best practice and problems

When funding was offered by Foras na Gaeilge to publish a weekly newspaper in Irish, a condition of the contract was provision of an electronic version free of charge on the web a number of days after the 'hard copy' publication.

www.gaelsceal.ie

The Oireachtas na Gaeilge Irish language media awards (roughly analagous to the Welsh Eisteddfodd), which celebrate excellence in journalism in the Irish language now have a new competition for best 'blog'.

A solely **web-based radio broadcaster** has been broadcasting in Irish with limited funding from the Department of Community, Equality and Gaeltacht Affairs. This broadcasts a narrow range of chart-based programming (with lyrics almost exclusively in English and continuity announcements in Irish) and because of its mode of transmission operates without a licence. As a consequence of this and its target audience of teenagers its potential listenership is limited to those with mobile devices (primarily smartphones and tablets) and broadband access. The project is thus heavily dependent on hardware which offers a range of other entertainments, and its success is likely to depend on its ability to adapt to changing technologies.

www.rrr.ie

An intermediary development involving old and new media is an on-line book club where a new title is announced monthly on a website and sold (hard copy) via the site. Local book clubs meet in selected locations (details on the website) to discuss the selected book but individuals can also review and discuss the books on an on-line forum. This approach uses technology to facilitate more use of the language and improving language skills via socialising and building networks of speakers.

www.clubleabhar.com

The project above indicates the lack of e-books in the Irish language. At the moment only two of the Irish language publishers produce e-books and even these do not provide them as an option for all new titles. The slow uptake of the related hardware – primarily Amazon's Kindle – may seem an unlikely barrier to making e-books commercially viable, but when the smaller size of the Irish language book market is considered, the hardware barrier proves critical.

4. An additional note on broadcasting

Broadcasting is probably the most prevalent use of technology is the area of language policy which probably impacts on daily life in Ireland (Watson 2003). While not automatically considered as part of the ICT area, the related technologies which support broadcasting and which have grown around it – particularly around TG4, as set out below – and which are in development (e.g. translation memories and speech synthesis) are likely to afford broadcasting the potential for even greater influence in the support of language such as Irish. For example Ireland's *20-Year Strategy for the Irish Language 2010-30* mentions that "subtitling options will be substantially increased in order to offer the option to have subtitles in Irish, English, or both, or no subtitles, thus significantly reinforcing the accessibility of TG4 to learners and non-proficient users of Irish as well as fluent speakers" and does so in the context of speech recognition, translation technology and speech synthesis.

The *20-Year Strategy for the Irish Language 2010-2030* also mentions a number of developments in the **Broadcasting Act 2009** which are intended to enhance the use and status of Irish in broadcasting (and thus everyday life), including: allowing more favourable charges, terms and conditions in respect of archive schemes by public service broadcasters for the purpose of Irish language broadcasts; increase in the allocation of licence fee money from RTÉ to the Broadcasting Funding Scheme (from 5% to 7%), of which TG4 is a main beneficiary; the continuation of a "free hour" of Irish language television from RTÉ to TG4 (valued at circa €10m); the deepening of RTÉ's remit in relation to the Irish language; the fact that Irish language programmes are now free from the "peak hours" restriction in the case of the Broadcasting Funding Scheme; the fact that TG4 has been given specific powers to provide on-line non-linear services in Irish; and; the fact the Minister for Communications, Energy and Natural Resources is to consider the multi-annual funding requirements of TG4.

Raidió na Gaeltachta, which originally began broadcasting in 1972 as a community radio station for the Gaeltacht (Irish-speaking regions) continues to fulfil that role but also serves the wider Irish language community throughout Ireland – and beyond, via the Astra 2D satellite and web streaming. Since 2005, the station has adopted an 'alter ego' of youth-focused programming after 8pm, primarily of pop, world, and eclectic music. The lyrics of songs played after this watershed need not be in Irish, but the continuity announcements are always in Irish, of course.

Two community radio stations operate fully through Irish on the island of Ireland, **Raidio na Life** (since 1993) in Dublin and **Raidió Fáilte** (since 2006) in Belfast. Both receive funding from Foras na Gaeilge. While having distinct local characters, the two stations co-operate and swop programmes on a regular basis. Both stations stream content on the web. Both stations also train broadcasters and producers and many of those who trained in the elder station are now household names through subsequent careers in other national media. This all helps to enhance the status of the language in the eyes of young adults in particular as something modern, attractive and glamorous.

TG4 is a national Irish language television broadcaster which was orignially called Teilifís na Gaeilge when it was established in 1996. Not all of its content is in the Irish language and it has used minority and specialist programming to attract new audiences and create awareness of the channel. Approximately five hours per day of Irish language content are broadcast including a comprehensive news service, a highly popular soap opera, a high quality arts magazine programme and a wide range of children and youth programming, some dubbed and some original. This synergy has had the effect of Irish language soundtracks being offered as options on DVDs of popular children's programmes such as Dora the Explorer, Spongebob Squarepants and so forth. The effect of TG4, then has been to support the normalization of the Irish language in broadcasting context, in the domains of popular culture and and everyday life for the general public but particularly for young viewers.

A secondary effect of TG4 has been the emergence of a cluster of companies working in the area of broadcast technologies (e.g. independent programme production, dubbing, subtitling) which operate predominantly through the medium of Irish and have provided employment opportunities in the creative sector for those in the Gaeltacht and other Irish speakers. As a result of Raidió na Life and TG4 in particular, it may well be the case that it easier for a young person to make a career as a broadcaster, producer or technician in the Irish broadcast media if he or she has Irish.

The national broadcaster RTÉ has a long history of integrating Irish into its output, particularly its news service and continuity announcements. This is true in particular of the television channel **RTÉ1** and the radio channel **RTÉ Raidió One**. In Northern Ireland, **BBC Northern Ireland** has a dedicated Irish language section on its website with listing of television, radio and web-based material available in Irish, some of it directed towards supporting language learning (as, unlike the situation in the Republic, Irish is not a part of the core curriculum in the education system in Northern Ireland).

5. References

Ó Riagáin, P. (1997): *Language policy and social reproduction: Ireland 1893-1993.* Oxford: Oxford University Press.

Watson, I. (2003): *Broadcasting in Irish.* Dublin: Four Courts Press.

Catia Cucchiarini / Linde van den Bosch

Medium-sized languages and the technology challenge: the Dutch language experience in a European perspective

1. Introduction

During the last decade the language policy of the Dutch Language Union (DLU, in Dutch Nederlandse Taalunie) has focused, among other things, on strengthening the position of Dutch in language and speech technology. Our approach is not technology or research driven, but user driven, i.e. oriented towards the language community as a whole and its communicative needs. The general aim is to guarantee the full integration of Dutch in modern ICT applications, at a level of excellence comparable with that of the big languages which surround our language area (English, French and German). From a language policy perspective this HLT policy is considered as a crucial contribution to the general aim of keeping Dutch a fully fledged language that can be used in all occasions and environments.

In this paper we present our policy and discuss some of the more important initiatives in the light of what is considered to be relevant for EFNIL and its member organisations. In particular, we address the following questions:

- what can be learned from the Dutch language experience?
- how could national language resources be integrated into a multilingual technical language infrastructure?

The remainder of this paper is organized as follows. In Section 2 we briefly introduce the Dutch Language Union. We describe its geographical and topical areas of activity, the nature of this organization, its policy and some of its most important achievements in the 30 years of its existence. In Section 3 we explain the rationale behind the DLU's involvement in HLT and the approach it has chosen. In Section 4 we describe a selected number of relevant HLT initiatives that were set up by the DLU. Section 5 is devoted to the lessons we learned through more than ten years of HLT policy and to our perspectives for the future. We end with some concluding remarks in Section 6.

2. The Dutch Language Union (DLU)

The Dutch Language Union is a joint effort of the Netherlands, Belgium and Surinam to promote the Dutch language, Dutch language teaching, the literature in the language and to support the Dutch language as such (infrastructure). As a living language, Dutch is constantly evolving so as to remain suited to the demands of our times. Although this happens largely by itself, it occasionally needs a little "push" by the parties working together to keep the Dutch language a vital, modern language. To achieve this for the entire Dutch-speaking world, in 1980 the Netherlands and Belgium signed the Treaty concerning the Dutch Language Union, in which the two countries agreed to pursue a common policy on the Dutch language. Owing to the Belgian state reform (federalisation), Flanders became the official partner of the treaty. This cross-border language area treaty is the only one of its kind in the world.

2.1 The Dutch language area

The Dutch language area is principally comprised of the Netherlands, Flanders and Surinam.

- The Netherlands is virtually 100% Dutch-speaking. Its capital city is Amsterdam, and its seat of government is The Hague, where the Dutch Language Union also has its official place of establishment.
- Belgium is a multilingual country, with Dutch being spoken in the northern region (Flanders), French spoken in the south (Wallonia) and a small German-speaking area in the east. Brussels, the capital of Belgium and of Europe, is officially both French and Dutch-speaking. The Dutch Language Union also has a small office in Brussels, responsible for the activities for Dutch as a foreign language.
- Surinam is a country in northern South America. It is a former colony of the Netherlands, and uses Dutch as its language of government and education.

2.2 The Dutch Language Union: a governmental, intergovernmental and international organisation

The policy of the Dutch Language Union is established by the Committee of Ministers (Comité van Ministers), a commission comprising the Dutch and Flemish ministers for education and culture and a representative from Surinam.

The Interparliamentary Commission (Interparlementaire Commissie), comprising Dutch and Flemish representatives, oversees the policy.

The Council for Dutch Language and Literature (Raad voor de Nederlandse Taal en Letteren), comprising experts and prominent language users, advises the policymakers.

The General Secretariat (algemeen secretariaat), which prepares and implements policy, works closely with individuals and organisations from within the language region and beyond.

The Dutch Language Union is also an intergovernmental organisation: it was founded in 1980 by the Dutch and Belgian governments. Surinam joined as an associate member in 2004.

The union also cooperates with the Caribbean islands that have Dutch as an official language

2.3 2010: 30th anniversary of the Dutch Language Union

As the Dutch Language Union Treaty was signed by the Netherlands and Belgium in 1980, 2010 marks the 30th anniversary of our organization. The Dutch Language Union's motto is 'Dutch without barriers'. It signifies the Dutch Language Union's desire to help all Dutch speakers continue to be able to use their language for every purpose that a language can serve. The major areas in which the Dutch Language Union has devoted its efforts in the past 30 years are the language itself, Dutch in electronic applications, Dutch language teaching (both teaching in Dutch and the teaching of Dutch as a second language), literature, promoting the position of Dutch in Europe and around the world and last, but not least, providing a single, uniform, official spelling for the Dutch language.

As the Dutch Language Union is a relatively small organisation, these activities have been carried out in close co-operation with other professional organisations and associations both within and outside of the Dutch language area. This is a key characteristic of the way we work. It is thanks to such cooperation that we are today able to look back on the past 30 years, and conclude that a great deal has been achieved, since the DLU was founded in 1980:

- In total there are more than 30,000 students of Dutch as a foreign language across the world, and Dutch is taught at 180 universities in 40 different countries;
- Books by Dutch and Flemish authors have been translated into 100 languages;
- Close cooperation links have been established with Surinam, Curacao, Sint-Maarten, Aruba, South Africa and Indonesia;
- Advice on a range of Dutch language and linguistic issues is freely available to the public. In 2009, 5.5 million items were consulted, and 6,300 new questions were submitted and answered;
- The DLU website, “Taalunieversum”, receives over 17 million visitors a year;
- Numerous digital Dutch language resources have been made available to researchers and to the general public, as will be explained in the remainder of this paper. These resources are now being managed and maintained for future use.

3. The DLU and Human Language Technologies (HLT)

As explained in the previous section, the initiatives by the Dutch Language Union cover all aspects of language policy. Each one is aimed at creating the right conditions to make it easier for Dutch speakers to use their language in as many different situations as possible. It is ultimately not the governments of the Netherlands, Flanders and Surinam, who are the DLU's most important ‘clients’, but the people who use Dutch to communicate.

In the digital world communication largely takes place through and with computers or other electronic devices. The DLU acknowledged the growing importance of Human Language Technologies (HLT), which make it possible to use natural language in information and communication technology applications, and realised it had an important role to play in guaranteeing that such technologies would become available for Dutch.

3.1 Rationale

According to the DLU embracing HLT would be the way to ensure that Dutch speakers keep using their mother tongue in all daily life situations. Taking this commitment to HLT seriously involves the development of HLT applications for a specific language, and requires the availability of a digital language infrastructure (comprising basic software tools, language and speech data, corpora and lexicons) for that language.

During the last decade the language policy of the Nederlandse Taalunie (NTU, Union for the Dutch Language) has focused on strengthening the position of Dutch in language and speech technology. Our approach is not technology or research driven, but user driven, i.e. oriented towards the language community as a whole and its communicative needs.

The general aim is to guarantee the full integration of Dutch in modern ICT applications, at a level of excellence comparable with that of the big languages which surround our language area (English, French and German). From a language policy perspective this HLT policy is considered as a crucial contribution to the general aim of keeping Dutch a fully fledged language that can be used in all occasions and environments.

As Dutch is a so-called medium-sized language and companies are not always willing or able to invest in developing HLT for a language with a relatively small market, government support was needed. On the other hand, the development of HLT is considered essential, if a language is to survive in the information society. It was against this background that the DLU set up a number of initiatives aimed at strengthening the position of Dutch in human language technologies.

3.2 Approach

The approach to stimulating language and speech technology that has been adopted for the Dutch language is comprehensive in many respects. First of all, because it is based on co-operation between government, academia and industry both in Belgium and in the Netherlands. Co-operating saves money and effort, boosts the status of the language and means not having to reinvent the wheel over and over again. Second, because it encompasses the whole range from basic resources to applications for language users. Third, because it concerns the whole cycle from resource development to resource distribution and (re)use.

4. HLT initiatives by the Dutch Language Union

DLU activities in the field of HLT date back to 1998, when a first explorative survey was carried out. Subsequently, different initiatives were set up in cooperation with various partners in the Netherlands and Flanders. Co-operation is specially required in HLT, because the market for Dutch HLT products is relatively small so it is necessary to share the high investments, this also increases efficiency and it makes it possible to establish a common agenda. Our partners in HLT initiatives are:

- Dutch Ministry of Culture, Education and Science,
- Netherlands Organization for Scientific Research,
- Flemish Fund for Scientific Research,
- Flemish Department of Economy, Science and Innovation,
- Dutch Ministry of Economic Affairs.

In this section we do not present all HLT initiatives that have bee launched over the years. We limit ourselves to discussing three of them: the **HLT Platform Project** (1999-2003) which paved the way for two other important HLT initiatives, the **STEVIN programme** (2004-today) and the **HLT Agency** (2004-today).

4.1 The HLT Platform Project

In 1999 a decision was taken by the Dutch and Flemish governments to work closely together in matters concerning HLT for Dutch. The Nederlandse Taalunie took the initiative to install an HLT Platform, bringing together all Flemish and Dutch government bodies involved. Within the framework of the HLT Platform project a number of action lines were carried out which culminated in concrete achievements in 2003.

4.1.1 Raising awareness

A first action line was aimed at stimulating cooperation between all parties involved (Dutch and Flemish industry, academia and policy institutions), at raising awareness and at disseminating the results of HLT research so as to stimulate market take-up. Part of the activities were carried out within the framework of the European Euromap project. In 2003 it was clear that this action line had helped create transparency and structure in the HLT field in the Netherlands and Flanders, and had clearly improved communication between interested partners. A co-operative framework was now available that provided a forum for discussing, exchanging and sharing experiences, best practices, information, data and tools. This success was partly due to the participation of DLU as the National Focal Point (NFP) in the Euromap project.

4.1.2 HLT infrastructure

A second action line aimed at defining the BLARK (Basic LAnguage Resources Kit), the basic elements required to create a suitable HLT infrastructure for the Dutch language. In addition, it aimed at determining which of these essential elements were already available for Dutch and which ones were missing (Cucchiarini et al. 2001). This resulted in priority lists for language and speech technology specifying which parts of the BLARK had to be developed (Binnenpoorte et al. 2002).

A complementary study commissioned by the Dutch Ministry of Economic Affairs investigated the functioning of the HLT innovation system and its contribution to sustainable growth in the Netherlands and Flanders, to identify the optimal form of financial support for the HLT sector. The results indicated that the HLT sector had economic potential in the Dutch language area and that the optimal form of government intervention should envisage three lines of activities: realizing the prioritized HLT resources; strengthening innovation oriented strategic research in academia in response to industry needs and stimulating the demand of HLT products.

These preparatory activities laid the basis for the STEVIN programme, which was eventually launched in 2004 under the auspices of the DLU.

4.1.3 Management, maintenance and distribution of HLT resources

The action line aimed at developing a blueprint for the management, maintenance and distribution of language resources was intended to identify the necessary requirements for the re-use of digital language resources developed with government money. A Blueprint for management, maintenance and distribution of digital materials developed with public funds was prepared by a team of language technology experts from the Institute for Dutch Lexicology (INL) and speech technology experts from other institutes, under supervision of the DLU (Binnenpoorte et al. 2002; Beeken/Van der Kamp 2004). This document also made recommendations for organising a structural form of co-operation in this respect, which eventually materialized in the HLT Agency, a central repository for HLT resources which was set up and financed by the DLU and hosted by the Institute for Dutch Lexicology in Leyden, the Netherlands (with an auxiliary branch in Antwerp, Belgium).

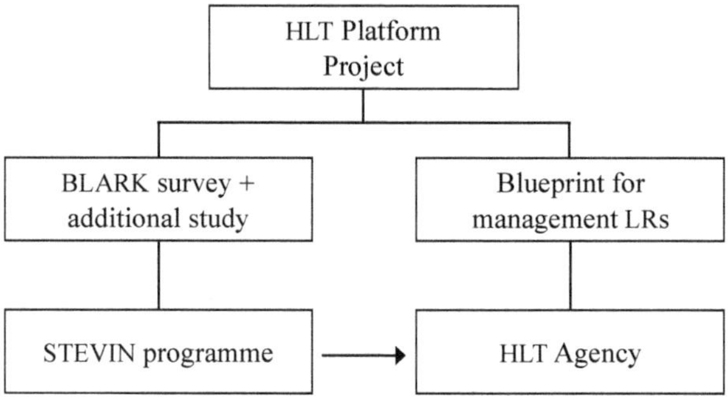

Figure 1: The relationship between the three HLT initiatives

4.2 The STEVIN programme

The respective Dutch and Flemish policy institutions acknowledged the recommendations that resulted from the various action lines, and budgets were assigned for a comprehensive HLT Programme, STEVIN. STEVIN is a Dutch acronym that stands for 'Essential Speech and Language Technology Resources'. Simon Stevin was a 16th century applied scientist who worked both in Flanders and the Netherlands and who, among other things, introduced Dutch terms for mathematical and physical concepts. In line with the priorities identified in the preparatory phase, the STEVIN programme aimed at realizing the prioritized HLT resources, strengthening innovation oriented strategic research in academia in response to industry needs and stimulating the demand of HLT products. In addition, it will strengthen the economic and cultural position of the Dutch language in the modern ICT-based society

4.2.1 STEVIN programme management structure

The STEVIN programme is jointly financed by the Flemish (Department of Economy, Science and Innovation) and Dutch governments (Ministry of Education, Culture and Science, Ministry of Economic Affairs and the Netherlands Organisation for Scientific Research). STEVIN runs until 2011 with a total budget of 11.4 million euros. STEVIN is coordinated by the Dutch Language Union and supervised by a board of representatives of the funding bodies (STEVIN Board). A Programme Committee, including both academic and industrial representatives, is responsible for scientific and content related issues (D'Halleweyn et al. 2006). An International Advisory Panel of highly-respected

HLT-experts evaluates the submitted R&D proposals. A Programme Office, a joint collaboration of the Netherlands Organisation for Scientific Research and the Dutch innovation agency AgentschapNL, takes care of the operational matters (see Figure 2).

Academic institutions and companies submit proposals that are first assessed and ranked independently by the International Advisory Panel and then by the Programme Committee. Evaluation criteria are quality, innovative features and economic aspects of the project proposal, contribution to the STEVIN Programme, proper treatment of IPR, use of standards, prevention of duplication. Based on the Programme Committee's recommendations, the STEVIN Board finally formulates a binding advice to the Dutch Language Union as to which projects should be funded.

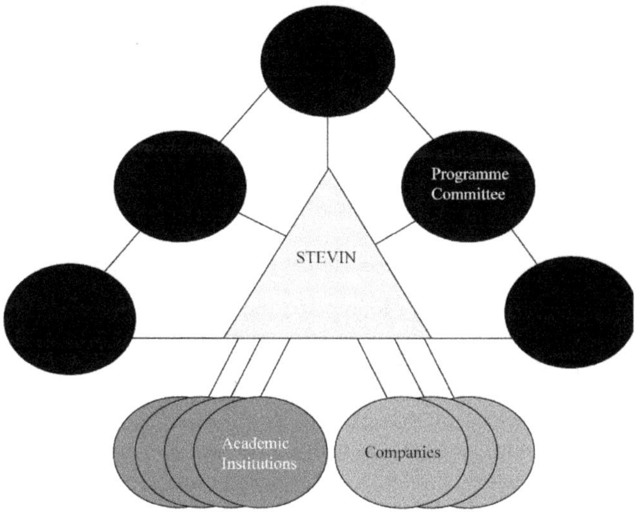

Figure 2: Management structure of the STEVIN Programme

4.2.2 Strategic research, resource development, and application development

Various calls for strategic research, resource development, and application development were launched in STEVIN. Cross-border consortiums were stimulated by increasing the standard bench fee by 50%. In total, 19 projects have been funded addressing basic HLT resources development, strategic research and application-oriented research:

1. Automata for deriving phonemic transcriptions of Dutch and Flemish names (AUTONOMATA);
2. Coreference Resolution for Extracting Answers (COREA);
3. Dutch Language Corpus Initiative (D-Coi);
4. Identification and Representation of Multi-word Expressions (IRME);
5. Extension of CGN with speech of children, non-natives, elderly and human-machine interaction (JASMIN-CGN);
6. Detecting and Exploiting Semantic Overlap (DaESO);

7. Dutch Parallel Corpus (DPC);
8. Large Scale Syntactic Annotation of written Dutch (Lassy);
9. Missing Data Solutions (Midas);
10. Northern and Southern Dutch Benchmark Evaluation of Speech recognition Technology (NBest);
11. STEVIN can PRAAT;
12. Speech Processing, Recognition & Automatic Annotation Kit (SPRAAK);
13. Combinatorial and Relational Network as Toolkit for Dutch Language Technology (Cornetto), a lexical resource for the semantic processing of Dutch;
14. Autonomata, Transfer of Output (Autonomata TOO);
15. Dutch lAnguage Investigation of Summarization technologY (Daisy);
16. Development and Integration of Speech technology into COurseware for language learning (DISCO);
17. Dutch Online Media Analysis (DuOMAn);
18. Parse and Corpus based Machine Translation (PaCo-MT);
19. Stevin Nederlandstalig Referentiecorpus (SoNaR), an annotated written Dutch corpus.

4.2.3 Raising awareness and stimulating the demand of HLT products

An important priority of STEVIN is to improve the visibility of the HLT sector, promoting cooperation, information exchange, and dissemination of research results. The former partners of the HLT Platform now meet in the board of the STEVIN programme. Within STEVIN, a substantial budget is allocated for 'accompanying measures', e.g. conferences, demonstration projects and network subsidies. The already existing cooperation is maintained and intensified through instruments that have proven to be successful, such as the STEVIN website, newsletters, conferences, workshops and seminars.

To narrow the gap between technology and the market and to address the end user conferences have been organized – a Dutch-Flemish counterpart of LangTech (2002 in Berlin, 2003 in Paris) – in the Taal in Bedrijf (intentionally ambiguous between "Language in Business" and "Language in Action") series, to bring together HLT and related-fields companies, as well as current and potential users of speech and language technologies. To attract as many different potential professional users of HLT as possible, business cases from sectors such as media, education, health care, transportation and logistics, tourism and recreation, public administration, telecom, and finance were presented.

To set an example of successful HLT applications and thus stimulate the demand of Dutch HLT applications, so-called **demonstration projects** were funded within STEVIN.

Essential characteristics of such projects are that they make use of "proven technology", that they try to access new markets for already established products or that they port established technologies to new domains. In total, 14 demonstration projects have been funded, which vary from a spoken dialogue system to optimize information provision to citizens and a speech-driven license plate retrieval tool for the police, to an auditory training system for children wearing cochlear implants.

To enhance the visibility of HLT among students and to attract them to HLT, three **educational projects** were funded aimed at making students between the age of 15 and 20 aware of the possibilities of language and speech technologies. In addition, **masterclasses** were organised on the following two topics: a) HLT and Dislexia and b) HLT for government bodies and public services.

4.2.4 Evaluations of the STEVIN programme

To be able to measure the impact of the STEVIN programme on the HLT sector, a benchmark study was carried out at the onset of the programme to establish a baseline for evaluation. In 2008, a scientific midterm programme review was carried out by the STEVIN International Assessment Panel (Spyns/D'Halleweyn 2010).

In 2010 the STEVIN Programme Committee conducted an internal evaluation of the programme, while a final evaluation of STEVIN was carried out by an external agency, the Technopolis Group (for further details, see www.stevin-tst.org/programma/#evaluaties).

The evaluations indicated that STEVIN largely achieved its goals, but this does not imply that all target areas are now fully covered. Owing to budgetary and timing constraints not all areas could be addressed, but the various projects and activities are an excellent concrete and justified translation of the STEVIN objectives. The programme has also managed to address the various target groups: companies and knowledge institutes in the Netherlands and Flanders. Other findings will be discussed in the section on Lessons Learned further on in this paper.

4.3 The HLT Agency

4.3.1 A central repository for digital Dutch language resources

The HLT Agency is a central repository for digital language resources based within an existing language planning institute of major importance, i.e. the Instituut voor Nederlandse Lexicologie (INL, Institute for Dutch Lexicology).

The resources that are developed within the STEVIN programme are subsequently handed over to the HLT Agency which takes care of their future lifecycle. This is a completely different situation from the one existing before the HLT Agency was established. At that time it was not uncommon that official bodies such as ministries and research organisations financed the development of LRs and no longer felt responsible for what should happen to those materials once the projects were completed. However, materials that are not maintained quickly lose value. Moreover, unclear intellectual property right (IPR) arrangements can create difficulties for exploitation.

To ensure that HLT resources developed with public funding become available for interested users (academia and companies) the Nederlandse Taalunie, as the owner of a number of these resources, took the initiative to set up the HLT Agency. The aim was to combine the infrastructures required for different projects, thus reducing the costs for equipment, data, software, licences, experts, and personnel, and at the same time to ensure optimal visibility and accessibility by offering resources through a one-stop-shop supplier.

In addition, to prevent HLT resources developed with public funding from lying unused on the shelf, it is necessary to make sure that they stay usable, which may entail debugging or updating to new platforms. All these activities concerning management, maintenance and distribution are carried out by the HLT Agency, which is hosted by the Institute for Dutch Lexicology. Further information on the activities of the HLT Agency, has been provided in previous publications (Beeken/van der Kamp 2004; Boekestein et. al 2006; Van Veenendaal et al. 2010).

4.3.2 IPR Issues

To enable the use and re-use of the results produced by STEVIN projects, a particular IPR-arrangement has been set up. The materials (software, data etc.) must be handed over to the Dutch Language Union so they can be made available to third parties through the Dutch HLT Agency ('TST Centrale', www.tst.inl.nl). The Dutch HLT Agency helps resolve IPR issues, is responsible for the management, maintenance and distribution of materials, and also acts as a servicedesk. For this reason, the HLT Agency is involved in the evaluation and negotiation procedures concerning the STEVIN projects. Through these IPR arrangements it can be ensured that all developed resources will become available for the whole language community in the Netherlands and Flanders.

4.3.3 Evaluations of the HLT Agency

Although it is clear that the existence of the HTL Agency has considerable advantages, we are interested to know whether and how the services offered by the HTL Agency could be improved. To this end evaluations are regularly carried out.

In 2007 a three-fold evaluation was carried out consisting of a self evaluation by the HLT Agency, a digital user inquiry by the Dutch Language Union and interviews with a selected group of users, project partners and suppliers held by an external evaluation committee. The main results of the evaluation were incorporated by the HLT Agency in a plan for improvement. The main focus was on increasing the visibility of the Agency in the field and improving collaboration and communication with suppliers and project partners.

In 2010 a similar evaluation was carried out which again indicated that a central repository for the maintenance and distribution of available Dutch language resources is highly appreciated, that IPR issues deserve continuous attention in the future, and that marketing strategies should be developed to stimulate the re-use of available resources.

These evaluations are also important to keep partners and users involved and to stay informed about the needs of the field. Other findings will be discussed in the section on Lessons Learned further on in this paper.

4.4 The European Dimension

While it should have become clear by now that the DLU stands for the Dutch language, it is also important to point out that it does not operate in a vacuum, but rather in a complex, multilingual context. As a consequence, the DLU is also concerned with the relationship between the Dutch language and other languages and/or language varieties. This is particularly important in the field of HLT and the DLU has been involved in European HLT initiatives from the early stages of its commitment to HLT. For this reason, the DLU has participated in projects such as Euromap and ENABLER and is now involved in FLaReNeT, CLARIN-EU, the CLARIN-ERIC and META-NET. In addition, since 2000 the DLU has been presenting its HLT policies and results at the various LREC conferences (Cucchiarini et al. 2000; Cucchiarini/D'Halleweyn 2002, 2004; D'Halleweyn et al. 2006; Spyns et al. 2008; Spyns/D'Halleweyn 2010; Van Veenendaal et al. 2010).

5. DLU HLT Policy: Lessons Learned and Future Perspectives

In the Introduction we mentioned two important questions we would address in this paper:

(a) What can be learned from the Dutch language experience?

(b) How could national language resources be integrated into a multilingual technical language infrastructure?

In this section we attempt to answer these questions.

5.1 Lessons Learned

The general impression is that the HLT approach that has been adopted in the Dutch language area has been successful in many respects. The Dutch-Flemish cross-border cooperation within the STEVIN Programme and the HLT Agency has significantly contributed to building a full-fledged Dutch language technology infrastructure. The comprehensive approach that combines stimulating research and development, creating a landing site for the results, and raising awareness of these results among prospective users has turned out to be fruitful and effective. Also the co-operation between government, academia and industry appeared to be successful and the recommendation is that it should be intensified in future initiatives.

The implementation of the STEVIN programme with a Board, a Programme Committee, an International Advisory Panel and a Programme Office might have seemed somewhat heavy at first sight, but in fact it has provided a sound structure for dividing responsibilities and making conscientious decisions.

The availability and maintenance of the developed resources through one central repository, the HLT Agency, is highly appreciated and strongly encouraged in the future.

IPR issues have properly been taken care of, but deserve continuous attention in the future. In this respect we would like to stress that the importance of IPR issues cannot be overestimated. They play a crucial role and should be properly covered through the whole lifecycle of languages resources, from their creation to their distribution. In our initiatives we noticed that sometimes it can be very difficult to explain this to providers of language material or potential users. For instance, the rationale behind the condition that materials developed in STEVIN projects (software, data etc.) should be handed over to the Dutch Language Union was purely to ensure that these materials would become available to the whole language community. However, this was often misinterpreted as being a specific requirement of the DLU for its own benefit, which of course was not. In addition, when dealing with IPR issues, it is necessary to take account of requirements and desiderata from various stakeholders in the language community, for instance also those of industry.

Finally, another lesson we have learned is the importance of the European dimension when dealing with HLT. Operating in a European context is important to meet with important HLT stakeholders in the various European countries to exchange ideas and best practices, coordinate efforts, reach consensus, and involve the community at large.

In addition, through European cooperation it is possible to create shared multilingual repositories of language data, metadata and tools by linking and aligning already existing resources in various languages, thus promoting the re-use of resources and improving sustainability and portability of language materials and technologies. This form of exchange can facilitate not only the production of multilingual language resources, but also the development of advanced technologies and innovative services in multiple languages.

European projects like Euromap, ENABLER, FLaReNeT, and more specifically CLARIN-EU and META-NET are good examples of how this can be achieved.

CLARIN (www.clarin.eu/external/) aims at facilitating research in the Social Sciences and Humanities by creating an innovative research infrastructure for e-Research and e-Science which employs language and speech technologies and data that are accessible and interoperable. META-NET (www.meta-net.eu/) with its initiative META-SHARE, aims at establishing a sustainable network of repositories of language resources, tools, web services with the corresponding metadata which can be made available for uniform search and access to eventually create a language technology marketplace for HLT researchers and developers, language professionals, and commercial players (see contribution by Uszkoreit, this volume).

For these reasons, the Dutch Language Union intends to take part in the CLARIN ERIC and will continue participating in and contributing to interesting European HLT initiatives like those mentioned above, either directly or indirectly through the HLT Agency.

5.2 Future Perspectives

A number of field studies were carried out by the Dutch Language Union to investigate new sectors in which HLT could play an important role. The surveys looked into the specific needs of different sectors and target groups particularly related to DLU policy such as Dutch language education, public administration and people with communicative disabilities.

A first study, Human language technologies and communicative disabilities, was carried out in 2005 (Rietveld/Stolte 2005). It was aimed at identifying the specific HLT-based tools that language users with communicative disabilities require to improve their communication capabilities, i.e. tools that assist verbal dialogue, reading and writing, and communication with machines. The long-term goal is to try to improve the position of these specific groups of users of Dutch. The study showed a world of very diverse desires, requirements, and possibilities – which helped explain why communicative disabilities arouse so little interest in the business sector. The diversity of disorders and requirements makes it impossible to develop products that everyone can use.

In 2009 a second study was conducted to determine how the development of HLT applications for people with communicative disabilities could be stimulated (Ruiter et al. 2010). Similar studies were carried out for the education sector and government organizations. The results of these investigations will be used as a basis to shape our HLT policy in the coming years.

In addition, we have being exploring the possibilities for a new Dutch-Flemish HLT programme that should address fundamental research, strategic research and application-oriented research and at the same time promote the re-use and re-purposing of available language resources and technologies for the Dutch language.

6. Concluding Remarks

In this paper we have outlined the HLT policy that has been developed and adopted in the Dutch language area by the Dutch Language Union together with a number of crucial Dutch and Flemish partners. We have explained the vision, rationale, approach and results of this 10-year endeavour. We hope that our efforts in developing a model to make a language "technology-ready" and the lessons we have learned from this experience may prove useful to other language communities that face the challenge of surviving in the digital era.

7. Acknowledgements

We would like to express our gratitude to our colleagues of the Dutch Language Union, the HLT Agency and the whole STEVIN team for their valuable cooperation

8. References

Beeken, J.C./van der Kamp, P. (2004): The Centre for Dutch Language and Speech Technology (TST Centre). In: Lino, M.T./Xavier, M.F./Ferreira, F./Costa, R./Silva, R. (eds.): *Proceedings of the 4th International Conference on Language Resources and Evaluation.* Paris: ELRA, 555-558.

Binnenpoorte, D./Cucchiarini, C./D'Halleweyn, E./Sturm, J./de Vriend, F. (2002): *Towards a roadmap for Human Language Technologies: the Dutch-Flemish experience. Proceedings of LREC2002.* Las Palmas de Gran Canaria.

Boekestein, M./Depoorter, G./van Veenendaal, R. (2006): Functioning of the Centre for Dutch Language and Speech Technology. In: *Proceedings of the 5th International Conference of Language Resources.* Genoa: LREC, 2303-2306.

Cucchiarini, C./Daelemans, W./Strik, H. (2001): *Strengthening the Dutch Language and Speech Technology Infrastructure, notes from the Cocosda Workshop 2001, Aalborg, 2 Sept. 2001.* 110-113.

Cucchiarini, C./D'Halleweyn, E. (2002): *A Human Language Technologies Platform for the Dutch language: awareness, management, maintenance and distribution.* Proceedings of LREC 2002, Canary Islands, Spain.

Cucchiarini, C./D'Halleweyn, E. (2004): The new Dutch-Flemish HLT Programme: a concerted effort to stimulate the HLT sector. In: *Proceedings of LREC 2004, Lisbon, Portugal*. 105-108.

Cucchiarini, C./Van Hoorde, J./D'Halleweyn, E. (2000): NL-Translex: Machine Translation for Dutch. In: *Proceedings of LREC 2000, Athens, Greece*. 1775-1780.

D'Halleweyn, E./Odijk, J./Teunissen, L./Cucchiarini, C. (2006): The Dutch-Flemish HLT Programme STEVIN: Essential Speech and Language Technology Resources. In: *Proceedings of LREC 2006, Genoa, Italy*. 761-766.

Rietveld, T./Stolte, I. (2005): *Taal- en spraaktechnologie en communicatieve beperkingen*. Den Haag: Nederlandse Taalunie.

Ruiter, M./Rietveld, T./Cucchiarini, C./Krahmer, E./Strik, H. (2010): Human Language Technology and communicative disabilities: requirements and possibilities for the future. In: *Proceedings of the 7th International Conference on Language Resources and Evaluation (LREC 2010), Valletta, Malta*. 2839-2846.

Spyns, P./D'Halleweyn, E./Cucchiarini, C. (2008): The Dutch-Flemish comprehensive approach to HLT stimulation and innovation: STEVIN, HLT Agency and beyond. In: *Proceedings of the 6th International Conference on Language Resources and Evaluation, Marrakesh, Morocco*. 1511-1517.

Spyns, P./D'Halleweyn, E. (2010): Flemish-Dutch HLT Policy: evolving to new forms of collaboration. In: *Proceedings of the 7th International Conference on Language Resources and Evaluation (LREC 2010), Valletta, Malta*. 2855-2862.

Van Veenendaal, R./Van Eerten, L./Cucchiarini, C. (2010): The Flemish-Dutch HLT Agency: a comprehensive approach to language resources lifecycle management & sustainability for the Dutch language. In: *Proceedings of the Workshop Language Resources: From Storyboard to Sustainability and LR Lifecylce Management at the 7th International Conference on Language Resources and Evaluation (LREC 2010), Valletta, Malta*. Valletta: LREC, 1-5.

Anna Dąbrowska / Tadeusz Piotrowski

Information Computer Technologies and the Polish language

Streszczenie

Technologie komputerowe i informatyczne stosowane są w Polsce przede wszystkim w celu korzystania z Internetu, komunikowania się, zdobywania informacji. Ich wykorzystanie bardziej specjalistyczne dopiero ostatnio staje się powszechniejsze dzięki zwiększającym się umiejętnościom użytkowników komputerów, aczkolwiek cały czas pozostawia to wiele do życzenia. Zasoby internetowe związane z tekstami w języku polskim to przede wszystkim korpusy tekstów współczesnych (np. Narodowy korpus języka polskiego tworzony dla Wielkiego słownika języka polskiego i niewielkie korpusy tworzone dla projektów naukowych, np. korpus błędów popełnianych przez cudzoziemców uczących sie języka polskiego) i historycznych (np. Cyfrowa Biblioteka Druków Ulotnych). W instytutach Polskiej Akademii Nauk czy też na Politechnice Wrocławskiej prowadzone są prace nad komputerową analizą współczesnego języka polskiego (analiza morfosyntaktyczna i semantyczna); istnieją też narzędzia kontrolujące pisownię, gramatykę i styl tekstu (Language Tool).

W ramach zachowania dziedzictwa narodowego zostało zdygitalizowanych wiele dawnych tekstów, w tym słowników i encyklopedii, dokumentów i dzieł literackich, historycznych opracowań naukowych (np. gramatyki języka polskiego). Polska Biblioteka Cyfrowa i Biblioteka Narodowa „Polona" oraz kilkanaście bibliotek regionalnych udostępniają w formie cyfrowej zbiory dzieł dotyczących Polski. Istnieją i coraz bardziej rozwijają się biblioteki cyfrowe, również rynek książek elektronicznych (e-booków). W zasobach internetowych nie ma, niestety, wielu informacji dotyczących samego języka polskiego (np. gramatyk, ćwiczeń gramatycznych i stylistycznych, innych pomocy dydaktycznych). Najobszerniejszym opracowaniem jest amatorska gramatyka G. Jagodzińskiego. Niewiele jest też możliwości nauki języka polskiego jako obcego.

Artykuł wspomina też w dużym skrócie wpływ narzędzi elektronicznych (komputera, telefonu komórkowego) na język polski, np. unikanie diakrytyków, wprowadzanie skrótów (wiąże się to również z wpływem języka angielskiego na współczesną polszczyznę).

Information computer technologies are commonly used in Poland for routine tasks, such as use of the Internet, and, as a result, for easy interpersonal communication or in using information services, such as library catalogues. More advanced technologies were earlier developed by computer specialist centres in Poland, but it is only fairly recently that their work has been known to the public at large, especially to linguists and other academics and non-academics dealing with Polish. This paper is a very brief survey of those technologies that can be potentially used by lay persons, who use resources and tools that are commonly known, i.e. in Poland predominantly on the Windows platform.

It also has to be said that the traditional divide between the humanities and the sciences is extremely sharp in Poland. As a result most arts students and scholars use computer technologies at a very basic level and are simply not aware of new possibilities opened up by them. This also results from the scope of studies, narrowed down to traditional "philological" courses. It follows from this that more advanced uses of text processing tools, for example, meet formidable psychological barriers, which can be seen in the facts that the establishment of large corpora of Polish started very late and that they are still not widely used. This also means that there are few studies that are based on corpus research.

Without any doubt the most important current resource, with accompanying suites of tools, is the National Corpus of Polish, which now contains more than 1.5 billion running (text) words (as on August 8, 2011). The corpus is being made for the Wielki Słownik Języka Polskiego (a large non-commercial academic dictionary of Polish), under preparation, and originally was a compilation of existing large corpora of several institutions, with the Instytut Języka Polskiego PAN as a coordinator. These institutions are Instytut Podstaw Informatyki PAN (Institute of Computer Sciences at Polish Academy of Sciences), Wydawnictwo Naukowe PWN (Polish Scientific Publishers PWN) and Zakład Językoznawstwa Komputerowego i Korpusowego, Instytut Filologii Angielskiej Uniwersytetu Łódzkiego (Department of Computational and Corpus Linguistics, English Department, the University of Łódź) (http://nkjp.pl/). At present the corpus can be described as opportunistic, though it aims at being in part at least representative. It contains a subcorpus of speech. The corpus is marked-up for inflection, by two schemes. The site has a working demo of the whole corpus, and, interestingly, it can be accessed from two subsites, each of which has texts with a different mark-up and different tools. One can use not only concordancing facilities, but also look up collocations or time profiles.

There are more specialist, small corpora worked on at various universities. One example is the corpus at Wrocław University (Polish Department), which collects errors made by students of Polish as a foreign language. It has 14,400 errors, recorded in typical sentential contexts. They are used in descriptions of those difficulties of Polish in grammar or in the lexicon that students have most problems with. This corpus is supplemented on a regular basis.

There is not much interest in corpora of historical periods of Polish. The most important one is the corpus of Old Polish (texts that can be dated from before 1500), which, unfortunately, contains only a selection of the most significant texts (Biblioteka Zabytków Polskiego Piśmiennictwa Średniowiecznego Instytucie Języka Polskiego PAN w Krakowie, 2006; http://kupujmy.eu/product_info.php?products_id=63). This is available on DVD-ROM, which contains both graphical images of the texts and the transliterated text, with the relevant editorial description. The transliteration can be also downloaded, free of charge, from the website of the Institute of Polish, Polish Academy of Sciences (http://www.ijp-pan.krakow.pl/index2.php?strona=korpus_tekst_star). Another historical corpus is Digital Library of Polish and Poland-Related News Pamphlets from the 16th to the 18th Century (http://cbdu.id.uw.edu.pl/cgi/set_lang?langid=en&fromurl=http://cbdu.id.uw.edu.pl/), which contains DjVu images (without the text layer) of texts in various languages.

As mentioned above, natural language processing has been studied in several centres in Poland. Linguists are perhaps better acquainted with The Linguistic Engineering Group in Warsaw (headed by Adam Przepiórkowski), which is part of the Department of Artificial Intelligence at the Institute of Computer Science, Polish Academy of Sciences and with The WrocUT Language Technology Group G4.19 (headed by Piasecki), at the Department of Artificial Intelligence, Institute of Informatics, Wroclaw University of Technology.

Both groups work on development of tools to process Polish and, specifically, the Warsaw group was one of the first to develop a large corpus of Polish, free of charge, and applications to process Polish texts. A number of them have been released on the GNU General Public License, including a powerful application to work with corpora, Poliqarp (http://poliqarp.sourceforge.net/), or a Polish morphosyntactic tagger, TaKIPI. Unfortunately, these cannot be used "off the shelf" as they often require programming skills. Therefore it is unlikely that they will exert any influence on the "traditional" linguistic community. The Wrocław group works on similar applications. They are initially concerned with developing a Polish WordNet, a network of lexical-semantic relations, and an electronic thesaurus with a structure modelled on that of the Princeton WordNet. In contrast to other WordNets, it is based on extraction of items related semantically from a corpus, and is also aimed at automatic language processing (http://plwordnet.pwr.wroc.pl/main/?lang=en).

The most widespread application used to work with text is Microsoft Word, which is most often used like a typewriter, even in very complex projects for which it is clearly not suitable (for example to compile dictionaries). Word is available with the suite of commonly used programs to help produce Polish text: a spelling checker, a thesaurus and a grammar and style checker. Macintosh computers also have a corresponding suite (when Microsoft Office is not used). While it is deplorable that Microsoft, thanks to questionable selling practices, managed to oust from the market native Polish applications, with their own correction tools, OpenOffice is gaining its share of the Polish market and it has its own standard linguistic tools for Polish. OpenOffice can be used with a powerful correction tool for several languages, which was developed in Poland: LanguageTool (www.languagetool.org/). It can be used for Polish, English, German, Russian, etc., and, apart from a spelling module, it is a style and grammar checker, exceeding the quality the (Microsoft) product for Polish. Moreover, it can be used for strictly linguistic tasks, such as the morphological tagging of a corpus, and it was in fact used for tagging the one billion word National Corpus of Polish.

The most widely known – and used – linguistic publication is a dictionary. At present most commercial general dictionaries, both monolingual and bilingual, are available in digital versions. This includes the largest contemporary dictionaries of Polish, such as *Uniwersalny słownik języka polskiego PWN*,[1] *Multimedialny* (*Inny słownik języka polskiego*[2]), and bilingual dictionaries, for example *Oxford-PWN* or *Nowy słownik Fundacji Kościuszkowskiej*[3] for English and Polish. Most often these dictionaries are offered both as standalone applications on DVD-ROMs and as paid up services on web pages (for a monolingual dictionary cf. http://usjp.pwn.pl/, for bilingual ones: http://oxford.pwn.pl/ or http://www.kosciuszkowski.org/). The largest publisher of dictionaries in Poland, PWN, also offers a number of simplified monolingual dictionaries online at http://sjp.pwn.pl/ http://so.pwn.pl. Simple monolingual and bilingual dictionaries can also be accessed by users of mobile networks.

It is quite interesting that apparently publishers do not want to issue digital versions of specialist dictionaries, for example those of synonyms, idioms, or collocations. One specialist dictionary of interest, especially to non-native speakers of Polish is *Słownik gra-*

---

1 Ed. by Stanisław Dubisz, Warszawa: PWN 2003; CD-ROM.
2 Ed. by Mirosław Bańko, Warszawa: PWN 2000; CD-ROM.
3 Ed. by Jacek Fisiak et al., Kraków: Universitas 2008.

matyczny języka polskiego[4] on CD-ROM, which includes inflection patterns and all inflectional forms of most words in Polish (with about 244,000 entries it is perhaps the largest list of contemporary Polish lexemes; cf. http://sgjp.pl/).

Dictionaries also play an important role in the projects of digital preservation of the national heritage and at present most significant historic Polish dictionaries and encyclopaedias can be accessed on Internet pages, at least in part. Because there is little cooperation between various libraries and individuals interested in digital storage, some of these are available in several copies, for example the monumental encyclopedia of geographical entities, *Słownik geograficzny Królestwa Polskiego i innych krajów słowiańskich*,[5] or the first monolingual dictionary of Polish, which is in fact also a multilingual translation dictionary, in six volumes, *Słownik języka polskiego* by Linde[6] (the above dictionaries at http://poliqarp.wbl.klf.uw.edu.pl/). Other notable nineteenth century dictionaries are: *Słownik warszawski*[7] (http://poliqarp.wbl.klf.uw.edu.pl/), still the largest Polish dictionary and *Słownik wileński*[8] (http://swil.zozlak.org/?prototyp=). Most of the pages at the sites referred to do not contain only images, but their text can be searched and concordances generated.

In addition, contemporary historical dictionaries, of various periods, are either being transferred to the digital medium, such as the huge unfinished dictionary of the 16th century, *Słownik polszczyzny XVI wieku*[9] (http://poliqarp.wbl.klf.uw.edu.pl/slownik-polszczyzny-xvi-wieku/ or http://kpbc.umk.pl/publication/17781), or are compiled from scratch in the digital medium (the one of the 17th and the 18th centuries, at http://xvii-wiek.ijp-pan.krakow.pl/pan_klient/). On the other hand, the most significant dictionary of the 20th century, edited by Witold Doroszewski,[10] was available for some time only on CD-ROM as low-quality images of pages because of unsolved copyright issues. Apparently there is not much interest in the digitization of other metalinguistic books, such as grammars, with the exception of historic nineteenth century texts, for example *Gramatyka* by Onufry Kopczyński (http://babel.hathitrust.org/cgi/pt?id=nyp.33433016467197) or those by Józef Muczkowski (http://babel.hathitrust.org/cgi/pt?id=uc1.b86970).

Dictionaries can be found at digital libraries, which in general collect significant texts in Polish or relating to Poland. After a period of uncontrolled development, work on digitization is now coordinated on a national scale by librarians. There are at least several dozen digital libraries in Poland, two national in scope (Polska Biblioteka Internetowa, www.pbi.edu.pl/index.html and Cyfrowa Biblioteka Narodowa "Polona", www.polona.pl/dlibra), nine regional ones, most often hosted by university libraries, and numerous local ones (cf. www.bg.umcs.lublin.pl/nowa/literat.php). A number of projects are under way.

---

4 Saloni, Z./Gruszczyński, W./Woliński, M./Wołosz, R. (2007): *Słownik gramatyczny języka polskiego*, Warszawa: Wiedza Powszechna.

5 T. 1-15, pod red. Filipa Sulimirskiego, Bronisława Chlebowskiego, Władysława Walewskiego, Warszawa (1880-1914).

6 Samuel Bogumił Linde (1807-1814): *Słownik języka polskiego*, t. 1-6. Warszawa.

7 A widely used name for: Karłowicz, J./Kryński, A./Niedźwiedzki, W. (1900-1927): *Słownik języka polskiego*, t. 1-8. Warszawa.

8 A widely used name for: *Słownik języka polskiego* (1861), t. 1-2. Wilno: Wyd. Maurycy Orgelbrand.

9 *Słownik polszczyzny XVI wieku*, t. I-XXXIV (1966-). Wrocław/Warszawa: Ossolineum and Instytut Badań Literackich PAN.

10 Doroszewski, W. (ed.) (1958-1969): *Słownik języka polskiego*, v. 1-12. Warszawa: PWN.

There is an agreed de facto standard of software in Poland, so called dLibra Digital Library Framework, developed since 1999 locally in Poznań, and based on DjVu technology, which uses graphical images, with an optional text layer. A number of libraries use this platform (cf. Digital Library of Wielkopolska, www.wbc.poznan.pl/dlibra). While there are more and more texts available in digital libraries (the Wielkopolska Library has more than 100,000 items), their quality, especially metadata, leaves much to be desired. Thanks to the interest in mobile access to digital texts, several companies now offer their own ebooks and sell dedicated readers (cf. www.eclicto.pl/ or www.empik.com/ebooki).

At present the Internet is very often the first and the most important source of information about a topic, and it is interesting what one can find there about the Polish language. Unfortunately, there is not so much informational content (if one does not take into account general reference works, such as Wikipedia), most web pages are in Polish and have been created by non-specialists, who often have a prescriptivist attitude to their language. In what follows we will disregard pages created by non-native Polish specialists, such as the one by Oscar Swan, the University of Pittsburgh (http://polish.slavic.pitt.edu/), which contains, for example, a course on Polish, a grammar and a bilingual dictionary, which can be downloaded free of charge.

A traditional grammar, quite detailed, in Polish and English, was written by Grzegorz Jagodziński, a biologist; it can be found at http://grzegorj.private.pl/gram/pl/gram00.html. It contains also reviews and various thoughts on linguistic matters. While there are practically no serious descriptions of Polish, there are a number of linguistic counselling services (poradnie językowe), which answer questions about "correct usage" on the web. They evolved from phone services and are usually run by universities or publishers (a tentative list of those services can be found at www.poradniajezykowa.us.edu.pl/index.php?action=inne_por).

What can usually be found on the web, in Polish, is various descriptions of particular points or areas in the language,[11] usually aimed at students from primary or secondary schools; they are often called *cribs*.[12] One can also find notes for exams in descriptive grammar (http://gramatyka.wordpress.com/home/). As usual, their value is uneven.

There is a survey of Polish rural dialects on the web, produced by specialists in the field, with descriptions of dialects, examples of texts and recordings (www.gwarypolskie.uw.edu.pl/index.php?option=com_frontpage&Itemid=1). These pages are in Polish only.

A person who would like to learn Polish using web resources will not find rich resources. Courses that can be found are usually basic ones, and were predominantly created in international projects (e.g., www.oneness.vu.lt, www.slavic-net.org), some were created by non-specialists, for example the person mentioned above, Grzegorz Jagodziński, offers a very traditional course of Polish for beginners,[13] based on memorizing metalinguistic description. There are no courses for more advanced learners.

---

[11] For example: www.sciaga.pl/tekst/55419-56-imieslowy_sciaga, www.sciaga.pl.

[12] For example: http://www.bryk.pl/teksty/gimnazjum/j%C4%99zyk_polski/gramatyka/24908-podstawowe_wiadomo%C5%9Bci_z_gramatyki_j%C4%99zyka_polskiego.html, http://ruczjak.webpark.pl/gramatyka.htm.

[13] http://grzegorj.w.interia.pl/kurs/index.html.

On the Web page of the School of Polish Language and Culture, University of Silesia, one can find[14] some programs for teaching or testing skills in Polish: *Grampol* (for intermediate learners) and *Frazpol* (for teaching idiomatic expressions). To teach or practise spelling one can use applications for teaching native Polish children.[15]

While any change in a language is very slow, there are some tendencies that can be seen in the use of Polish under the influence of the computer, the Internet and mobile phones. These tendencies are seen above all in informal texts, and informal uses of the language. On formal occasions Polish text will have the features of pre-computer texts. One conspicuous tendency, in part inherited from the early stages in the development of both hardware and software, is the omission of Polish diacritics (for example, earlier text messages, i.e., SMSs, that used diacritics were far longer than those without them). However, at present there are no technical problems with diacritics and this tendency can be attributed to a certain fashion: diacritic-less text is probably considered to be more colloquial, more trendy, etc. While obviously loss of diacritics can lead to misunderstanding of the message, usually context, linguistic or non-linguistic, is sufficient for disambiguation.

Another tendency in economizing the written form occurs when sequences of characters are shortened – this is perhaps also motivated by more complex morphological and phonological changes in Polish – by a widespread use of clipping, in which typically only the final syllables are elided, and the resulting structure is disyllabic (e.g. *spokojnie* >*spoko*). Earlier clipping in Polish was not used very often. It can be found not only in single words but also in phrases (typically in highly conventional ones, e.g. *na razie*> *nara*). Also proper names can be affected by this process. The occurrence of other devices can be attributed to the influence of English, rather than computers, such as use of acronyms (often in English), emoticons, etc.

One important factor, which can exert a powerful influence on Polish speakers, results from various forms of social communication in the Internet, in which non-standard Polish is used. In writing Poles can use their linguistic creativity, which has been stifled in the predominantly highly prescriptive models used in schooling. They can also see that in fact they can quite efficiently communicate using those forms, in contrast to what prescriptivists usually say. Finally, non-standard forms can spread widely and quickly over the networks, thus perhaps accelerating language change.

References

Bień, J.S. (2006): Kilka przykładów dygitalizacji słowników. In: *Poradnik Językowy* 8, 5-63.

Godzic, W. (2000): Język w Internecie: czy piszemy to, co myślimy? In: Bralczyk, J./Mosiołek-Kłosińska, K. (ed.): *Język w mediach masowych*. Warszawa: Upowszechnianie Nauki – Oświata „UN-O", 178-185.

Grzenia, J. (2007): *Komunikacja językowa w Internecie*. Warszawa: Wydawnictwo Naukowe PWN.

---

[14] http://www.sjikp.us.edu.pl.

[15] Np. http://www.dyktanda.net/; http://www.tylkoprogramy.pl/ortografia.php.

Piotrowski, T. (2005): Digitization of Polish historic(al) dictionaries. In: *Преглед НЦД* (*Review of the National Center for Digitization*) 6, 4, 95-102. www.komunikacija.org.yu/komunikacija/casopisi/ncd/6/index_e.

Piotrowski, T./Szafran, K. (2005): The dictionary of Polish of the 16th c. and the computer: from paper to (structured) file. In: Kieler, F./Kiss, G./Pajs, J. (eds.): *Computational lexicography*. Budapest: Hungarian Academy of Science, 171-180.

Przepiórkowski, A./Górski, R.L./Lewandowska-Tomaszczyk, B./Łaziński, M. (2009): Narodowy Korpus Języka Polskiego. In: *Biuletyn PTJ*, LXV, 47-55.

Maria Gavrilidou / Penny Labropoulou / Stelios Piperidis

National Report on Language Technology in Greece

1. Introduction

The present document reports on Language Technology related activities in Greece. After a general introduction to LT and its benefits, it presents the evolution of the field in Greece and the current state of affairs, with an extensive reporting on Language Resources and Technologies developed for Greek. The report concludes with the presentation of ongoing infrastructural initiatives operating at the European level with the participation of Greek institutes.

2. Language Technology in use

Language Technology (LT, also referred to as Human Language Technology, HLT) covers a wide range of software components, data, tools and technologies, techniques and applications aimed at processing human natural language. Typical examples of such tools are tokenizers and sentence splitters, morphological analyzers, part of speech taggers and lemmatizers, syntactic analyzers, etc. The term Language Resources (LRs) denotes language data in digital format, usually of considerable size, for use by any type of research and development targeting linguistic study and language technology applications, as well as by all fields where language plays a critical role. Typical examples of LRs are spoken, written or multimodal/multimedia corpora, lexica, grammars, terminological thesauri or glossaries, ontologies etc. Nowadays, the term is extended to cover basic language processing tools used for the collection, preparation, annotation, management and deployment of LRs.

The change of perspective from the native speaker's intuition to original data and the analysis of language in actual use has been a landmark in linguistic research. Language data collection had started as a tendency in the '50s, but was led to success by the dramatic improvements in hardware technology and the advent of the web. Besides the constant need for general language and domain specific data, technologies that help quickly and efficiently analyze huge bulks of data are of critical importance.

LT is a valuable aid in many fields where research is based on language material, whether language is the object of research or the means that carries information for the research; even simple procedures such as the compilation of the list of words of a given text and its comparison with the word-list of a general language corpus can lead to insightful observations which would be missed by traditional methodologies. LT reduces the amount of time needed for the initial processing of the research material, leaving, thus, more time to researchers for the qualitative and interpretative processing of the data. Additionally, the use of LT facilitates access to secondary material, such as literature on the research subject (e.g. intelligent full-text search aiming to locate specific sections of interest).

Most importantly, LT can play a crucial role serving the needs of laymen in all aspects of their everyday life, as it enables communication across languages, and increases access to information and knowledge for users of any language. For instance, the use of LT in the access of language resources offers many advantages to the public: natural language queries are friendlier to the lay user than specialized interfaces; machine translation systems integrated in search engines produce a rough translation ("gisting translation") allowing the users to have an idea about the content of a foreign language text, although they are usually unable to convey a complete understanding of it. It is also clear, however, that not all LT tools and applications are mature enough to provide high-level services and in a user-friendly way.

3. Historical overview of LT in Greece

Greece has a thirty-year tradition in LT research and development, starting with the EUROTRA project in the mid-80's. EUROTRA was a very ambitious EU-funded project aiming to create a fully automatic high quality translation system for all of the originally seven and, later, nine European official languages. Although the project did not succeed in fulfilling the set goal, its main legacy (apart from the lexica and grammars produced) lies in the creation and training of groups of LT experts in all the involved countries.

At approximately the same time, EU-funded projects have inaugurated speech processing research in Greece, focusing on speech synthesis at first.

The decade 1990-2000 saw a critical increase in the amount of public funds invested in LT in the country, besides the EU funds. Several national programmes resulted in the creation of resources, tools and infrastructure as well as small and medium-scale applications in the field of language and speech processing. The results included text and speech databases, speech processing tools, Natural Language Processing tools, Machine Translation tools and systems, but also multimedia, LT-aware educational material for the teaching of Greek as mother tongue and foreign language. During the same years, infrastructural programmes catered for the introduction of this educational material in primary and secondary schools. Programmes with dedicated funding for resource creation resulted in the production of lexicographic material, such as computational lexica for HLT, mono-/bi-/multi-lingual multimedia dictionaries for human users, pedagogical dictionaries for Greek, terminological resources for various domains etc. A few medium- and large-scale EU infrastructural projects have also contributed to the development of monolingual resources (corpora and computational lexica) with common specifications for all EU official languages.

Through national funding, the development of the Hellenic National Corpus (HNC, http:// hnc.ilsp.gr) was made possible. HNC, accessible through the web via an interface designed for non-expert users, boosted research on linguistics, lexicology and lexicography as well as education.

These pioneer endeavours of the 90's have inspired the construction of new textual, speech, but also multimodal/multimedia resources, for general language as well as for specialized domains. Regarding general language text corpora, for instance, two endeavours, which saw the light in subsequent years (the first by the Centre for the Greek Language and the second by the University of Athens) made available more Greek language resources. Relevant initiatives and results are presented in the following section.

During the next decade, 2000-2010, the national programmes mainly addressed the wider sector of Information and Telecommunications Technologies, although specific activities targeted to LT have also been launched. Their objective was the development and enhancement of the LT infrastructure (e.g. creation of digital corpora and computational lexica) as well as applications in the general framework of human-machine interaction (e.g. voice-enabled dialogue systems for information extraction, intelligent human-machine interfaces, authoring aids, optical character recognition for manuscripts, automatic subtitling of multimedia content, multimedia search etc.). Obviously, the monolingual dimension was prominent in the nationally funded projects; a few bi-/multilingual resources and applications have also been produced, with English as the second language primarily. Additionally, bilateral cooperation programmes for the Balkan region have resulted in the creation of a set of resources and applications incorporating also languages from the area (Bulgarian, Serbian, Romanian, Albanian, etc.).

Recently, Greece has faced new challenges, as the volume of digital (textual and multimedia/multimodal) content has increased rapidly. Many digitization projects nationally funded, aiming at the preservation and the promotion of Greek cultural heritage, have created new requirements on the LT use and, thus, new impetus on related R&D. The results of these projects are (or will be) available over the Internet in the form of digital libraries. Researchers now have access to all types of data through their computers, but the amount of information available is so huge and so dispersed, that, without the appropriate tools, it becomes unmanageable. Furthermore, the use of language resources and tools is not extensive, not because of their quality, but because they are difficult to locate and sometimes even more difficult to use. In order to perform a specific task (e.g. to use a summarization tool, a morphological or syntactic analyzer, a speech synthesis tool etc.) the users have to know the exact tool needed and the organization or the person they need to contact in order to get the appropriate license, to review the terms of use, to download the tool or the data, to convert the format of the data to render it interoperable with the tool, to learn how to use it and so on. This situation can discourage the most dedicated researcher, let alone the ones that are not digitally literate and/or the general public that wishes to have access to digital cultural collections. Cultural informatics is a domain currently attracting LT interest.

As far as EU-funding on LT is concerned, the majority of projects currently on-going in Greece cater for application-oriented research in machine translation, information extraction, data mining, semantic web-based technologies, cognitive systems etc. Greek is not necessarily the focus of these projects, but one of the languages used as test-bed for the applications. As for data resources, the focus is on multilingual lexica and, more recently, on conceptual resources (e.g. ontologies, semantic lexica) as well as corpora; these resources are mainly domain-specific, given that most of the projects target small and medium-scale applications.

4. Current LT activities in Greece

Constant funding through national and EU sources as outlined in the previous section has resulted in a steady, increasing and dynamic evolution of LT research and development in Greece. Thus, human resources employed in the LT area have increased over the last few years, with the advent of new research groups and units in universities and research organizations dedicated to LT research. The private sector has also invested on LT; a small (but important for the dimensions of the country) number of private companies are active in the field, some of which are spin-off companies of research centres that engage in the areas of speech recognition and synthesis, machine translation, media monitoring, ePublishing, eLearning and intelligent content analysis.

A key parameter for the progress of LT has been its introduction in higher education: over the years it has been introduced in the form of modules in the curricula of under- and postgraduate studies in universities, in linguistics and technological departments alike (obviously taught from different perspectives); in addition, a post-graduate two-year interdepartmental course, summer schools and seminars dedicated to LT methodologies and applications constitute an important asset in the dissemination of LT know-how.

LT for a less-widely spoken language like Greek poses additional challenges. Notably, whereas some of the research and development work carried out in Greece is based on English data-sets and/or uses language-independent algorithms, the majority of the research endeavours has focused on Greek, attempting to model linguistic phenomena, to create Greek training data and to develop language-sensitive applications. This is reflected in the high number of research groups who are active in the country as well as abroad, trying to tackle language processing problems from the morphographemic and phonetic level to technological solutions for access to information and content.

In fact, LT research and development concerning the Greek language has spread over the years in a multitude of areas. Taking a closer look at the way it has evolved in Greece, we can discern the main driving forces: the LT domain per se (engaged in Natural Language Processing and speech related research), research in theoretical linguistics (mainly focusing on the analysis of written and spoken language), the use of LRs and LTs in language learning and, more recently, applications for the cultural domain. It is under this prism that we can explain the range and variety of research activities in which Greek LT researchers are involved.

As evidenced from the following summary, the community has moved on from the more "traditional" word/sentence-based research to new challenges (web content, various modalities, emotional language etc.). The following should be seen as points of interest rather than a full synopsis of all research activities of the LT community in Greece.

Important progress has been made in the *LR building domain*. The processes of manual collection, typing and/or OCRing, conversions from typeset material for the construction of corpora, manual selection and encoding for the construction of general language and domain specific lexica etc. are complemented and increasingly replaced by new methods and techniques. The development of (semi-)automatic tools catering for knowledge acquisition from various sources (texts, images, video etc.) are exploited for LR construction where possible: for instance, lemma and term extraction from mono and bi-/

multilingual text corpora, ontology building from textual content, web crawling methods used for spotting candidate texts for the construction of monolingual and bi-/multilingual corpora (both parallel and comparable), new OCRing methods for manuscripts. As a consequence, manual effort is more efficiently spent on the more challenging tasks (e.g. annotation with semantic and pragmatic information). Moreover, most of these techniques and methods are integrated in LT applications and systems serving end-user needs (e.g. keyword extractors for the automatic construction of indexes and thesauri to be used in accessing cultural collections).

As far as *speech* is concerned, both speech recognition and analysis are the objects of extensive research. Current interests of the community include voice interactive systems, speech-only user interfaces, speech synthesis from documents and web content, emotional speech synthesis, implementation of prosodic features etc., going even beyond speech to research on sound and music.

In the wider areas of *text mining, information extraction and knowledge acquisition*, the focus is on cross-lingual information retrieval, sentiment analysis, textual entailment and processing, automatic text categorization, text genre detection (including web genres), authorship attribution, spam filtering, multimedia information processing (image/video and/or audio processing for information extraction, automatic metadata extraction and fusion from various modalities), exploitation of cognitive modeling techniques, etc.

Natural language generation activities currently include research in document summarization, image-based summarization, user-adaptive management and presentation of information, monolingual and multilingual subtitling, question answering systems, spoken dialogue interaction etc.

Machine translation research addresses both aids for human translation (e.g. translation memories) and fully automatic machine translation (e.g. corpus-based machine translation approaches exploiting mono- and bi/multilingual corpora).

Developing *assistive technologies for disabled persons* (with visual and/or hearing impairments but also with learning difficulties) is the objective of several research groups in the country.

Finally, research into the use of LT for the benefit of the specialized public but also of the broad public is ongoing: for instance, in educational software and applications, authoring aids (e.g. spelling and style checkers, controlled language applications), eGovernment applications etc.

5. LRTs for the Greek language

As a result of the research efforts described above, there is a significant number of LRs for Modern Greek; most of these are available for educational and research purposes. More specifically:[1]

---

1 This section presents a synopsis of results from various surveys on LRT for Greek, the most recent of which has been conducted in the framework of the preparatory stage for the Greek counterpart of the CLARIN project (cf. section 6). The results of this survey can be found at www.clarin.gr/clarinmaps (site in Greek, accessed 29/3/2011).

- as far as *textual data* are concerned:
  - there are three *general language corpora* of considerable size, namely: (a) the Hellenic National Corpus (HNC, http://hnc.ilsp.gr/), which was compiled in the early 90's but continues to be enriched; it currently includes 47 million words solely of written texts from various sources and it can be accessed via a web interface; (b) the Corpus of Greek Texts (CGT, http://sek.edu.gr/index.php?en) comprising around 30 million texts, including transcribed oral texts; the corpus is available for downloading; and (c) the newspaper corpora of the Centre for the Greek Language, of a total of 10 million words, made available through the Portal for the Greek Language (http://www.greek-language.gr/greekLang/modern_greek/tools/corpora/index.html);
  - *domain specific corpora* of small and medium size, an important proportion of which are bi-/multilingual (with English as the most frequent other language), are also available via the internet and/or distributed by the creators, covering a wide range of domains (e.g. biomedicine, health, tourism, press, literature, academic speech etc.);
  - *dialectal* material that has been collected and transcribed in the framework of linguistic research activities;
  - an important number of *cultural text collections* has become available following a digitization programme funded by the Greek state over the last few years. Although most of these texts have been digitized as images and necessitate OCR processing in order to be fully processable by LT tools, the accompanying metadata descriptions can benefit from LT.
- *linguistically annotated resources* include aligned bi-/multilingual text corpora, aligned transcriptions of audio data and text data annotated with various types of linguistic information; the annotated text corpora include morpho-syntactically tagged ones, some of which are manually disambiguated and validated, a treebank and various corpora annotated with semantic information (e.g. ontological class, named entities, event type etc.); obviously, the deeper level annotations are manually performed while morpho-syntactic tagging is usually automatic;
- most recently, a small but increasingly significant number of *multimedia/multimodal resources* has been produced; most of these resources, mainly video with accompanying audio and/or text equivalents, have been annotated with various types of modality-dependent information (e.g. speaker turn, gesture annotation etc.), while their textual counterparts are also linguistically processed (e.g. morpho-syntactically, semantically tagged);
- as far as *lexical/conceptual resources* are concerned, there are a few bi-/trilingual lexica of small and medium size intended both for computer and human use, three large monolingual morphological computational lexica, various small-size computational lexica endowed with syntactic and semantic information, usually developed for specific applications (e.g. ontologies, lists of acronyms and named entities, lexica with event types, semantic classes etc.) and a number of terminological/domain-specific lexical resources (e.g. for biomedicine, science etc.);

- available LTs can be classified in two broad categories:
  - *tools and software components that can be used to manage and process resources* (e.g. grammar/lexicon authoring tools, annotators etc.): here, we include morpho-syntactic taggers, chunkers, dependency parsers, lemmatizers and stemmers, manual annotation aids for text and multimodal/multimedia resources, named entity recognizers, text aligners for bilingual texts etc.; most of these are available for academic research and can be accessed via the internet and/or by permission of the creators; some of these tools address the Greek language, either employing a lexical/corpus resource of Greek or having been developed by the use of statistical techniques on Greek training data; the use of these tools is primarily intended for LT research and applications but it can also be extended to serve needs of end users with appropriate tuning/customization (e.g. lemmatizers deployed to facilitate lemma-based search, named entity recognizers to mark person and place names etc.);
  - *LT applications/technologies/systems* that can be used *for the benefit of the end user*: here we include authoring aids (e.g. spelling and syntactic checkers), speech recognizers, speech synthesizers, statistical information extraction tools, term extractors, speech transcribers, language detectors, summarizers, machine translation tools, etc.

A significant set of LRTs catering for Greek Sign Language (multimedia lexica, corpora, terminological resources etc.) has been compiled during the last decade.

Finally, important digital text resources but also tools and systems (OCRing tools, morphosyntactic taggers etc.) for older variants of Greek (ancient, medieval, early modern Greek etc.) are at the heart of research projects in Greece as well as abroad (cf. Perseus, http://www.perseus.tufts.edu/hopper/ and TITUS, http://titus.fkidg1.uni-frankfurt.de/framee.htm?/search/query.htm#Etabelle, two large repositories including ancient Greek resources).

6. Current initiatives for the promotion of LT

In the previous sections, we have given an overview of the LT field in Greece and the LRs that exist for the Greek language. However, although it is obvious that the field has progressed a great deal in the last years, the impact and the significance of LT for research but also for everyday life has not actually reached crucial audiences, that is, researchers at large, the broad public and, last but not least, the policy makers. The main drawbacks are:

- fragmented scenery as regards the availability of LRs:
  - although most of these are supposedly available for research and/or educational purposes, they are mainly distributed through the creators themselves and quite often they are poorly "advertised" (i.e. dissemination of their existence is at best limited to specialized conferences); interested users have to search the internet in various web sites and/or communicate with all LT institutes to find the resources they need;
  - moreover, access and usage rights are not always clear, so, even when they find them, users are not sure if they can indeed use these LRs;

• finally, technical issues also need to be tackled before LRs are used: some resources can only be accessed through specific tools that users do not have; in other cases, the operation of the tools is scarcely documented and/or too difficult to be understood by LT illiterate users; or, even in cases where resources and relevant processing tools are both available, they are not compatible and require some customization.

The infrastructure that puts resources together and sustains them is still largely missing; interoperability of resources, tools and frameworks at the organizational, legal and technical levels has recently come to be recognized as perhaps the most pressing current need for language processing research.

– lack and/or improvements of specific tools and datasets: although most of the basic processing tools and data resources have been developed, there is still need for extensions, enrichment and/or improvements thereof and development of new ones, especially for higher level processing (e.g. semantic annotation, discourse processing, sentiment analysis, etc.); recording of existing tools and resources in surveys like the one presented here is the first step towards the solution of this problem; however, identification of the gaps and prioritization thereof in accordance to user needs must be made in a well organized way, as well as attracting the funds that will support their development.

Bridging the gap between the LRT community and the research community at large is the task of certain initiatives that have been launched lately at the European and at national levels. The European projects META-NET and CLARIN have the aim to prepare the ground and to provide the necessary infrastructure that will offer services based on LT to the research community and to the public. A third initiative, FLaReNet, on the other hand, has a different scope than the other two: it addresses the policy makers, its results being mainly recommendations based on extensive analysis of the field according to several parameters.

More specifically, META-NET (A Network of Excellence forging the Multilingual Europe Technology Alliance, www.meta-net.eu) is a Network of Excellence that brings together researchers, commercial technology providers, private and corporate LT users, language professionals and other information society stakeholders. It constitutes a concerted, substantial, continent-wide effort in LT research and engineering which aims to create an open distributed facility for the sharing and exchange of resources, to build bridges to relevant neighbouring technology fields, as well as to prepare the strategic research agenda of the field for the years to come.

META-NET is supporting these goals by pursuing three lines of action:

– fostering a dynamic and influential community around a shared vision and strategic research agenda (META-VISION),
– creating an open distributed facility for the sharing and exchange of resources (META-SHARE),
– building bridges to relevant neighbouring technology fields (META-RESEARCH).

META-SHARE is a sustainable network of repositories of language data, tools and related web services documented with high-quality metadata, aggregated in central inventories allowing for uniform search and access to resources. It targets existing but also new and emerging language data, tools and systems required for building and evaluating new technologies, products and services. In this respect, reuse, combination, repurposing and re-engineering of language data and tools play a crucial role. META-SHARE will eventually be an important component of a LT marketplace for HLT researchers and developers, language professionals (translators, interpreters, content and software localization experts, etc.), as well as for industrial players, especially SMEs, catering for the full development cycle of HLT, from research through to innovative products and services. META-SHARE will start by integrating nodes and centres represented by the partners of the META-NET consortium. It will gradually be extended to encompass additional nodes/centres and provide more functionality with the goal of turning into an as largely distributed infrastructure as possible.

Similar to META-NET but catering for the Social Sciences and Humanities researchers, the European project CLARIN (Common Language Resources and Technology Infrastructure, www.clarin.eu) is structured as a network of organizations that offer LRT for all European languages. It is a research infrastructure that aims to make LRs and LTs available though web services to researchers with little or no technical experience; services include all aspects of resource creation and use (technical, legal, administrative etc.).

When finalized, the infrastructure will constitute a platform on which

- LRT providers will be able to upload their resources and their technologies, to describe them according to a common metadata schema, to get help on legal issues such as licensing or property rights;
- LRT consumers (Social Sciences and Humanities researchers, users, developers, etc.) will profit from unified access to data and tools which physically might exist in different distributed repositories and will be able to: harvest metadata in the process of LRTs identification; browse samples or whole resources; sign usage licenses; save the resources on their computers; run a tool and save the results of the process etc.

The participation of Greece in this network will cater for the integration in the infrastructure of LRs and tools developed for the Greek language. Given that CLARIN will serve as a dynamic, constantly updated atlas of LRTs, it will constitute a valuable tool that will register the gaps that need to be tackled in what concerns the Greek language and that will evaluate the performance of the data and technologies offered for Greek in the domain of Social Sciences and Humanities.

In the framework of the national counterpart of the project, CLARIN-EL, a charting of the field has been initialized, which has recorded user needs and current practices, information on existing resources, tools, LRT organizations and research teams;[2] the national network has also been drafted. The vision of CLARIN-EL is to gather the resources and technologies that have been developed for Greek in one virtual repository and to transform them into web services which are characterized by interoperability, stability, accessibility and extensibility and which will be available to the users.

---

2 The results of the CLARIN-EL survey have fed the current report.

The mission of the third initiative that aims at the unification of the LRT scenery, FLaReNet (Fostering Language Resources Network, www.flarenet.eu) is to identify priorities as well as long-term strategic objectives and provide consensual recommendations in the form of a plan of action for EC, national organizations and industry. Its outcomes are essentially of directive nature, aimed at policy makers at all levels. FLaReNet analyses the sector along various dimensions: technical, scientific but also organizational, economic, political and legal. It aims to bring together major experts from different areas, reach consensus, make the community aware of the results and disseminate them in a fine-grained, pervasive way. Work in FLaReNet is inherently collaborative.

These concerting actions have as a goal to help the egression of LRT from the boundaries of the scientific domain and its percolation through other domains, including everyday life. They aspire to introduce the benefits of LRT use to the researcher but also to the lay-man, whose work, whether scientific or not, may be facilitated and accelerated and its quality enhanced. The active participation of Greek LT research institutes in these initiatives is of paramount importance to the progress of the field in the country.

Thibault Grouas

Présentation de la Recommandation "Langues et internet" du Forum des droits sur l'internet

Abstract

Internet Rights Forum is an organization supported by the French government, working on the rights and uses issues related to the Internet. Its mission is to inform the public and organize cooperation between public authorities, private companies and users on these subjects.

Through this cooperation process, the players have the opportunity to reach a consensus point on each subject, facilitating the respect of the adopted rules. It also allows the implementation of, in addition to State regulation (rules, laws, international agreements), new means coming from self regulation like best practices, technical means, efficient networks to share information, etc. This process does not aim at discrediting State intervention, as only states can transform the coregulation results into legal frameworks.

Internet Rights Forum began work on internet accessibility in 2007 and set up a dedicated workgroup with a sustainable development approach. It first focused on eAccessibility, and published its first Recommendation on that specific topic in 2008.[1] The next step of these works was focused on languages on the internet, which is another way to greatly enhance users accessibility on the internet.

In that regard, the Internet Rights Forum issued many recommendations[2] to the State, recommending a better use of 'plurilinguism': languages are in fact a very strong cultural and economic issue. The Internet Rights Forum recommended a complete reorganisation of the public translation services to implement the new objectives, amongst other recommendations.

The Internet Rights Forum also issued recommendations to private companies and end-users, some of them strategic or political, some of them technical. For instance, it recommended that the dot fr (*.fr*), operated by the French organization AFNIC, should be opened to non-ASCII characters and accept accented characters like *é*, *à*, *ô*, commonly used in the French language. It also recommended webmasters not to use pictures or flags to symbolize a language selection on a website, but the localized language name in full text.

The full text of the "Languages and the Internet" Recommendation is freely available on the Internet Rights Forum Website (French only): www.foruminternet.org/spip.php?action=redirect&id_article=2985.

Créé en 2001 avec le soutien des pouvoirs publics, le Forum des droits sur l'internet est un organisme indépendant de corégulation de l'internet. Il associe, dans une structure de gouvernance innovante, représentants de l'État, du secteur privé et de la société civile. Son domaine de compétence couvre l'ensemble des aspects de politique publique liés au développement de la société numérique sur le plan des contenus et des usages. Sans être un organe de supervision et dépourvu d'une capacité de décision en propre, le Forum assume cependant un rôle de facilitation.

1 Internet Rights Forum Recommendation on eAccessibility: www.foruminternet.org/spip.php?action=redirect&id_article=2809.

2 Internet Rights Forum Recommendation on Languages and the internet: www.foruminternet.org/spip.php?action=redirect&id_article=2985.

Une des missions premières du Forum des droits sur l'internet est d'organiser la concertation entre les acteurs de l'internet. Il s'agit de réunir en un lieu neutre et ouvert les acteurs du monde numérique pour fabriquer du consensus. Cet espace de dialogue permet notamment:

→ d'identifier les questions émergentes et de les porter à l'attention des différents acteurs;
– de faciliter les interactions et la concertation entre les différentes parties prenantes concernées par un sujet donné;
– de contribuer à l'élaboration de codes de conduite, de principes directeurs ou de cadres légaux relatifs au développement des réseaux numériques et à leur usage.

Dans le cadre de cette mission, le Forum a porté sa réflexion en 2007 sur le développement durable et ses interactions avec le monde numérique. Le groupe de travail consacré à l'étude de ces questions a, sur la demande de la Délégation interministérielle aux personnes handicapées (DIPH), rendu une première Recommandation relative à l'accessibilité numérique des sites internet en 2008.[3] L'accès à tous au patrimoine culturel, que constitue l'internet dans des conditions optimales, constitue l'un des piliers du développement de l'internet dans une optique de pérennité de l'information, et de qualité de l'accès à cette information.

La question de l'environnement culturel étant cruciale pour une politique de développement durable, la langue constitue assurément un sujet de préoccupation prioritaire, puisqu'elle est la première des expressions culturelles – un constat renforcé au sein de l'univers numérique. Le Forum a participé au premier symposium international sur le multilinguisme dans le cyberespace, qui s'est tenu à Barcelone en septembre 2009.[4] Il a permis de sensibiliser le public à ces questions et de créer un inventaire des outils et solutions disponibles. Il illustre l'impact de l'internet sur les réflexions liées au multilinguisme.

Le Forum a donc souhaité prolonger ces réflexions et s'est penché sur le sujet de la langue sur l'internet, qui est aussi un facteur majeur de l'accessibilité de tous aux contenus numériques puisque leur accessibilité passe non seulement par un respect attentif des différentes normes techniques et des recommandations pour l'accessibilité, mais aussi par une gestion linguistique des contenus adaptée aux publics qui sont visés. Plusieurs membres du Forum tels que l'Association française pour le nommage internet (AFNIC), l'association diversum ou encore le Centre national de recherche scientifique (CNRS) ont par ailleurs souligné leur intérêt pour ces travaux, et les pouvoirs publics ont largement soutenu cette initiative, notamment la Délégation générale à la langue française et aux langues de France (DGLFLF), qui a participé activement aux débats.

L'objectif principal poursuivi par le Forum dans ces travaux a été de montrer que la langue constituait un enjeu fortement stratégique en terme de rayonnement pour un pays, notamment pour la pensée scientifique, mais également un enjeu économique puissant

[3] Recommandation du Forum des droits sur l'internet "Internet et développement durable I : l'accessibilité des services de communication publique en ligne du secteur public": www.foruminternet.org/spip.php?action=redirect&id_article=2809.

[4] Site internet du Symposium international sur le multilinguisme dans le cyberespace: www.maayajo.org/spip.php?article103.

tant pour les nations que pour les acteurs économiques. C'est aussi bien sûr un enjeu culturel considérable, la langue permettant l'accès à l'information et les échanges entre les peuples.

Dans cette optique, le Forum a souhaité proposer aux pouvoirs publics des recommandations opérationnelles sur l'organisation du cadre juridique français et des services de l'administration pour une meilleure prise en compte des problématiques linguistiques. Il suggère ensuite aux acteurs privés une série de bonnes pratiques à suivre en matière de multilinguisme en ligne et de respect des normes techniques de l'internet, à partir des débats et des travaux du groupe de travail qui se sont déroulés au Forum entre février et novembre 2009. Ces recommandations visent à faciliter la mise en œuvre de bonnes pratiques linguistiques et du multilinguisme sur internet.

L'approche retenue par le Forum des droits sur l'internet dans ces travaux se veut résolument universelle et non pas focalisée sur le cadre national de la langue ou sur la défense de la seule langue française. Les problématiques qui y sont abordées et les recommandations qui en découlent ont donc vocation à nourrir la réflexion collective sur la langue bien au-delà de nos frontières, dans le cadre mondial que constitue l'internet.

Le Forum recommande notamment

→ une meilleure prise en compte de la langue comme enjeu stratégique, notamment par les pouvoirs publics en ce qui concerne la traduction des sites officiels, des normes juridiques, des publications scientifiques, des marchés publics et des standards techniques, afin d'assurer une meilleure visibilité à la pensée française;

→ la nécessité de mettre en place un véritable dispositif public de la traduction piloté au niveau interministériel et doté de compétences et de ressources plus étendues;

→ de valoriser l'effort national et communautaire de recherche sur les technologies de la langue et de mieux utiliser ces technologies dans le cadre de l'enseignement;

→ de consolider le dispositif d'enrichissement de la langue française en rationalisant son fonctionnement et en apportant diverses améliorations techniques à la plateforme FranceTerme;

→ de mettre en Suvre une plate-forme internet collaborative et ouverte à tous les internautes, dédiée à l'enrichissement de la langue française, la terminologie et la néologie, en articulation avec le dispositif existant;

→ de généraliser l'usage du jeu de caractères Unicode et ses normes d'encodage les plus récentes sur l'internet;

→ de permettre le dépôt de noms de domaines en caractères étendus ou "IDN" sur le domaine de tête *.fr*;

→ de réaliser une norme technique pour les claviers français;

→ pour les exploitants de sites internet, de veiller à un bon étiquetage des contenus publiés, de matérialiser le choix des langues par des liens en toutes lettres dans la langue parlée par ses locuteurs et de privilégier la neutralité de la page d'accueil.

Après dix mois de travaux en 2009, la Recommandation "Langues et internet", fruit du groupe de travail constitué autour de cette thématique, a été proposée pour avis aux membres du Forum. Elle a ensuite été adoptée par son conseil d'orientation le 22 décembre 2009 puis publiée en ligne sur le site internet du Forum,[5] où elle est librement accessible.

La communication du Forum autour de ces travaux a été prolongée par les membres de son groupe de travail, ce qui a permis une diffusion plus large dans les milieux spécialisés. Peu visible dans la presse généraliste et notamment chez les grands médias nationaux, elle a cependant été reprise de façon beaucoup plus marquée chez les professionnels et les spécialistes du sujet, comme dans les publications numériques liées au domaine culturel ou littéraire.

Les recommandations visant plus spécifiquement l'enseignement et le bon usage des technologies de la langue dans le cadre scolaire ont été les plus reprises sur l'internet, notamment dans les revues destinées au monde de l'Éducation (EducNet[6] par exemple). Sur ce point précis, il était recommandé d'améliorer l'apprentissage des outils linguistiques mis à disposition des élèves et, notamment, des correcteurs orthographiques et grammaticaux, qui peuvent faciliter le travail de relecture, mais en aucun cas le remplacer.

Cette présentation très synthétique ne reprend que certains des points les plus saillants de la Recommandation "Langues et internet". Pour la découvrir plus en détail, nous vous invitons à consulter le document en ligne à l'adresse suivante:

http://www.foruminternet.org/spip.php?action=redirect&id_article=2985

[5] Recommandation "Langues et internet" du 22 décembre 2009: www.foruminternet.org/spip.php?action=redirect&id_article=2985.

[6] La langue et internet :Recommandation du Forum des droits sur l'internet. L'éducation est concernée: www.educnet.education.fr/veille-education-numerique/janvier-2010/la-langue-et-internet-recommandation-du-forum-des-droits-sur-l-internet/.

Einar Meister

Human Language Technology developments in Estonia

Lühikokkuvõte

Eesti keel on üks väiksema kõnelejate arvuga keeli Euroopa Liidus ja seetõttu on keeletehnoloogiline arendustöö eesti keele jaoks majanduslikult ebaotstarbekas, kuid keele tuleviku seisukohast äärmiselt oluline. Keeletehnoloogia arendamiseks Eestis on käivitatud mitmeid ettevõtmisi. Uurimistöid alustati juba 1960ndatel aastatel ja tänaseks on keeletehnoloogia saavutanud tunnustatud positsiooni. Artikkel annab ülevaate keeletehnoloogia arengust Eestis keskendudes peamiselt riiklikule programmile "Eesti keele keeletehnoloogiline tugi (2006-2010)". Tutvustatakse programmi eesmärke, ülesehitust ja juhtimist ning mitmete projektide tulemusi. Lisaks käsitletakse aastateks 2011-2017 kavandatud keeletehnoloogia jätkuprogrammi, spetsialistide järelkasvu ning teadustulemuste rakendamisega seotud probleeme.

Abstract

Estonian is one of the smallest official languages in the EU and therefore in a less favourable position on the Human Language Technologies (HLT) market, although this is extremely important for survival of the language. To promote HLT developments in Estonia national initiatives have been undertaken. HLT research in Estonia was started in the early 1960s and by today has gained a recognized position. The paper gives an overview of developments in the field of HLT focussing on the National Programme for Estonian Language Technology (2006-2010). The management of the programme and projects covering different areas of language technology are introduced. In addition, the follow-up programme for 2011-2017 and the issues of human resources and cooperation with industry are discussed.

1. Introduction

Linguistic and cultural diversity are core values of the European Union protected by EU legislations as well as promoted by several funding instruments. The report "Human Language Technology for Europe" compiled within the TC-STAR project states that for Europe, Human Language Technology (HLT) is an economic, political and cultural necessity since the European Union is a multilingual society by design (Lazzari 2006). Despite the fact that all EU languages are declared equal, however, as the report states, there are primary, secondary and even tertiary languages of commercial relevance; especially languages with a small number of speakers are at a disadvantage. Indeed, the official languages of the EU differ to a great extent from the point of view of existing technological support as well as availability and diversity of reusable language resources. This unbalanced situation is a result of multiple factors including the strength and number of academic HLT research groups in different countries, differences in national-level funding (both the public sector and industry) for research and technology development, as well as the disadvantageous funding practice of recent EU Framework programmes where most funding went to commercially attractive languages; in addition, the subsidiarity principle does not allow EU funding schemes to offer more favourable opportunities for HLT development of smaller languages (Krauwer 2005, 2006).

In recent years, several EU-level activities have been initiated in order to promote the development and wider use of HLT, for example, the CLARIN project (www.clarin.eu) for creating a Europe-wide infrastructure for common language resources; the FLaReNet project (www.flarenet.ee) aiming at developing a common vision of the field of language resources and technologies and fostering a European strategy for consolidating the HLT sector; META-NET (www.meta-net.eu), a Network of Excellence building the Multilingual Europe Technology Alliance in order to join efforts towards furthering language technologies as a basis for the technological foundations of a multilingual European information society. Protecting the linguistic diversity and building the technological support for all official EU languages is certainly expensive (23 official languages, 506 language pairs) – the necessary investments should be shared with the European Commission and the Member States, in full agreement with the concept of "subsidiarity" (Mariani 2009).

In several EU countries diverse national level initiatives are undertaken in order to facilitate and coordinate research and development of HLT for national languages, e.g., in France (Mariani 2009), the Netherlands (Spyns/D'Halleweyn 2010; Odijk 2010), Sweden (Elenius et al. 2008), etc.; some effort has been made also for the languages without national state, e.g., Catalan (Melero et al. 2010).

In Estonia, the National Program for Estonian Language Technology (2006-2010) (NPELT) was launched in 2006. NPELT was a government supported funding initiative aimed at developing HLT for the Estonian language to the level that would allow functioning of Estonian in the modern information society. NPELT funded HLT-related R&D activities including the creation of reusable language resources and development of essential language-specific linguistic software (up to the working prototypes) as well as bringing the relevant language technology infrastructure up to date. The resources and prototypes funded by the national program are declared public. In 2011, the follow-up program for Estonian Language Technology for the years 2011-2017 was approved.

The current paper gives an overview of the HLT developments in Estonia starting with a retrospect from the 1960s, then NPELT (2006-2010) will be introduced and finally the perspectives of the HLT developments within the follow-up program for 2011-2017 will be discussed.

2. HLT evolution in Estonia[1]

HLT development in Estonia can be characterized as an evolutionary process starting in the early 1960s when the first machine translation experiments were carried out and the analysis of legal texts using a computer was initiated at the University of Tartu. In the same decade two research units were established in Tallinn – the laboratory of experimental phonetics at the Institute of Estonian Language and the research group on speech analysis and synthesis at the Institute of Cybernetics.

In the 1970s studies on speech recognition and human-machine dialogue modelling were initiated and the transition to computer-based production of dictionaries was started. Experimental studies in Estonian phonetics and developments in speech analysis and synthesis techniques allowed the building of microprocessor-controlled formant synthesizers to begin.

[1] The provided brief overview of the HLT evolution in Estonian does not claim to be exhaustive and unbiased, it is rather the author's personal (insider) view of the main processes and development trends.

In the 1980s several text-to-speech systems for Russian and Estonian were developed at the Institute of Cybernetics and at the Institute of Estonian Language and exploited as output devices in automated control systems or as message readers for the blind. The research group on computer linguistics at the University of Tartu was formed with the main focus of study on morphology, syntax, semantics and human-machine dialogue.

After 1991, when Estonia re-established its independence, the whole system of academic research structure in the country was reorganised and new financing schemes were introduced. The restructuring of the political and economic system was accompanied by a remarkable decrease in the number of academic personnel – several researchers and engineers moved to governmental institutions and business, especially to the IT sector, where a large number of SMEs was established.

For the academic groups in the HLT area surviving the reforms, new opportunities for international cooperation opened up in the mid-1990s – Estonian research groups were able to join several EU projects such as EuroWordNet, BABEL, GLOSSER, TELRI, TELRI-II, etc. In addition to different corpus projects (both text and speech) carried out in the 1990s, a number of electronic dictionaries were made available via the Internet and a speller for Estonian was developed and commercialized by Filosoft Ltd (a spin-off company of Tartu University).

In the first decade of the 2000s HLT research in Estonian made substantial progress – the scope of research was remarkably broadened, involving areas such as morphologic, syntactic and semantic analysis, lexical resources and tools, speech synthesis and recognition, dialogue models, information retrieval, machine translation, web-based access to different resources and tools, and the amount as well as diversity of different reusable speech and text resources increased significantly.

The progress in Estonian HLT in the last decades was achieved through activities of academic groups who in parallel with academic research put a lot of effort into explaining the role of HLT in the information society and the need for developing language-specific resources and software. A number of concerted initiatives were successful and resulted in funding of different research projects from nationwide programmes or promoted international cooperation in the HLT field, for example:

- the Estonian HLT programme supported by the Estonian Informatics Centre (1997-2000); within this programme the first Development Plan for Estonian Language Technology was compiled in 1999;
- the EU FP5 project eVikings II (2002-2005) contributed to the development of the Roadmap for Estonian HLT 2004-2011 (Meister/Vilo 2008);
- the national programme "Estonian Language and Cultural Heritage" (1999-2003) funded some HLT projects;
- the national programme "Estonian Language and National Memory" (2004-2008) had a specific sub-programme for Estonian HLT (2004-2005).

Not all initiatives were fully successful, for example, the application for the Centre of Excellence in HLT (2003) was successful in the first round but failed in the final round, and the application for the Estonian Language Technology Development Centre (2005) was accepted for financing, but failed due to withdrawal of the main industrial partner.

However, all these initiatives played an enlightening role among decision-makers and contributed to the forming of a positive attitude in the society as well as paving the way for the national HLT programme.

In 2004 the Development Strategy of the Estonian Language 2004-2010 was compiled by the Estonian Language Council and approved by the Estonian Government. It involved a chapter on Estonian HLT which served as a base for the development of the National Programme for Estonian Language Technology. The programme for 2006-2010 was compiled by the joint effort of local HLT experts and the Ministry of Science and Education and approved in 2006.

3. National Programme for Estonian Language Technology (2006-2010)

The National Programme for Estonian Language Technology (NPELT) was a government-supported funding initiative aimed at developing Estonian language resources and language-specific software (up to working prototypes) in order to enable Estonian to function in the modern information technology environment. NPELT involved two main action lines:

Action line 1 for supporting projects of reusable language resource collection, including different **text corpora** (written language corpus, multi-lingual parallel corpora, resources for interactive language learning, etc) and **speech corpora** (emotional speech, spontaneous speech, dialogues, L2 speech, radio news and talk shows, etc).

Action line 2 for research of **methods** and development of **software prototypes** in a wide range of HLT areas such as speech recognition and synthesis, machine translation, information retrieval, lexicographic tools, syntactic and semantic analysis, dialogue modelling, rule-based language software, variations in speech production and perception, etc.

3.1 Steering committee

The management of the programme was carried out by a steering committee of 9 members including HLT experts and representatives of the ministries, and a programme coordinator. The steering committee was responsible for the evaluation of project proposals and progress reports according to established criteria, making funding proposals, surveying the developments in the HLT field on the national and international scale, etc. General rules adopted by the committee included the following:

- financing of projects based on open competition,
- groups are requested to provide annual progress reports,
- evaluation of projects based on well-established criteria,
- international standards/formats need to be followed,
- the developed prototypes and language resources should be put in the public domain, only in exceptional circumstances access could be based on clear license agreements.

3.2 Project evaluation criteria

Two types of evaluation criteria were developed: (1) criteria for new project applications, and (2) criteria to assess the annual progress of on-going projects. The funding decision of a new project was based on the average ratings of eleven features (sub-criteria) including the relevance of the proposal in the context of the programme, methods applied to achieve the goals of the project, competence and experience of the project team, whether the results of the project were useful for other projects, etc. In the case of ongoing projects the evaluation was based on annual progress reports which had to provide detailed information on how well the project had proceeded; objective measures were applied where possible (mainly in the case of resource projects).

3.3 Financing of the programme

The programme was financed out of the government budget, in 2006 and 2007 ca 0.5 M€ per year, ca 1.1 M€ in 2008, and ca 0.8 M€ per year in 2009 and 2010. According to the guidelines of the programme, ca 33% of total financing was used for projects focussed on the development of language resources, and ca 66% for research and software development; administration costs were limited to ca 1%.

3.4 Funded projects

The number of funded projects was slightly increased from year to year: 2006 – 17 projects, 2007 – 20 projects, 2008 and 2009 – 23 projects, and 2010 – 24 projects. Most of the projects were long-term projects spanning the years from 2006 to 2010, but also a few short-term projects (1-2 years) were funded. The projects covered a wide range of topics and were carried out mainly by three key players working in the field of HLT (see www.keeletehnoloogia.ee/projects):

1. University of Tartu, represented by three groups: (1) Research Group on Computer Linguistics, (2) Phonetics, and (3) Bioinformatics. Their projects were focused on:
   - morphology, syntax, semantics, and machine translation,
   - corpora of written and spoken language, dialogue corpora, parallel corpora, lexical and semantic database (thesaurus, Estonian WordNet), phonetic corpus of spontaneous speech,
   - rule-based language software, information retrieval, interactive Web-based language learning.
2. Institute of the Estonian Language, represented by the Research Group on Language Technology, had three projects:
   - corpus-based speech synthesis for Estonian,
   - Estonian emotional speech corpus,
   - lexicographic tools.
3. Institute of Cybernetics at Tallinn University of Technology, represented by the Laboratory of Phonetics and Speech Technology, carried out three projects:
   - automatic speech recognition in Estonian,
   - variability issues in speech production and perception,
   - speech corpora including radio news and talk shows, lecture speech, foreign-accented speech.

In addition, there were other institutions and companies responsible for single projects:

- Tallinn University – Estonian Interlanguage Corpus,
- Estonian Literary Museum – electronic dictionary of idiomatic expressions,
- Filosoft – corpus query on the Estonian language website keeleveeb.ee,
- Eliko – prototype of a Controlled Natural Language module for knowledge-based systems.

3.5 Some project examples

3.5.1 Intelligent user interface for databases (University of Tartu)

The project was aimed at the development of a user interface which enables adaptation to different problem domains and access to different databases. Using minor readjustment, the interface can be tuned to new problem domains. Users enter their query in Estonian and get an answer also in Estonian, in form of a text or as synthesized speech. In the dialogue manager a general model for controlling information dialogues was implemented, which takes into account general regularities of practical dialogues. The Estonian dialogue corpus (Gerassimenko et al. 2008) served as a basic resource for modelling domain-specific conversations. Some other resources for processing of Estonian were integrated into the interface: morphological analysis and generation, spell checking and correction of erroneous forms, automatic recognition of named entities (proper nouns, temporal expressions), and text-to-speech synthesis. Two test applications, user interfaces to a movie schedule database and a dentist database have been developed (www.dialoogid.ee).

Some references: Treumuth (2010); Hennoste et al. (2009); Koit et al. (2009); Koit/Roosmaa/Õim (2009); Koit (2009).

3.5.2 Resources and software for syntactic analysis (University of Tartu)

Syntactic analysis is an important component in different HLT applications including automatic grammar correction, dialogue systems, automatic text summarization, machine translation, etc. The aim of the project was to develop a rule-based syntactic parser for Estonian (based on Constraint Grammar) and its implementations such as a grammar checker for written and spoken language and a prototype for automatic summarization of newspaper texts.

The developed parser gives a shallow surface oriented description of the sentence where every word is annotated with a tag corresponding to its syntactic function (in addition to morphological description). The prototype of grammar checker involves two modules: (1) morphological disambiguation, and (2) syntactic parsing. It gives ca 5% false alarms and misses about 7% of errors.

The prototype of automatic summarization implements different statistic and linguistic methods in order to find the sentences in a text which best represent the content of the analyzed text. The current version is tuned to process news texts on the web (http://lepo.it.da.ut.ee/~kaili/estsum/).

Some references: Lindström/Müürisep (2009); Müürisep/Nigol (2009); Müürisep/Nigol (2008a, b).

3.5.3 Corpus query on the Estonian language website keeleveeb.ee (Filosoft Ltd.)

To enable the use of the Estonian Reference Corpus (www.cl.ut.ee) via www.keeleveeb.ee a convenient query system, allowing the search for lemmas and morphosyntactic categories, was developed. The Estonian Reference Corpus (Kaalep et al. 2010) has been morphologically tagged and disambiguated and clause boundaries have been automatically tagged. The query system to this corpus makes use of all these tags, and in addition, it can be used in conjunction with queries to the dictionaries.

The language portal www.keeleveeb.ee hosts 30 specialised dictionaries, containing over 200,000 concepts. All these dictionaries can be queried simultaneously. In addition, the very same query can also obtain answers from 30 dictionaries hosted elsewhere on the Web, thus linking 60 dictionaries into a single virtual database.

3.5.4 Lexicographer's workbench (Institute of the Estonian Language)

In the project an interactive, web-based working environment for lexicographers was developed. The system called EELex represents a toolset for dictionary management implementing both universal and Estonian-based language resources and linguistic software. EELex makes dictionary work easier and faster, and raises its quality. The dictionaries compiled in or transferred to EELex represent universal reusable language resources with standard XML mark-up, necessary for lexicographers and language technologists. EELex takes care of formatting, punctuation, sorting, referencing, access rights to different sections of the entry and to different working stages etc. Nowadays all dictionaries produced by the Institute of the Estonian Language are compiled using EELex. In addition to the professional system, a public version of the system (http://exsa.eki.ee/) allows dictionary development via Internet for everyone.

Some references: Langemets et al. (2006, 2010).

3.5.5 Research and development of methods for Estonian speech recognition (Institute of Cybernetics at Tallinn University of Technology)

The project is focused on the research, development and testing of methods for Estonian speech recognition and the implementation of speech recognition prototype systems in different domains. The main tasks of the project involved (1) determining optimal basic lexical units for Estonian LVCSR (such as syllables, (pseudo-)morphemes, data-driven units), (2) developing statistical language modelling techniques using the determined lexical units, (3) applying of acoustic model adaptation techniques, (4) developing methods and algorithms for large/unlimited vocabulary speech recognition systems, (5) implementing speech recognition prototype systems.

Main outcomes:

- Complete system for large vocabulary speech recognition of long speech recordings, including speech/non-speech segmentation, speaker diarization, and multi-pass speech recognition, involving unsupervised adaptation techniques.
- Current word error rates: 14.3% for dictated broadcast news, 28.6% for broadcast conversations, 37.1% for conference presentations.

- Web interface (http://bark.phon.ioc.ee/tsab/) for browsing transcribed speech. Supports synchronized listening to speech and viewing its transcriptions, search in transcriptions, viewing related transcripts.
- Speech recognition system for the radiology domain, 9.8% WER with speaker independent models, faster than real time.

References: Alumäe/Kurimo (2010a, b); Ruokolainen/Alumäe/Dobrinkat (2010); Alumäe/Meister (2010); Alumäe, T. (2008).

3.5.6 Centre of Estonian Language Resources

In order to guarantee the availability of the language resources and software prototypes developed in different projects funded by NPELT a project for setting up the Centre of Estonian Language Resources at the University of Tartu was initiated in 2008.

Existing natural language resources can be used by different end users only if they are well documented, archived and publicly accessible. In order to achieve this goal there needs to be an infrastructure to manage and coordinate different activities, from elaborating the corresponding language technology standards to drawing up the contracts/licence agreements necessary for the use of these language resources.

On the European scale, the ESFRI project CLARIN (Common Language Resources and Technology Infrastructure, www.clarin.eu) aims at establishing the infrastructure for documenting, archiving and sharing common language resources. The University of Tartu is the official representative of Estonia among the 36 partners of CLARIN and the Centre of Estonian Language Resources should become a local node of the pan-European infrastructure.

It should guarantee that the existing language resources will not remain only at the disposal of the creators of these resources but will ultimately reach all the interested parties all over Europe, e.g. linguists, teachers, creators of software systems and their applications, civil servants, etc.

In 2010, the Centre of Estonian Language Resources was included in the list of objects of the Estonian Research Infrastructures Roadmap (approved by Government Order No 236 of June 17, 2010) (see https://www.etis.ee/portaal/includes/dokumendid/teekaart.pdf). The Centre is established and will act as a consortium including the University of Tartu, the Institute of Cybernetics at Tallinn University of Technology, and the Institute of the Estonian Language as the main partners.

4. National Programme for Estonian Language Technology (2011-2017)

NPELT 2006-2010 has been definitely successful and has resulted in a remarkable increase of the amount and diversity of language resources and language-specific prototypes. However, the quality and quantity of prototypes and resources is not yet sufficient to enable exploitation of the current technology in end user applications and e-services. Therefore, a follow-up programme was compiled in 2010 and approved by the Minister of Science and Education in January 2011. The follow-up programme is proposed for the period 2011-2017 and supports HLT activities in five action lines:

1. Research and development of language-specific methods and prototypes (speech synthesis and recognition, prosody models for speech synthesis, audiovisual speech synthesis, syntactic analysis adapted to spoken language, semantic analysis, dialogue management, dialogue systems for different domains, analysis of affective speech, tools for translation and terminology management, machine translation, etc.);
2. Development of reusable language resources (text, speech and multimodal corpora, electronic dictionaries and databases, corpus management and access systems, etc.);
3. Support for the Centre of Estonian Language Resources (standardization, licensing, quality control, archiving and documentation of language resources, etc.);
4. Integrated software and application (dialogue systems in specific domains, applications for users with special needs, computer-aided language learning, user interfaces to public services, etc.);
5. Specific projects carried out on demand of the steering committee or to fulfil public needs.

The two first action lines are similar to those of the previous programme; the third one was introduced to support the functioning of the Centre of Estonian Language Resources. Action lines 4 and 5 are new instruments introduced to extend the flexibility of funding schemes. The aim of action line 4 is to promote the use and integration of the existing language resources and prototypes into different applications demonstrating the possibilities of HLT. Action lines 1, 2 and 4 are of bottom-up type, i.e. project applications are proposed by eligible research groups or institutions and the steering committee makes funding decisions based on competition.

Action line 5 is a top-down scheme and is an instrument at the disposal of the steering committee to control the HLT developments more actively. Project tasks and technical requirements are defined by the steering committee or by a public authority and the best bid will be selected.

5. Development of human resources

In Estonia, there exists a critical mass of researchers and engineers working in different HLT areas, and the University of Tartu provides curricula in computational linguistics and in language technology. To improve the quality of doctoral studies in linguistics and language technology and to meet the growing need for HLT experts, the Doctoral School in Linguistics and Language Technology (DSLTT) was launched at Tartu University for 2005 to 2008. The activities of the school have strongly contributed to the effectiveness of many students' doctoral studies; about 10 PhD theses in HLT areas have been prepared and defended with DSLLT support.

In 2009, two new doctoral schools were launched for the period 2009-2015:

- **Doctoral School in Information and Communication Technologies** at Tallinn University of Technology – involves also HLT students from Tartu University;
- **Doctoral School in Linguistics, Philosophy and Semiotics** at Tartu University – involves also students of general linguistics with specialization in computer linguistics.

Estonian language technology researchers are also engaged in the Estonian centre of excellence called **Estonian eXcellence in Computer Science** (EXCS) to be financed over the period 2008-2015. The centre involves the research staff of the Institute of Cybernetics at Tallinn University of Technology, Cybernetica AS, and the University of Tartu representing a major part of the computer science research conducted in Estonia. The general objective of the centre of excellence is to consolidate and advance computer science in 6 areas of recognized strength: programming languages and systems, information security, software engineering, scientific and engineering computing, bioinformatics and human language technology. The specific objectives are to enhance the research potential of the groups by facilitating collaboration, to increase the impact of research results and popularize them in society, and to ensure the sustainability of the groups. This will be achieved by carefully planned coordination and joint actions, targeted at creating a thriving and highly reputed research environment attractive for young researchers.

However, there is a need to improve the study opportunities and attract more students in the speech processing field – currently no systematic teaching is provided in the area of speech analysis, synthesis and recognition.

6. Small and Medium Enterprises (SMEs)

The market situation in Estonia does not attract ICT companies' investments into language-specific HLT developments – there are only ca 1.4 million speakers of Estonian in the world. However, a few small private HLT companies exist:

- **Filosoft** (www.filosoft.ee) – a spin-off company of Tartu University established in 1993, provider of several software products (speller, hyphenator and thesaurus for Estonian, speller and hyphenator for Latvian) and dictionaries for several platforms (MS Windows, Mac OS X, Unix). The company runs the language portal Keeleveeb (www.keeleveeb.ee) offering free access to different on-line dictionaries, software and corpora.
- **Keelevara** (www.keelevara.ee) was founded in 2004 in order to provide on-line access to several professional electronic dictionaries and lexicons, access to some dictionaries is free.
- **Tilde Eesti** (www.tilde.ee) is a branch of the Latvian company Tilde (www.tilde.lv), established in 1991. Tilde's products cover localized fonts, Latvian and Lithuanian language support, proofing tools, electronic dictionaries, multimedia products, etc. Tilde Eesti is focused mainly on software localisation and translation services.

HLT developments in academic groups typically end up with a prototype which is not yet suitable for an end user application – product development needs a lot of additional work that is beyond the capabilities and interests of an academic researcher. There is a need for an intermediate unit between academy and industry, a development unit which is able to evolve a laboratory prototype into an applicable technology.

In Estonia the competence centres' programme was launched by Enterprise Estonia aiming to bridge the gap between scientific and economic innovation by providing a collective environment for academics, industry and other innovation actors. The competence centres are established as independent state supported research organizations. Two of eight existing competence centres are potential intermediary units able to carry out industry-oriented applied research and development in HLT field:

- Software Technology and Applications Competence Centre (STACC, established in 2009) – a joint initiative between the University of Tartu and Tallinn Technical University and the leading IT companies and users of Estonian software and knowledge-based technology (including e.g. Cybernetica AS, Regio AS, Webmedia AS, Logica Eesti AS, eHealth Foundation, Skype Technologies OÜ, Swedbank AS). STACC aims to conduct applied research in software technology by working with suppliers and users of technology; among other topics STACC is applying different language technology methods for the analysis of medical text corpora.
- Competence Centre in Electronics, Information and Communication Technologies ELIKO – established in 2004 by Tallinn University of Technology and private companies (including Artec Group OÜ, Apprise OÜ,Cybernetica AS, Modesat Communications, Regio AS, Smartdust Solutions OÜ, Smartimplant OÜ and others). ELIKO is focussing mainly on the development of complex embedded hardware and software systems, but has also done some research in the area of Controlled Natural Language.

It is expected that language resources and language-specific software prototypes developed within NPELT and within the follow-up programme and made available via the Centre of Estonian Language Resources will attract SMEs' and competence centres' interest, leading to the development of end users applications for Estonian market.

7. Summary

The national programme for 2006-2010 has resulted in a remarkable advancement in Estonian HLT. The programme has been successful and has fulfilled most of the expectations. The amount of written and spoken language resources and software prototypes as well as new knowledge and experience created in different projects have strengthened the technological bases for the development of innovative HLT-applications in coming years. To further the HLT progress in Estonia the follow-up programme for 2011-2017 has been launched. It is focused on the development of more advanced software prototypes and new languages resources as well as on the implementation and integration of the software prototypes in public services and commercial applications. The dedicated national initiatives together with international cooperation in EU networks such as CLARIN and META-NET, etc should contribute to the achievement of technological level which allows functioning of Estonian in the modern information society equally with big languages.

8. References

Alumäe, T. (2008): Comparison of different modeling units for language model adaptation for inflected languages. In: Gelbukh, A. (ed.): *Computational Linguistics and Intelligent Text Processing: 9th International Conference, CICLing 2008, Haifa, Israel, February 17-23, 2008. Proceedings*. (= Lecture Notes in Computer Science 4919). Berlin/Heidelberg/New York: Springer, 488-499.

Alumäe, T./Kurimo, M. (2010a): Efficient estimation of maximum entropy language models with N-gram features: an SRILM extension. In: *Proceedings of INTERSPEECH 2010 Spoken Language Processing for All: 26-30 September 2010*. Chiba: ISCA, 1820-1823.

Alumäe, T./Kurimo, M. (2010b). Domain adaptation of maximum entropy language models. In: *48th Annual Meeting of the Association for Computational Linguistics: Proceedings of the Conference, Workshops and Associated Events: Uppsala, Sweden, July 11-16, 2010*. Stroudsburg, PA: Association for Computational Linguistics, 301-306.

Alumäe, T./Meister, E. (2010): Estonian large vocabulary speech recognition system for radiology. In: Skadina, I./Vasiljevs, A. (eds.): *Human Language Technologies: The Baltic perspective. Proceedings of the Fourth International Conference Baltic HLT, Riga, Latvia, October 7-8, 2010*. (= Frontiers in Artificial Intelligence and Applications 219). Amsterdam: IOS Press, 33-38.

Elenius, K./Forsbom, E./Megyesi, B. (2008): Language resources and tools for Swedish: A survey. In: Calzolari, N. et al. (eds.): *Proceedings of the Sixth International Conference on Language Resources and Evaluation: May 26-June 1, 2008, Marrakech, Marocco*. Paris: European Language Resources Association.

Gerassimenko, O./Hennoste, T./Kasterpalu, R./Koit, M./Rääbis, A./Strandson, K./Valdisoo, M./ Vutt, E. (2008): Annotated dialogue corpus as a language resource: An overview of the Estonian Dialogue Corpus. In: Shirokov, V. (ed.): *Prikladna lingvistika ta lingvistichni tehnologii: Megaling 2007, Ukraina, september 2007*. Kiev: Dovira, 102-110.

Hennoste, T./Gerassimenko, O./Kasterpalu, R./Koit, M./Rääbis, A./Strandson, K. (2009): Towards an intelligent user interface: Strategies of giving and receiving phone numbers. In: Matoušek, Václav (ed.): *Text, Speech and Dialogue. Proceedings of the 12th International Conference, TSD 2009, Pilsen, Czech Republic, 13-17 September 2009*. (= Lecture Notes in Computer Science 5729). Berlin/Heidelberg/New York: Springer, 347-354.

Kaalep, H.-J./Muischnek, K./Uiboaed, K./Veskis, K. (2010): The Estonian Reference Corpus: Its composition and morphology-aware user interface. In: Skadina, I./Vasiljevs, A. (eds.): *Human Language Technologies: The Baltic perspective. Proceedings of the Fourth International Conference Baltic HLT, Riga, Latvia, October 7-8, 2010*. (= Frontiers in Artificial Intelligence and Applications 219). Amsterdam: IOS Press, 143-146.

Koit, M. (2009): Experiments on automatic recognition of dialogue acts. In: Karpov, A. (ed.): *Proceedings of SPECOM 2009: 13th International Conference Speech and Computer, St. Petersburg, 22-25 June 2009*. St. Petersburg: Institution of the Russian Academy of Sciences/ St. Petersburg Institute for Informatics and Automati, 533-538.

Koit, M./Gerassimenko, O./Kasterpalu, R./Rääbis, A./Strandson, K. (2009): Towards computer-human interaction in natural language. In: *International Journal of Computer Applications in Technology*, 34 (4), 291-297.

Koit, M./Roosmaa, T./Õim, H. (2009): Knowledge representation for human-machine interaction. In: Dietz, Jan L.G. (ed.): *Proceedings of the International Conference on Knowledge Engineering and Ontology Development, Madeira (Portugal), 6-8 October 2009*. Setubal: INSTICC, 396-399.

Krauwer, S. (2005): How to survive in a multilingual EU? In: Langemets, M./Penjam, P. (eds.): *Proceedings of The Second Baltic Conference on Human Language Technologies*. Tallinn: Institute of Cybernetics and Institute of the Estonian Language, 61-66.

Krauwer, S. (2006): *Strengthening the smaller languages in Europe. Proceedings of the 5th Slovenian and 1st International Language Technologies Conference, October 9-10, 2006, Ljubljana, Slovenia*. Internet: http://nl.ijs.si/is-ltc06/proc/01_Krauwer.pdf (accessed on 11.06.2007).

Langemets, M./Loopmann, A./Viks, Ü. (2006): The IEL dictionary management system of Estonian. In: de Schryver, G.-M. (ed.): *DWS 2006: Proceedings of the Fourth International Workshop on Dictionary Writing Systems: Pre-EURALEX workshop. Turin, 5th September 2006*. Turin: University of Turin, 11-16.

Langemets, M./Loopmann, A./Viks, Ü. (2010): Dictionary management system for bilingual dictionaries. In: Granger, S./Paquot, M. (eds.): *eLexicography in the 21st century: New challenges, new applications. Proceedings of eLex 2009, Louvain-la-Neuve, 22-24 October 2009*. Louvain-la-Neuve: Presses universitaires de Louvain, Cahiers du CENTAL, 425-430.

Lazzari, G. (2006): *Human Language Technologies for Europe. ITC IRST/TC-Star project report*. Internet: http://tcstar.org/pubblicazioni/D17_HLT_ENG.pdf.

Lindström, L./Müürisep, K. (2009): Parsing corpus of Estonian dialects. In: Bick, E./Hagen, K./Müürisep, K./Trosterud, T. (eds.): *Proceedings of the NODALIDA 2009 workshop Constraint Grammar and robust parsing, Odense, 14.05.2009*. (= NEALT Proceedings Series 8). Tartu: Tartu University Library, 22-29.

Mariani, J. (2009): Research infrastructures for Human Language Technologies: A vision from France. In: *Speech Communication* 51, 569-584.

Meister, E./Vilo, J. (2008): Strengthening the Estonian language technology. In: Calzolari, N. et al. (eds.): *Proceedings of the Sixth International Conference on Language Resources and Evaluation: May 26-June 1, 2008, Marrakech, Marocco*. Paris: European Language Resources Association.

Melero, M./Boleda, G./Cuadros, M./España-Bonet, C./Padró, L./Quixal, M./Rodríguez, C./Saurí, R. (2010): Language technology challenges of a 'small' language (Catalan). In: Calzolari, N./Choukri, K./Maegaard, B./Mariani, J./Odijk, J./Piperidis, S./Rosner, M./Tapias, D. (eds.): *Proceedings of the Seventh International Conference on Language Resources and Evaluation, LREC 2010, 17-23 May 2010, Valletta, Malta*. Valletta: European Language Resources Association, 925-930.

Müürisep, K./Nigol, H. (2008a): Towards better parsing of spoken Estonian. In: Čermak, F./ Marcinkevičiene, R./Rimkute, E./Zabarskaite, J. (eds.): *Proceedings of the Third Baltic Conference on Human Language Technologies. Kaunas, Lithuania, October 4-5, 2007*. Vilnius: Vytautas Magnus University, Institute of the Lithuanian Language, 205-210.

Müürisep, K./Nigol, H. (2008b). Where do parsing errors come from: The case of spoken Estonian. In: Sojka, P./Horak, A./Kopecek, I./Karel, P. (eds.): *Text, Speech and Dialogue. Proceedings of the 11th International Conference, TSD 2008, Brno, Czech Republic, 8-12 September 2008*. (= Lecture Notes in Computer Science 5246). Berlin/Heidelberg/New York: Springer-Verlag, 161-168.

Müürisep, K./Nigol, H. (2009): Shallow parsing of transcribed speech of Estonian and disfluency detection. In: Vetulani, Z./Uszkoreit, H. (eds.): *Human Language Technology. Challenges of information society. Third Language and Technology Conference, LTC 2007, Poznań, Poland, October 5-7, 2007*. Berlin/Heidelberg/New York: Springer-Verlag, 165-177.

Odijk, J. (2010): The CLARIN-NL Project. In: Calzolari, N./Choukri, K./Maegaard, B./Mariani, J./Odijk, J./Piperidis, S./Rosner, M./Tapias, D. (eds.): *Proceedings of the Seventh International Conference on Language Resources and Evaluation, LREC 2010, 17-23 May 2010, Valletta, Malta*. Valletta: European Language Resources Association, 48-53.

Ruokolainen, T./Alumäe, T./Dobrinkat, M. (2010): Using dependency grammar features in whole sentence maximum entropy language models for speech recognition. In: Skadina, I./Vasiljevs, A. (eds.): *Human Language Technologies: The Baltic perspective. Proceedings of the Fourth International Conference Baltic HLT, Riga, Latvia, October 7-8, 2010*. (= Frontiers in Artificial Intelligence and Applications 219). Amsterdam: IOS Press,73-79.

Spyns, P./D'Halleweyn, E. (2010): Flemish-Dutch HLT policy: Evolving to new forms of collaboration. In: Calzolari, N./Choukri, K./Maegaard, B./Mariani, J./Odijk, J./Piperidis, S./Rosner, M./Tapias, D. (eds.): *Proceedings of the Seventh International Conference on Language Resources and Evaluation, LREC 2010, 17-23 May 2010, Valletta, Malta*. Valletta: European Language Resources Association, 2855-2862.

Treumuth, M. (2010): A Framework for Asynchronous Dialogue Systems. In: Skadina, I./Vasiljevs, A. (eds.): *Human Language Technologies: The Baltic perspective. Proceedings of the Fourth International Conference Baltic HLT, Riga, Latvia, October 7-8, 2010*. (= Frontiers in Artificial Intelligence and Applications 219). Amsterdam: IOS Press, 107-114.

Pirkko Nuolijärvi / Toni Suutari

The landscape of the Finnish language research infrastructure

Abstract

Languages are a basic part of cultural heritage and the language collections and archives are an essential research infrastructure for humanities. Nowadays, there is an intensive co-operation between Finnish national institutes within the larger European context. This paper presents two nationwide projects in Finland working for the better use of language resources. These projects, FIN-CLARIN and National Digital Library belong, to some extent, also to the work of the Research Institute for the Languages of Finland, which is responsible for the nationally remarkable language collections.

Tiivistelmä

Kielet ovat kulttuuriperinnön perusta, ja kielenaineskokoelmat ja arkistot ovat humanistisille tieteenaloille tärkeä infrastruktuuri. Nykyisin Suomen kansalliset laitokset tekevät tiiviisti yhteistyötä keskenään ja myös laajemmin Euroopan mitassa. Artikkelissa esitellään lyhyesti Suomen kaksi laajaa kansallista hanketta, joissa työskennellään kieliresurssien paremman käytön edistämiseksi. Näissä hankkeissa, FIN-CLARINissa ja Kansallisessa digitaalisessa kirjastossa, on mukana myös Kotimaisten kielten tutkimuskeskus, joka vastaa kansallisesti merkittävistä kieliaineistoista.

Sammandrag

Språk är grunden för vårt kulturarv, och språksamlingar och arkiv utgör väsentlig infrastruktur för humanistisk forskning. Nuförtiden samarbetar de nationella institutionerna i Finland intensivt med varandra och med andra europeiska institutioner. I den här artikeln presenteras kort två omfattande finländska nationella projekt som båda har som mål att främja en bättre tillgång till språkresurser. De här två projekten, dvs. FIN-CLARIN och Det nationella digitala biblioteket, ingår också i arbetet på Forskningscentralen för de inhemska språken, som är den institution, som ansvarar för det nationellt viktiga språkmaterialet.

Languages are a basic part of cultural heritage and the language collections and archives are an essential research infrastructure for humanities. During the past decade Finnish society has become more aware of this matter. The state has provided funds for more work in this area than ever before and there is an organized and systematic cooperation of various institutes, building new ways to maintain and develop the culturally remarkable infrastructures.

At the moment, there are a number of projects working for the better use of language resources in Finland. This work means that there is intensive co-operation between national institutes within the larger European context. In this context, we will briefly describe two nationwide projects. The work in the Research Institute for the Languages of Finland is also, to some extent, involved with these projects, FIN-CLARIN and the National Digital Library.

First, we will briefly describe the mentioned projects and secondly, present the electronic databases of the Research Institute for the Languages of Finland.

1. FIN-CLARIN as a Finnish part of the European CLARIN

One of the priorities of European research policy is to develop research infrastructures. As mentioned in a number of chapters in this volume, the European Strategy Forum on Infrastructures (ESFRI) has drawn a roadmap for European research infrastructures. CLARIN (Common Language Resources and Technology Infrastructure) is one of the some 34 infrastructures chosen for the ESFRI roadmap. The goal of CLARIN is to provide access for all scholars to language materials and tools all over Europe.

In 2008, Finland's Ministry of Education and Culture provided funds for the Federation of Finnish Learned Societies for the mapping of research infrastructures at national level. This work concerned research infrastructures in all areas and, as a result, 20 projects were proposed for the roadmap of new infrastructures that are to be significantly developed. Thirteen of those projects are associated with European research infrastructures proposed by ESFRI. One of the associated projects is FIN-CLARIN (*Kansallisen tason infrastruktuurit: nykytila ja tiekartta* 2009), funded by the Ministry of Education and Culture as well as the Academy of Finland and the University of Helsinki.

FIN-CLARIN is the Finnish Language Resource Consortium and it is committed to building the Finnish language resource infrastructure and making it an integral part of the European CLARIN infrastructure. FIN-CLARIN as well as CLARIN will solve three problems which presently prevent the efficient use of existing language materials and tools: First, even if digital material exists, it is difficult to find out where the material is located. Hence, common metadata for various materials are needed. Secondly, even if the user finds the material, it is difficult to know how to get permission to use it. Hence, standardized licensing types and a common system for authorization and authentication are needed. Thirdly, even if the user gets the permission to use the material, the parts of it are in different formats and not compatible with each other or with the tools available. Hence, standardizing formats and interfaces are needed. (For more about FIN-CLARIN see http://www.ling.helsinki.fi/finclarin/ and https://kitwiki.csc.fi/twiki/bin/view/FinCLARIN.)

Topics of FIN-CLARIN are: relevant standards and guidelines for resources; accessing and acquiring resources from other sources; collecting and using text, speech, lexical and other resources; developing methods and tools to better utilize and use the resources; intellectual property rights (IPR) of the resources and training and education of related topics.

The Finnish Language Resource Consortium will build its activities around the CSC (the IT Center for Science) Language Bank, which will be the main depository of resources, tools and knowledge. CSC is funded by the Finnish state. There are a number of participants in FIN-CLARIN, universities and the Research Institute for the Languages of Finland.

The preparatory phase that has been performed by CLARIN ended in 2010. FIN-CLARIN will continue its work by implementing the recommendations produced by CLARIN in close collaboration with the European META-NET project and its northern part META-NORD.

In addition, several other research projects operate in close collaboration with FIN-CLARIN, e.g., the Finnish Treebank project, the Finnish WordNet and the HFST project (*Helsinki Finite-State Transducer Technology*) at the Department of Modern Languages, University of Helsinki (www.ling.helsinki.fi/finclarin/intro.html).

To sum up, the main task of FIN-CLARIN is to make the use of materials easier for both researchers and laymen. The whole project is made from the users' point of view.

2. National Digital Library

The information society has radically changed the environment of the various types of collections: archives, libraries and museums. During the last decade, significant investments have been made in digitizing traditional collections and distributing the materials online. In addition, the organizations must accumulate existing digital materials. The main archives, libraries and museums have an obligation to preserve materials in digital format for a long period of time.

The National Digital Library (NDL) is implemented in the project launched by the Ministry of Education and Culture with 35 Finnish organizations, e.g. scientific and public libraries, museums, archives and other organizations and key interest groups. It is one of the key electric research and culture infrastructures currently under construction in Finland.

The aim of the project is to improve accessibility and long-term preservation (LTP) of the electronic materials of libraries, archives and museums. It offers new possibilities for information seeking and ensures that the information remains in active use in the future as well. The project also contributes to the European Union's objectives concerning the digitisation of cultural materials and scientific information as well as their digital availability and long-term preservation (www.kdk.fi/en).

There are four support services that should be provided within the scope of the NDL:

- permanent actionable identifiers of digital objects (such as URN identifiers);
- an authority database, i.e. a system that interconnects the names of persons and organizations in different languages and forms;
- maintenance of the standard portfolio;
- services related to competence development.
  (*The National Digital Library – collaborating and interoperating* 2011, 14)

There are different types of material: publications, government publications, museum materials, archival documents and manuscripts, radio and TV programs, audio and video recordings of various types. Naturally, the rules and practices for describing these materials vary. Also the technical capabilities of the organizations and their present solutions for managing, using, distributing and preserving materials vary significantly.

The public interface gives access to the electronic information resources and services of libraries, archives and museums. The web service makes it easy to gain access to materials on any given subject matter, such as pictures, documents, newspapers, research, video and audio recordings. Aim is to launch the service in 2012.

Through the public interface, the materials of libraries, archives and museums come to form a whole. The public interface is intended to enable users to find the information they need through one interface, irrespective of which organization has produced the information. Hence, the information seeker no longer needs to know who owns or manages the materials. It is enough to want to gain knowledge or experiences. The information resources from various organizations can be found in one service and with one search. It helps information seekers not only to find the information they need but also other pertinent information. The user can also receive the electronic services connected with the materials from the same address.

Organizations will continue to be responsible for the production, cataloguing and management of their own digital resources. The public interface will facilitate access to the diverse resources of libraries, museums and archives for research, teaching and other information acquisition. Organizations will be able to customize the public interface for their own unique requirements and will also be able to create default views for different groups of users. (See www.kdk.fi/en/public-interface.)

The role of the long-term preservation sub-project (see e.g. Merenmies 2010) of the National Digital Library project is to coordinate the development of the long-term preservation of cultural heritage content data objects. The users of the centralized long-term preservation solution are primarily those responsible for the preservation of published and other kinds of material cultural heritage operating within the sector of the Ministry of Education and Culture, e.g. the National Archives, the National Library, and the Institute for the Languages of Finland.

The basis for designing the centralized long-term preservation solution is to offer archives, libraries and museums a system that is reliable, versatile and provides the required preservation services such as the controlled migration of the preserved content.

An expert group of long-term preservation in NDL was established in spring 2011. This includes representatives from archives, libraries and museums. CSC, the IT Center for Science, will be the organization responsible for the first phase of the long-term preservation system implementation project. This phase will be completed by the end of 2014. In the second phase of the project, which according to plans will start in 2015, will include a transition from the project phase into permanent system administration and full-scale use. The LTP system should be operational by 2016, at the earliest.

One of the main benefits of the NDL project is the unification of work processes, data structures and systems in archives, libraries and museums including the production and distribution of administrative metadata required for long-term preservation. Organizations will need to have a collection policy and clear operating principles guiding the compiling, management and preservation of digital collections within the framework of legislative and other obligations. The objective is that the national data resources will be widely available to the use of entire society. (See www.kdk2011.fi/images/stories/KDK_PAS_jarjestelma_metatiedot_v0.9.pdf.)

National Digital Library – Enterprise Architecture by the Finnish National Digital Library project steering group describes how the various elements – organizational units, people, processes, information and information systems – relate to each other and function as a whole. Enterprise architecture is subdivided into four areas as follows:

- Business architecture: the project's services, stakeholders and processes;
- Data architecture: the key glossaries being used, the central information resources and the relationship between information categories and systems;
- Application architecture: the content of the information system portfolio;
- Technical architecture: the technology portfolio, reference architectures and interfaces.

A centralised long-term preservation solution for the digital materials will secure transitions between generations of systems, software and equipment, keeping digital information coherent and understandable for future users. Even in the long-term preservation system, the ownership of materials will remain with the organization who stored them. The system will be designed to allow the preservation of electronic data resources for research in the future.

The National Digital Library is the most extensive cooperation project between libraries, archives and museums so far in Finland. During the project, cooperation both between and within the library, archive and museum sectors has increased and intensified. (*Putting data into use* 2011; see also www.minedu.fi/OPM/Julkaisut/2011/Kansallinen_digitaalinen_kirjasto.html?lang=fi&extra_locale=en.)

4. Electronic archives and collections held by the Research Institute for the Languages of Finland

The Archives and Collections of Linguistic Corpora and Collections of Electronic Linguistic Corpora of the Research Institute for the Languages of Finland belong to the national infrastructures (*Kansallisen tason tutkimusinfrastruktuurit. Nykytila ja tiekartta* 2009, 26). As mentioned above, the institute is one participant of both projects, FIN-CLARIN and National Digital Library.

The extensive archives and collections (www.kotus.fi/collections) held by the Research Institute for the Languages of Finland have been assembled over more than a century. Besides the material held in paper form, there are also audio and video recordings and an ever increasing volume of electronic data. An on-line data service named 'Kaino' was launched in December 2006. This includes Finnish texts dating back as far as the 1500s as well as a separate Atlas of Place Names and etymological data on the Saami languages (Álgu – Origins of Saami Words). The Finland-Swedish data is mostly available in the electronic and manual archives of Svenska Litteratursällskapet i Finland (The Society of Swedish Literature in Finland) or in the data bank of the University of Gothenburg in Sweden.

At present, there is a number of electronic data in the Research Institute for the Languages in Finland (http://kaino.kotus.fi/korpus). A large part of the data is available for everybody. The electronic freely accessible on-line data service is 2011 as follows:

Finnish:

- Corpus of Old Literary Finnish 1543-1809;
- Corpus of Early Modern Finnish 1809-1899;
- Modern Finnish Lexicon by Research Institute for the Languages of Finland;
- Corpus of Finnish Literary Classics 1880s-1930s;
- Corpus of Proverbs and Other Colloquial Expressions;
- New Year Speeches of the President of the Republic of Finland 1935-2007;
- Etymological Reference Database;
- Atlas of Place Names;
- Toponymic Database, 162,774 place names;
- Collection Database of Audio Recordings Archive.

Languages related to Finnish:

- Álgu – Origins of Saami Words;
- Etymological Reference Database;
- Dictionary of Karelian;
- Vepsian Word List.

The freely accessible on-line data service includes other materials, and it increases continuously.

Another part of the electronic data requires user authorization. It includes materials as follows:

Finnish:

- Corpus of the Finnish Language = Finnish Text Collection (access via CSC, Language Bank), contains written Finnish from 1990s;
- Corpus of Magazines and Periodicals 20th century;
- Syntax Archive Data: The data is owned by the Research Institute for the Languages in Finland and the School of Languages and Translation Studies (Finnish Language) at the University of Turku. The Syntax Archive Data contains dialects from 132 Finnish parishes (one hour from each parish) and literary Finnish (40 units);
- Lexical Data from the Archive of Modern Finnish;
- Headwords in the Dictionary of Modern Finnish (= Nykysuomen sanakirja 1-6, 1951-1961);
- Oulu Corpus, a representative sample of the Finnish language in the 1960s media (access via CSC, Language Bank, www.csc.fi/english/research/software/oulu);
- Texts from the Samples of Finnish Dialects Collection, text and audio (access via CSC);
- Corpus of Entries from the Dictionary of Finnish Dialects.

Finland Swedish:

- Finland Swedish Text Corpus = Finnish-Swedish Text Collection 1997-2000 (access via CSC, Language Bank),
- Swedish-Finnish Parallel Text Corpus 21th century (CSC, Language Bank).

The Research Institute for the Languages of Finland has also other types of digital data, which requires user authorization: audio and video recordings, manuscripts and photos.

The list of the databases of the Research Institute for the Languages of Finland will increase and develop in the future. This work is funded in the frame of the budget of the institute, but, however, it is supported by the experts in the national projects, FIN-CLARIN and National Digital Library.

5. References

Kansallisen tason infrastruktuurit: nykytila ja tiekartta. (= Opetusministeriön julkaisuja 2009:1). Helsinki: Opetusministeriö. www.minedu.fi/OPM/Julkaisut/2009/Kansallisen_tason_tutkimusinfrastruktuurit._Nykytila_ja_tiekartta.html?lang=fi&extra_locale=en.

Merenmies, M. (2010): *The National Digital Library Initiative Long-term Preservation Project. Final Report. 8th European Conference on Digital Archiving, Geneva, 28-30 April 2010.* www.kdk.fi/en.

Putting data into use. A roadmap for the utilization of electronic data in research. (= Reports of the Ministry of Education and Culture, Finland 2011:4). Helsinki: Opetus- ja kulttuuriministeriö.

The National Digital Library – collaborating and interoperating. (= Publications of the Ministry of Education and Culture 2011:26). Helsinki: Opetus- ja kulttuuriministeriö. www.minedu.fi/OPM/Julkaisut/2011/Kansallinen_digitaalinen_kirjasto.html?lang=fi&extra_ locale=en.

Anna Maria Gustafsson / Pirkko Nuolijärvi

Multilingual public websites in Finland

Abstract

This paper presents a case study of the websites produced by Finnish authorities. Our main task is to show how the public sector promotes or does not promote the use of the national and minority languages and other languages used in Finland on the internet, and how virtual information is offered in those languages. The data consist of websites of universities; ministries; Parliament; various public service institutions, e.g., Kela = the Social Insurance Institution of Finland; state research institutes; municipalities and a number of other state institutions. The investigation shows that the Finnish public sector and universities are multilingual, but mostly in Finnish, English and Swedish. If other languages are used, the information provided is quite limited. Some positive exceptions can be mentioned: the Ombudsman for Minorities and the Finnish Police with 17 languages on their websites, and with the Finnish Immigration Service with a website in 11 languages. In addition, many municipalities and the Finnish Immigration Service use a common Information Bank, an online service which supports immigrant integration by providing information on Finnish society and its services in 15 languages.

Tiivistelmä

Artikkelissa käsitellään Suomen viranomaisten ja korkeakoulujen verkkosivuja. Tarkoituksena on osoittaa, miten Suomen julkinen sektori suosii tai ei suosi kansalliskielten, vähemmistökielten ja muiden kielten käyttöä internetissä ja miten milläkin kielellä tarjotaan informaatiota verkossa. Aineisto koostuu yliopistojen, ammattikorkeakoulujen, ministeriöiden, eduskunnan, erilaisten julkisten palvelulaitosten, kuten Kelan, valtion tutkimuslaitosten ja eräiden muiden valtion laitosten sekä kuntien verkkosivuista.

Tarkastelu osoittaa, että Suomen julkisen sektorin ja korkeakoulujen verkkosivut ovat monikielisiä, mutta niillä on käytetty enimmäkseen vain suomea, englantia ja ruotsia. Muilla kielillä tarjotaan tietoa melko rajallisesti. Myönteisinä esimerkkeinä mainittakoon vähemmistövaltuutetun toimisto ja Suomen poliisi, jotka tarjoavat sivuillaan informaatiota 17 kielellä, sekä Maahanmuuttovirasto, joka käyttää sivuillaan 11 kieltä. Lisäksi monet kunnat käyttävät yhteistä Infopankkia, palvelusivustoa, joka tukee maahanmuuttajien kotoutumista tarjoamalla tietoa Suomen yhteiskunnasta ja palveluista 15 kielellä.

Sammandrag

Artikeln behandlar finländska myndigheters och högskolors webbplatser. Syftet är att visa på vilket sätt den offentliga sektorns webbplatser främjar eller låter bli att främja användningen av de nationella språken och minoritetsspråken liksom andra språk i Finland samt att visa på vilka sätt den offentliga sektorn erbjuder information på dessa språk. Materialet består av webbplatser för universitet, yrkeshögskolor, ministerier, riksdagen, offentliga serviceinstitutioner (t.ex. Folkpensionsanstalten), statliga forskningsinstitut, ett antal andra statliga institutioner och kommuner.

Undersökningen visar att den offentliga sektorn och universiteten i Finland är mångspråkiga, men de språk som förekommer på webbplatserna är oftast endast finska, engelska och svenska. Om andra språk än dessa förekommer är informationen relativt begränsad. Goda exempel är dock Minoritetsombudsmannen och den finska polisen som båda har information på 17 olika språk på sina webbplatser, liksom Migrationsverket i Finland som informerar på 11 olika språk på sin webbplats. På många kommuners webbplatser förekommer länkar till den så kallade Infobanken, som är en webbplats som stöder integrationen av invandrare genom att tillhandahålla grundläggande information om det finländska samhället på 15 olika språk.

The linguistic environment has changed during the past few decades in Finland, just as elsewhere in the world. Multilingualism in our country has increased, and people have contacts with more language groups and environments than ever before. Hence, using different languages is necessary in our real and virtual life.

The changes in the environment have also led the public institutions, e.g., state authorities into a situation where they have to shoulder more responsibility for providing the information needed by the multilingual public. The internet is one forum where the language policy of a country can be implemented. It is also a forum where a country's language policy, as it is put into practice by the authorities every day, can be displayed.

Our study is a tentative case study of the websites produced by Finnish authorities. Our main task is to show how the public sector promotes or does not promote the use of the national and minority languages and other languages used in Finland on the internet, and how virtual information is offered in those languages. Our purpose is to present the linguistic landscape of the Finnish public sector on the web, to investigate which languages the authorities use on their websites, and to discuss what kinds of matters the authorities present in different languages.

Our data consist of the websites of universities, ministries, Parliament, public service institutions, e.g., Kela (the Social Insurance Institution of Finland), state research institutes, some other state institutions, including the Academy of Finland, the Finnish Funding Agency for Technology and Innovation (Tekes), the National Archives Service of Finland, the National Library of Finland and the National Board of Antiquities, and municipalities. First, before describing the current language use on the websites, we will give some background information and look at the paragraphs in the general legislation regarding the languages of information in Finland. In addition, we will briefly refer to the current need for information in the language landscape of Finland.

1. Public services in legislation

According to the Finnish Constitution (Section 17), the national languages of Finland are Finnish and Swedish. The right of everyone to use their own language, either Finnish or Swedish, before courts of law and other authorities, and to receive documents in that language, is guaranteed by an Act. The public authorities should provide for the educational, cultural and societal needs of the Finnish-speaking and Swedish-speaking populations of the country on an equal basis. “On an equal basis” means, among other things, that the public authorities have to give information in both languages (Suomen perustuslaki/Finlands grundlag 731/1999).

The same content is also included in the Language Act (2003). A bilingual authority, be it a state authority or a bilingual municipal authority, must use both Finnish and Swedish in their information to the public. The information does not necessarily have to be equally comprehensive in both languages. There is a danger that it is possible to interpret the relevant paragraph in different ways, in practice so that Swedish is needed less (Kielilaki/Språklag 423/2003).

According to the Sami Language Act (2003), everyone has the right to use the Sami or the Finnish language, as he or she may choose, and the authorities in the Sami domicile area have to provide services in Sami languages. All three Sami languages, North Sami, Inari Sami and Skolt Sami, are included in the act, but none of these languages are accorded the same legal status as Finnish and Swedish. Skills to give information in Sami are necessary for the authorities in the Sami domicile area in the northernmost part of Finland (Saamen kielilaki 1086/2003).

Especially during the past few decades, the population speaking languages other than Finnish or Swedish as their first language has increased in Finland. This means that there are an increasing number of people who need information in their own languages or in languages they use as a second language. For example, in Helsinki, 10.2% of the total of 600,000 people speak other languages than Finnish or Swedish as their first language. In the whole country, 4% of the population have another first language than Finnish, Swedish or Sami. Hence, the information in many languages is needed in everyday life. The most widely used first languages are Russian, Estonian, Somali, English, Arabic, Kurdish, Chinese, Albanian, Thai, Vietnamese, German, Turkish, Farsi, Spanish, and French (OSF 2010).

There are no explicit paragraphs in the Finnish legislation concerning language use on the internet. With the exception of Finnish and Swedish, the authorities and institutes have to judge for themselves how and in which languages they offer information and guidance in the virtual world. One might ask if a separate language policy is needed for the internet. Richard Domeij, who has investigated the use of languages on the internet in Sweden, has made a proposal on how to make such a policy programme (cf. Domeij 2010, 35-39). Also, the Finnish language policy programme has emphasized that the internet is an important channel for offering information in the public sector (Suomen kielen tulevaisuus 2009, 214-216).

2. Information in higher education: universities and polytechnics

There are 16 universities in Finland. Aalto University, consisting of the School of Art and Design, the School of Economics and the Schools of Technology, together with the University of Helsinki, are bilingual (Finnish and Swedish). Åbo Akademi and Hanken School of Economics are Swedish-speaking universities. All the other 12 universities are officially monolingual Finnish. In addition, there are 25 polytechnics in Finland, mostly funded by the state and municipalities.

The languages used on the websites of Finnish universities and polytechnics are presented in table 1.

On the 16 websites of the Finnish universities and the 25 of the Finnish polytechnics, we found information in just 4 different languages. Finnish and English dominate, especially on the websites of the polytechnics; and there are 12 different websites providing information in three languages, Finnish, Swedish, and English – in varying degrees. Only one polytechnic in Helsinki offers information in 4 languages: the two national languages, English, and Russian.

Languages	Universities	Polytechnics
Finnish, English	**7**	**18**
Finnish, Swedish, English	**4**	2
Finnish, English, Swedish	2	1
Finnish, English, Russian	1	1
Swedish, Finnish, English	1	–
Swedish, English, Finnish	–	2
Swedish, English	–	–
Finnish, Swedish, English, Russian	–	1
Total	16	25

Table 1: The languages on the websites of Finnish universities and polytechnics in order of appearance

Lappeenranta University of Technology in eastern Finland also makes available web pages in Russian, but behind the links at the Russian page, we find English again. So, the information in Russian is limited as compared to that in English. Two polytechnics, one in Helsinki and one in Eastern Finland, also provide information in Russian, but this is not extensive.

Our investigation shows that the universities are mostly trilingual in Finnish, Swedish and English, and the polytechnics are bilingual, though not in the national languages, but rather in Finnish and English.

3. Languages used on the websites of state research and cultural institutes

There are 19 state research institutes in Finland analyzing and guiding various areas, e.g., climate, forest, agriculture, environment, health and welfare, economy, consumption, and language. The languages used on the websites of the Finnish research institutes are presented in table 2.

Languages	Institutes
Finnish, Swedish, English	**12**
Finnish, English, Swedish	**5**
Finnish, Swedish, English, German, Russian (Finnish Forest Research Institute)	1
Finnish, Swedish, English, Sami, Finnish Romani, Finnish Sign Language (Research Institute for the Languages of Finland)	1
Total	19

Table 2: The languages on the websites of the Finnish research institutes in order of appearance

As state institutes, all of the research institutes comply with the Language Act and provide information both in Finnish and in Swedish. Finnish and Swedish information is mostly available to a more or less equal degree. The third language is English. There are only two institutes which offer information in more than three languages.

The Finnish Forest Research Institute has comprehensive pages in, e.g., German. In addition, there is some information in Russian. This is necessary, because the Finnish forest industry and research have much cooperation with the German, Karelian, and Russian industries and researchers.

The Research Institute for the Languages of Finland offers information in Finnish, Swedish, English, the Sami languages, Finnish Romani and the Finnish Sign Language. Hence, there is information in and about all of the languages the institute works with.

The main research funding state institutes are the Academy of Finland and the Finnish Funding Agency for Technology and Innovation (Tekes). The cultural institutes are the National Archives Service of Finland and the National Library of Finland. The language spectrum on their websites is the following:

Academy of Finland: Finnish, English, Swedish;
The Finnish Funding Agency for Technology and Innovation: Finnish, Swedish, English, Chinese, Japanese;
The National Archives Service of Finland: Finnish, Swedish, English, Sami, Russian;
The National Library of Finland: Finnish, Swedish, English.

As usual, all of the four institutes offer information in Finnish, Swedish and English on their websites. The National Archives Services of Finland also offers information in Sami and Russian. Sami history and culture is part of Finnish history and culture, and there is a lot of material about the life of the Sami people even in the national collections. Russian archive materials, especially from the nineteenth century, are important for researchers of the political history of Finland.

The Finnish Funding Agency for Technology and Innovation has offices in China and Japan. Therefore, the funding agency also offers service in Chinese and in Japanese.

In summary, our results show that the national languages of Finland and English are the languages of web information in state research and cultural institutes. Other languages are available if there are clear economical and practical reasons to provide information in those languages, e.g., Russian, German, Chinese, and Japanese; or if there are cultural reasons for offering information in indigenous and minority languages like Sami, Romani, and the Finnish Sign language.

4. The languages used on the websites of Finnish state authorities

For this study we also looked at the language use on websites of 33 different Finnish authorities. These authorities include seven ministries, the Finnish Parliament, and the most common providers of public services in Finland, for instance the Finnish Food

Safety Authority, the Finnish Tax Administration, the Consumer Agency, the Social Insurance Institution of Finland, the Finnish Immigration Service, and the Finnish Police – in other words, authorities who deal with issues such as health, taxes, social insurance, consumer information, law and order, and security.

On the 33 websites of the Finnish state authorities we found information in 23 different languages. It is clear that Finnish, Swedish and English dominate as a whole, and all of the 33 different websites do, in fact, offer information in these three languages. Thus, one can draw the conclusion that the Finnish authorities are trilingual. All the ministry websites included in the study provide information in Finnish, Swedish, and English, exclusively. This trilingualism seems to constitute a policy – either written or unwritten – for all the Finnish ministries. Other languages used on the websites of Finnish state authorities are presented in table 3.

Language	**Number of websites**	**Language**	**Number of websites**	**Language**	**Number of websites**
French	**6**	Chinese	2	Inari Sami	1
Russian	6	German	2	Finnish Romani	1
Northern Sami	5	Kurdish	2	Portuguese	1
Estonian	4	Persian	2	Skolt Sami	1
Albanian	3	Spanish	2	Vietnamese	1
Arabic	3	Thai	2		
Sign language	3	Turkish	2		
Somali	3				

Table 3: Languages except Finnish, Swedish and English used on the websites of Finnish state authorities

The occurrence of 23 different languages might indicate that the Finnish state authorities are highly multilingual, at least on their websites. But in reality the use of many different languages is concentrated to just a few websites. In addition to Finnish, Swedish, and English, information in French, Russian, Northern Sami, and Estonian can be found on some of the websites. North Sami is the most widely spoken of all the Sami languages, and it can be found on five of the studied authorities' websites. The two other Sami languages, Skolt Sami and Inari Sami, are much smaller and they are almost non-existent on the websites. Information in all of the three Sami languages can nevertheless be found on one of the studied websites, i.e. the website of the Ombudsman for Minorities.

Even if the state authorities mostly offer information only in Finnish, Swedish, and English – or at least they give the impression that they offer information in these languages through the language links on the main page, there is still a chance that information in other languages may be found, as well. Some authorities occasionally present, for instance, press releases in other languages.

The most multilingual state authorities are presented in table 4.

Ombudsman for Minorities	**17**
Finnish Police	**17**
Finnish Immigration Service	**11**
Parliamentary Ombudsman	**9**
Emergency Response Centre	**8**

Table 4: Number of languages used on websites of state authorities

The most multilingual authority in our study is the Ombudsman for Minorities, which is not very surprising considering its task of advancing the status and legal protection of ethnic minorities and foreigners in Finland. The Finnish Police is also highly multilingual on its websites, where you can find information in 17 different languages. The third most multilingual authority in our data is the Finnish Immigration Service, followed by the Parliamentary Ombudsman and the Emergency Response Centre Administration, which gives information on their website on how and when to use the emergency number in eight different languages.

The 17 different languages used on the website of the Ombudsman for Minorities are Finnish, Swedish, English, all three Sami languages: Northern Sami, Inari Sami and Skolt Sami; Russian, Estonian, French, Spanish, Somali, Turkish, Albanian, Arabic, Chinese, Thai and Finnish Romani.

What have been usually called the traditional minority languages of Finland, i.e. the Sami languages, Finnish Romani, and the Finnish Sign language, are not widely used on the websites of the state authorities, which was an unexpected result for us. Sami is used on five different websites and the Sign language only on three. Finnish Romani is only used by the Ombudsman for Minorities.

5. Language spectrum on the websites of municipalities

In our study, we were also interested in the language use on the websites of the Finnish municipalities. In 2010, there were 342 municipalities in Finland; of these, 19 were monolingual Swedish speaking, of which 16 were in Åland. There were 31 bilingual municipalities; of these, 13 had a Swedish-speaking majority, and 18 had a Finnish-speaking majority. All the remaining 289 municipalities were monolingual Finnish-speaking municipalities.

Our study includes 55 of the Finnish municipalities. Our sample comprises both bilingual and monolingual municipalities, both small towns and cities, both university cities and municipalities from more rural areas of the country. We also found it important to include municipalities which are situated close to the Finnish-Swedish, Finnish-Sami, and Finnish-Russian language borders.

Finnish is found on 54 of these 55 municipality websites. The only exception is the municipality of Mariehamn in Åland, which is a Swedish-speaking municipality, just as all the municipalities in Åland. Swedish is found on 37 different municipality websites and English on 45 websites. Based on this, we can establish that English is more common than Swedish on the websites of Finnish municipalities.

The range of languages used on the municipality websites is not as wide as that of the authorities' websites. We found information in just ten different languages on the websites of the municipalities. Most languages are used by the municipalities of Helsinki, Lappeenranta, and Kuopio. Helsinki, being the capital city, has a vast number of different language groups living in the city and therefore needs to offer important information in many languages. Lappeenranta and Kuopio are both university cities in eastern Finland.

In addition to Finnish, Swedish, and English; Russian and German are fairly common languages on the websites of the municipalities. German and Russian are also almost the only other languages used frequently; all the other languages noted in our data only occur occasionally (see table 5).

Russian	**15**
German	**14**
French	4
Sami	3 (Utsjoki, Sodankylä, Inari)
Estonian	1
Norwegian	1 (Utsjoki)
Chinese	1

Table 5: Languages except Finnish, Swedish and English used on the websites of 55 Finnish municipalities

The North Sami language can be found on three websites: Utsjoki, Sodankylä and Inari in northern Finland, which is the Sami region; therefore these municipalities are obliged to offer information in the Sami languages.

There is considerably variation in both the amount of and the quality of information on the websites. Many of the websites of the municipalities *seem* to have information in other languages than Finnish and/or Swedish, based on the language links on the main pages. In reality, though, some of the links only lead to half a page of information in English or German for tourists, or they contain a brief historical overview of the municipality. This kind of information is clearly not intended exclusively for the inhabitants of the municipality, but mainly aims to attract visitors to the region.

Other municipalities, on the other hand, offer a lot of information, above all in English, clearly intended for new inhabitants, students or other people with a foreign mother tongue and living in the municipality. For instance, on the website of the municipality of Oulu, a university city in northern Finland, you can find comprehensive information in

English on, for example, day care, schools, social and health services and public safety. It is obvious that the municipality of Oulu finds it important to offer information in English to all the foreign students and researchers and immigrants living in the city.

Consequently, there are two kinds of information in foreign languages on the websites: general and municipal information for inhabitants with another mother tongue than Finnish or Swedish; and tourist information only aimed to attract visitors to the region. This difference in the quality of the information can be seen, for instance, in the headings and links used on the main page. Information intended for the inhabitants is usually titled "Municipal Information", "Immigrant's Guide", "New Inhabitants", or "Information for Foreigners", whereas tourist information or information for temporary visitors is called "Briefly in English", "Facts about ...", "Basic Fact", or in German: "Allgemeines" or "Die Gemeinde ...".

The municipality of Helsinki provides information in Finnish, Swedish, German, French and Russian through language links on the main page. In addition to these links, there is also one link called "Other languages" which leads the user to Infopankki, or the Information Bank. The Information Bank is an online service which supports immigrant integration by providing information on Finnish society and its services in 15 languages: Finnish, Swedish, English, Estonian, French, Russian, Somali, Serbo-Croatian, Turkish, Arabic, Persian, Chinese, Spanish, Albanian and Kurdish (Sorani). All the language versions are identical in format. The Info Bank offers basic information about permits, education and work, housing and social services, society, culture and leisure, and other important issues to immigrants everywhere in Finland, but particularly in the Info Bank's member municipalities. The website contains local information on the Helsinki Region (Helsinki, Espoo, Vantaa and Kauniainen), Turku, Tampere, Kuopio, Rovaniemi and the Province of Kainuu. The Info Bank is based on networking, cooperation and information exchange among the authorities, the third sector, immigrants and other partners.

6. Summary

There are clearly three dominating languages on the websites of the Finnish public sector and higher education: Finnish, Swedish, and English.

The websites of the universities and the polytechnics show how the language priorities in the academic society have changed: Finnish and English sites are always available, but not always Swedish. In fact, the polytechnics in Finland are bilingual in Finnish or Swedish and English. In general, Swedish is present in the academic environment less than we expected.

The state research institutes follow the Language Act closely – as is, of course, their duty – giving information in Finnish and Swedish, and, in addition, in English. There are differences in how Swedish sites have been constructed, but it is typical that there is less information in Swedish than in Finnish. Only two of 19 institutes also offer information in other languages.

The websites of the Finnish state authorities are trilingual. The use of different languages is concentrated to only a few sites. Finnish and Swedish are always present on the websites of state authorities and bilingual municipal authorities; the municipalities follow the Language Act very closely.

The traditional minority languages are not used much. One could ask oneself the following questions: Why does it look like this? Is it a Finnish "tradition" not to give information in these languages? Is it because of the status of the languages or the bilingualism of the minorities? Are the language minority groups pleased with this situation? Is this something that is going to change in the future? In the Sami area the use of Sami languages has already changed, even if there is still much to do in the real and virtual life.

There is more information in other languages than we expected. Even if as many as 23 languages are used on the websites of the authorities, it does not mean that the Finnish authorities overall are highly multilingual: the use of many different languages is, in fact, concentrated to only a few sites. The "average" Finnish authorities are trilingual.

The most multilingual authorities are those who are concerned with minorities or those who find it important to emphasize the use of everyone's own mother tongue. What we found slightly surprising was that the Finnish Police had information in so many different languages.

The results from the municipalities show that the municipalities comply with the Language Act, and do so very well. The bilingual municipalities often have identical information in both Finnish and Swedish; sometimes slightly less in the other national language, depending on which of them is the majority language in the municipality. The information that you find in other languages is often tourist information or general information on the municipality, such as history, population, and other kinds of statistics.

The municipalities whose websites offer citizens information which is clearly addressed to persons who do not have Finnish, Swedish or Sami as their mother tongue, are naturally the biggest cities and the university cities, i.e. municipalities where there are most foreigners, living there either permanently or temporarily.

Some municipalities also use the Information Bank, which is a good example of how useful information can be provided for persons with a different mother tongue than the official languages. It is also proof of what can be achieved through fruitful co-operation between authorities and municipalities in the virtual environment.

Even if our study is only a first – and quantitative – step to analyze the use of languages on the websites in the public sector, it has shown that, on the one hand, the Finnish virtual environment is mostly trilingual, and that, on the other hand, there are a number of institutions which offer service and information in several languages used by people living in Finland. We do not know if Finnish institutes and authorities are better or worse at offering information as compared with other countries, because there is no information available on the situation in other countries. It could be very interesting to compare the Finnish web landscape with the web landscapes of the authorities and institutions in other European countries.

7. References

Domeij, Richard (2010): *En språkpolitik för Internet.* Rapporter från Språkrådet 2. Stockholm: Språkrådet.

Kielilaki/Språklag [Language Act] 423/2003. Retrieved from www.finlex.fi.

OSF (2010) = Official Statistics of Finland (OSF): Population structure [e-publication]. Appendix figure 3: The largest groups by native language 2000 and 2010 . Helsinki: Statistics Finland. Access method: www.stat.fi/til/vaerak/2010/vaerak_2010_2011-03-18_kuv_003_en.html [referred: 21.03.2011].

Saamen kielilaki [Sami Language Act] 1086/2003. Retrieved from www.finlex.fi.

Suomen kielen tulevaisuus 2009. Kielipoliittinen toimintaohjelma. Kirjoittajat: Auli Hakulinen, Jyrki Kalliokoski, Salli Kankaanpää, Antti Kanner, Kimmo Koskenniemi, Lea Laitinen, Sari Maamies, Pirkko Nuolijärvi. (= Kotimaisten kielten tutkimuskeskuksen julkaisuja 155). Helsinki: Kotimaisten kielten tutkimuskeskus.

Suomen perustuslaki/Finlands grundlag [Constitution] 731/1999. Retrieved from www.finlex.fi.

Svelta Koeva

Natural Language Processing in Bulgaria (from BLARK to competitive language technologies)

1. Introduction

The meaning of the terms *Natural Language Processing* and *Computational Linguistics* can be interpreted in different ways. Linguistics, in contrast to the other sciences, began to use formal methods for description much later. If by "computational" we mean the application of formal methods for the description of linguistic data and the improvement of the accuracy and speed of analysis with the aid of specialized computer programmes, then modern linguistics is computational linguistics in the same way as modern physics, for example, might be called computational physics. Computational linguistics to the extent that we understand it has a wider meaning. In addition to the formal (to be understood as complete and consistent) description of natural language this concept also refers to Natural Language Processing. This means the development, on the one hand, of effective theoretical models and language technologies, while on the other hand – computational applications and systems to enhance the quality and effectiveness of communication at various levels – spelling and grammar checking; machine translation; categorisation and summarisation of documents, searching and extraction of information, transformation of written text into speech and vice versa; and much else. This understanding is synchronous with the definition "Computational linguistics (CL) is a discipline between linguistics and computer science which is concerned with the computational aspects of the human language faculty" (Uszkoreit 2000).

In this paper a brief overview of the history of Natural Language Processing in Bulgaria is presented, as well as a short survey over the basic language resources and some innovative research achievements.

2. The beginnings of Natural Language Processing in Bulgaria

The beginnings of Natural Language Processing in Bulgaria are connected with the Machine Translation in the Mathematical linguistics group led by Prof. Alexander Ludskanov in early 1970. The group began work at the Institute of Mathematics of the Bulgarian Academy of Sciences and developed a research programme devoted to the problems of Russian-Bulgarian machine translation as well as quantitative and statistical studies of Bulgarian language. The Institute of Mathematics and Informatics at the moment includes a Department on mathematical linguistics as well.

At the end of the 1980's a new section was formed – the Laboratory for linguistic modelling – which brought together leading researchers (logicians, mathematicians, linguists) from a range of Bulgarian research institution of the Bulgarian Academy of Sciences and the University of Sofia. Over a short period of time the laboratory won financing for a number of research projects from European institutions: LaTeSLav[1] (1991-1994) – aimed

[1] http://www.coli.uni-saarland.de/projects/lateslav1.html.

at developing a prototype of a grammar checker; BILEDITA[2] (1996-1998) – for the development of bi-lingual electronic dictionaries; GLOSSER[3] (1996-1998) – aimed at supporting foreign language training and others. In 1994 a number of researchers from the laboratory led by Prof. Yordan Penchev established a new unit at the Institute for Bulgarian (Bulgarian Academy of Sciences). In 2003 it was renamed as the Department for Computational Linguistics.

Since 1995 there has been a significant increase in the number of projects supported by European funds and nationally-financed projects, supported mainly by the Fund for Academic Research of the Ministry of Education, Youth and Science. The Multext-East[4] (1995-1997) extension of the previous Multext and EAGLES EU projects provided the Bulgarian language resources in a standardized format with standard mark-up and annotation, and these resources were later expanded and upgraded in the TELRI[5] I and II (Trans European Language Resources Infrastructure 1995-1998/1999-2001) and Concede[6] (Consortium for Central European Dictionary Encoding 1998-2000) projects.

In parallel with this, language resources are being developed at the University of Sofia (for example speech corpora), Plovdiv University (for example, electronic dictionaries), the New Bulgarian University (translation memory resources), South-West University (parallel corpora) and others.

A number of years ago five Bulgarian academic institutions founded a consortium to create and develop an integrated national academic infrastructure for language resources. Bulgarian institutions are also involved in the CLARIN[7] project. Other ongoing projects include those comprised by META-NET,[8] EUROPEANA[9] and ATLAS[10] aimed at developing the basic technologies and standards necessary to make knowledge on the Internet more widely available in the future.

In addition to many other smaller-scale funded projects, the above-mentioned projects have led to the development of competences in the field of Language Technology as well as a basic technological infrastructure of language tools and resources for Bulgarian. As a consequence over the past decade a number of important electronic language resources (dictionaries, corpora, lexical data bases) as well as programmes for their processing (spell checking, information extraction, word sense disambiguation, machine translation, etc.) have been developed.

3. Language resources

Electronic language resources (as well as methods for describing language data) for Natural Language Processing are radically different from traditional methods of working in

2 http://www.cis.uni-muenchen.de/projects/BILEDITA/leaflet_cover.html.
3 http://www.let.rug.nl/glosser/.
4 http://nl.ijs.si/ME/.
5 http://telri.nytud.hu/.
6 http://www.itri.brighton.ac.uk/projects/concede/.
7 http://www.clarin.eu/external/.
8 http://www.meta-net.eu/meta/about.
9 http://www.europeana.eu/portal/.
10 http://kms.atlasproject.eu/index.

linguistics. In order that it can be used in a wide range of computational applications, data within the electronic language resources has to be as complete and consistent as possible and the properties and relations between the units of which it is composed must be explicitly encoded.

The term 'language resources' refers to a large variety of electronic data which includes both written and spoken language forms. Depending on their structure, language resources can generally be divided into corpora, dictionaries (including terminological data bases, thesauri and ontologies), lexical-semantic networks, grammars and language models. The term 'language resources' also refers to large variety of language processing tools (tokenizers, taggers, lemmatizers, parsers and so on). The BLARK (Basic Language Resources Kit) concept was defined in a joint initiative between ELSNET (European Network of Excellence in Language and Speech) and ELRA (European Language Resources Association). BLARK is defined as the minimal set of resources that is necessary to do any precompetitive research and education at all (Krauwer 2003). BLARK includes many different resources, such as (mono- and multilingual) written and spoken language corpora, mono- and bilingual dictionaries, terminology collections and grammars, taggers, morphological analysers, parsers, speech analysers and recognisers, etc. ELDA[11] (Evaluations and Language resources Distribution Agency) elaborated a report defining a (minimal) set of Language resources to be made available for as many languages as possible.

3.1 Corpora

The following definition might be proposed as a compilation of the numerous and varied definitions of corpus: "A corpus is a large collection of language samples presented in such a manner as to allow for computational processing and selected on the basis of certain (linguistic) criteria, in order to represent an adequate language model" (Koeva 2010b, 9).

It could be said that some of the most extensively developed language resources in Bulgaria or for the Bulgarian language are corpora. There is a wide range of data for monolingual corpora and archives which reflect various periods in the development of the Bulgarian language, mainly connected with its current status (for example: Bulgarian National Corpus, BgSpeech[12] collection, BulTreeBank Text Archive, Corpus of Old Slavic Texts from the XIth Century[13] and others).

The Bulgarian National Corpus (Koeva et al. 2009) undoubtedly occupies central place amongst them. The Bulgarian National Corpus project began development at the Institute for Bulgarian of the Bulgarian Academy of Science at the beginning of 2009. The project is aimed at compiling and annotating a very large general corpus representative of the synchronous state of the Bulgarian language. The Bulgarian National Corpus reflects the conditions of the Bulgarian language from the middle of the XXth century (specifically from 1945 – the year of the last orthographical reform in Bulgaria) to the

---

[11] http://www.blark.org/.

[12] http://www.bgspeech.net/index_en.html.

[13] http://www.hf.ntnu.no/SofiaTrondheimCorpus/.

present day. At this present moment about 10% of the total number of texts are documents published between 1945 and 1989, and 90% are documents published between 1990 and 2011.

At the present moment the Bulgarian National Corpus has more than 420 million words and includes more than 11,000 samples. It is envisaged in the very near future that the volume of the Corpus will exceed 500 million words (1 billion words is an achievable aim).

Every document is accompanied with metadata in XML format containing information relating to: the author (authors) of the text, translator (translators) of the text (in the case of translated works), the year of first publication of the text, number of words in the text, genre category of the text, style and thematic area, text source, data of addition, additional commentaries, etc. The unified description of texts facilitates their processing and grouping in relevant subcorpora on the basis of various criteria (for example, author, date of creation, genre category, etc.). The corpus was automatically processed for sentence borders, part of speech tags, lemma and grammatical features of words, word senses (according to data from the Bulgarian wordnet). Recently shallow parsing is performed by means of detecting of phrase structure and assigning phrase boundaries, labels and heads.

The Bulgarian National Corpus is a language resource of national importance and provides a wide range of possibilities for theoretical and practical applications in a number of areas. Since mid 2009 the Bulgarian National Corpus has been publicly accessible on the Internet.[14]

The annotated corpus contains additional "interpretative and predominantly linguistic information" (EAGLES 1996). Separate levels of linguistic annotation can be defined (Leach 1997, 8-15), for example: morphological, morpho-syntactical, syntactical, semantic and discourse (EAGLES 1996), and annotated corpora are usually associated with more than one level of annotation. A number of Bulgarian annotated corpora should also be mentioned: for parts of speech (POS), word senses and dependency structure.

Bulgarian POS and sense annotated corpora are excerpts from the Bulgarian Brown corpus.[15] In the Bulgarian POS-annotated Corpus (+150,000 words) each word form is annotated by hand with the relevant part of speech and grammatical features, with which it is used in the context, selected from a majority of possibilities from the large Grammar dictionary of Bulgarian (Koeva et al. 2006). In the Sense-annotated corpus (+100,000 words) each lexical unit is linked manually with the most appropriate synonym set from the Bulgarian wordnet (BulNet) (Koeva 2010b). Unlike the bulk of sense-annotated corpora where only (sets of) content words are annotated, in the Bulgarian Sense-annotated corpus[16] each lexical unit has been assigned a sense.

The Dependency part of BulTreeBank represents the syntactic information (based on HPSG) encoded in BulTreeBank. It consists of two sets of sentences: grammar derived examples (1,500) and corpus-derived ones (10,000 sentences) (Osenova/Simov 2004).

---

[14] http://search.dcl.bas.bg.

[15] http://dcl.bas.bg/Corpus/home_en.html.

[16] http://dcl.bas.bg/semcor/en/.

It gives examples from sentences from Bulgarian grammar textbooks, newspapers, literature and other sources of texts. The main function of the three resources is to serve as training and test corpora in the development of basic programmes for automatic annotation at a morpho-syntactical level (tagger), semantic level (word sense disambiguation tool) and syntactical level (parser) with sufficient accuracy and coverage.

Corpora might contain texts from one language only or more than one language. These are accordingly monolingual and multilingual corpora. Multilingual corpora can be divided into translated (consisting of originals and translated equivalents), parallel corpora (consisting of originals and translated equivalents, sentence (and word) aligned – for example the multi-lingual corpus of documents from the European Parliament JRC-ACQUIS[17]) and comparable corpora (collection of thematically similar texts in one or more languages) – for example news translation on Hristo Botev Bulgarian National Radio.

The Bulgarian-X language parallel corpora already compiled or under development are mainly focused on other Slavic, Balkan and West European Languages. One of the aims of the short-term European SEE-ERA NET project *Building Language Resources and Translation Models for Machine Translation Focused on South Slavic and Balkan Languages* (Tufiş et al. 2009) was to develop parallel corpora for Bulgarian, Greek, Romanian and Slovene plus Czech, English, French and German excerpts from Acquis Communautaire (called SEE-ERA.net Administrative Corpus – SEnAC) and for Jules Verne's novel *Around the world in 80 days* translated into French, German, Spanish, Portuguese, Italian, Romanian, Russian, Serbian, Croatian, Bulgarian, Macedonian, Polish, Slovenian, Hungarian and Greek (called SEE-ERA.net Literary Corpus – SEnLC). The SEnAC resulted in 60,389 translation units, each containing one sentence translated in the 8 languages. The SEnLC total number of segments is 4,409 and the average number of words per language is about 60,000. The selected texts are tokenised, tagged, lemmatised and aligned at the sentence level for both corpora subparts and at the word level for the SEnAC.

In the scope of the project Multext-East the versions of Orwell's novel *Nineteen Eighty-Four* in six languages (Bulgarian, Czech, Estonian, Hungarian, Romanian, and Slovene) were tagged for part-of-speech and aligned to English (Dimitrova et al. 1998). Another project resulted in the development of a bilingual collection of cultural texts in Greek and Bulgarian (Ghouli et al. 2009). The corpus amounts to 700,000 tokens in total (350,000 tokens per language): the literature sub-corpus is about 550,000 tokens, the folklore and legend sub-corpus is about 150,000 tokens.

There are other projects aimed at compiling and processing parallel corpora (targeting Bulgarian as well) – i.e. the RuN Corpus (Grønn/Marijanovic 2010), a parallel corpus consisting (mostly) of Norwegian and Russian texts, extended recently with parallel texts in other European languages including Bulgarian); the Bulgarian-Polish-Lithuanian Corpus (Dimitrova et al. 2009); the ParaSol (Waldenfels 2006), known as the Regensburg Parallel Corpus – a parallel aligned corpus of translated and original belletristic texts in Slavic (Bulgarian among them) and some other languages, etc.

[17] http://langtech.jrc.it/JRC-Acquis.html.

Two basic approaches are implemented in the compilation of the Bulgarian-X language corpora: 1) extracting them from well known multilingual databases of parallel texts available on the Internet, i.e. Acquis Communautaire (Steinberger et al. 2006), and 2) compiling new collections of parallel documents. In the scope of the combination of the two approaches special efforts have been made towards the development of Bulgarian-English-X language parallel corpus. It consists of Bulgarian English parallel fiction texts (34,553,474 words in Bulgarian), European union law documents in 23 languages (30,082,860 words in Bulgarian) and news items in 9 Balkan languages and English (7,056,104 words in Bulgarian). The corpus is aligned at the sentence level, the Bulgarian texts are tagged and lemmatized.

The conclusion that can be drawn from this brief and not complete overview of parallel corpora available, where Bulgarian is one of the languages in focus, is that those corpora are not very extensive; they represent generally administrative or literally texts and they are built from the available texts on the Internet, rather than on a planned strategy for developing a balanced and representative parallel corpus.

3.1 Dictionaries and lexical-semantic networks

Dictionaries are other basic components in Natural Language Processing. Computational dictionaries are different from electronic dictionaries in which words are normally presented as lists of basic forms. The term 'computational' is used to mean a dictionary the format which allows for more complex processing – for example the generation of all word forms relating to a given lemma or the link of a lemma and the relevant grammatical features with a specific word form. The format, structure and content of computational dictionaries are designed to serve the various applications of the Natural Language Processing.

Large morphological dictionaries developed by a number of centres (Institute for Bulgarian, University of Plovdiv, Language Modelling Laboratory) have existed for a long time (Koeva 1998; Totkov et al. 1988; Paskaleva 1997). They allow for the automatic analysis and synthesis of word forms and thus provide the ability to construct a paradigm (all possible forms) of a given word, the recognition of a given form as a part of a paradigm and to ascribe the grammatical features. Some of them are used for the development of spell checkers. For example, applications that have been developed at an academic level for spell checking and hyphenating both for Windows and MacOS, for example ItaEst[18] and MacEst.[19] However, such non-commercial applications despite providing high level functionality for correctness and convenience, cannot be expected to develop quickly on the market. A series of commercial products called Slovnik Plus (spell checker, hyphenator, translation dictionary from and into English, electronic synonym dictionary for Bulgarian) and Slovnik Expert (grammar checker) are offered by Sirma Media.[20] Kirila Korekt 10, a product offering full compatibility with Windows 7 and MS Office (spell checker and hyphenator, grammar checker, stylistic appropriate-

[18] http://www.bacl.org/itaestbg.html.
[19] http://dcl.bas.bg/MacEst.html.
[20] http://www.sirma.com/?Sirma_Media.

ness recommendations, synonym dictionary with added antonyms and search and replace functions based on all forms of a given word) is distributed by BMG Ltd.[21]

Wordnet and FrameNet undoubtedly occupy an important place amongst lexical resources which have been very important for the creation of more complex applications in the area of Natural Language Processing. Wordnet and FrameNet have been successfully used in intelligent information search and information retrieval from documents in different languages, text categorisation and text summarisation, word sense disambiguation, machine translation, as well as in many other Natural Language Processing tasks.

The Bulgarian wordnet (Koeva 2010a) is a lexical-semantic network which nodes are synonym sets (so-called synsets) which contain words or multiword expressions (called literals), while arcs contain semantic, morpho-semantic, derivational and extra-linguistic relations between objects placed within the nodes (Fellbaum 1998). The meaning of the lexical nodes in wordnet is expressed by means of the relations to the other nodes in the network, on the one hand and through the properties of the nodes itself (implicitly through the synonym relation between the literals in the synonym set and explicitly through the interpretative meaning and examples of meaning), on the other. Wordnet is one of the most complete and consistent lexical resources (in comparison the literals in the Bulgarian wordnet are much greater in number than the word list in a standard spelling dictionary), at the same time the synonym sets from different languages are connected by means of inter-language equivalence relations, which are used as a basis for the development of the wordnet multilingual lexical-semantic network, the so called global wordnet. Wordnet combines the qualities of the existing language resources. It contains definitions and examples, like ordinary dictionaries, but also organises synonym sets into a conceptual network by means of the semantic relations which exist between them. At the moment the Bulgarian data base contains more than 33,000 synonym sets. The Bulgarian wordnet is approximately one quarter the size of the English wordnet and is one of the biggest in Europe. The European organisation ELDA disseminates the Bulgarian wordnet.

The Bulgarian FrameNet represents general semantic and language-specific lexical-semantic and syntactic combinatory properties of Bulgarian lexical units (the pairing of a word (either a single word or a multi-word expression) and word sense). The Bulgarian FrameNet database (Koeva 2010c) so far contains unique descriptions of over 3,000 Bulgarian lexical units, approx., one tenth of them aligned with appropriate semantic frames (Ruppenhofer et al. 2006). A lexical entry in Bulgarian FrameNet consists of a lexical unit, a semantic frame from the English FrameNet expressing abstract semantic structure, a grammatical class, defining the inflexional paradigm, a valency frame describing (some of) the syntactic and lexical-semantic combinatory restrictions (an optional component) and (semantically and syntactically) annotated examples.

The unique character of the Bulgarian FrameNet is determined by the fact that it defines classes of lexical units in relation to: their place in a given semantic frame at an inter-language level, their productivity in the formation of diathesis, semantic and syntactic alternations, the expression of general morpho-syntactic characteristics and the description of (combinations of) obligatory and permissible contexts.

[21] http://www.bmg.bg/LiveContent/English.aspx.

With regard to resources such as lexicons, wordnets and framenets in Bulgaria substantial resources have been developed in recent years, although their enlargement and cross-validation are subject to further work.

4. Basic language processing tools

The automatic pre-processing and annotation of texts is a necessary precondition for the majority of Natural Language Processing systems. The identification of word and sentence boundaries in the majority of cases includes the removal of ambiguity in the use of punctuation, i.e. when a given symbol designates the end of a sentence and when not. The tokenization is the process of identifying words, phrases, symbols, or other meaningful elements in a text called tokens (the simplest definition of a token is a sequence of symbols between blanks). Many of the interesting problems in the area of computational linguistics, as well as many of the most important applications for the natural language processing require an automatic system for correct association of words with suitable grammatical categories and their values – a tagger. In the most general terms, tagging (the analysing of words according to parts of speech and the relevant values of their grammatical categories) includes the inputting of ambiguous grammatical information and disambiguation. Usually taggers are associated with tokenizers and sentence splitters. Again, Bulgarian taggers developed by a number of centres (Institute for Bulgarian, University of Plovdiv, Language Modelling Laboratory) have existed for a long time (Koeva 2008; Doychinova/Mihov 2004; Chanev/Krushkov 2006).

Lemmatisation is closely connected with the tagging of parts of speech and consists of ascribing a lemma, i.e. the basic form of inflectional words, to each word in the text after the performance of a morpho-syntactical analysis, as well as the relevant grammatical characteristics which characterise the used form of the word.

In order for a parallel corpus to be useful, it needs to be processed with sentence and word alignment – the process of connecting pairs of words, phrases, terms or sentences in texts from different languages which are translated equivalents. Although there are manually aligned Bulgarian parallel corpora, automatic alignment of parallel corpora is used due to the large volumes of texts (Tufiş et al. 2009).

Recently a word sense disambiguation tool was developed for Bulgarian. The principal application of Bulgarian Sense-annotated corpus is in training and evaluation of a multi-component word sense disambiguation system currently under development. The corpus is used in almost every stage of the system creation and tuning. Currently, it uses 4 independent "weak" classifiers (two knowledge-based and two implementing Hidden Markov Models) and fifth weak classifier assesses the confidence for a particular sense according to its frequency in Sense-annotated corpus. The current version outperforms the calculated random sense baseline by 24 points with an overall precision of ~65% (vs ~40% for random sense).

5. Main areas of applications of language resources

The main areas in which language resources and technologies are applicable are searching and extracting information, categorisation and summarisation, automatic question answering and machine translation as well as speech synthesis and recognition.

Even big search engines like Google do not use all the options for "intelligent" searching, especially for languages like Bulgarian which have a relatively small number of native speakers and relative small amount on texts exposed on the Internet. Jabse.com is a Bulgarian search engine (Jabse is an acronym of: Just Another Bulgarian Search Engine). Jabse uses its own spider to recognize and correctly index various types of documents (including MS Word, Adobe pdf, MS Power point, Flash swf). It can process Cyrillic domains and possesses its own evaluation system to define the importance of pages and terms contained therein on the basis of a range of criteria, including the number of incoming links. Certain Bulgarian portals have crawlers similar to those used by global search engines designed to index sites included within their categories. These portals provide the most accurate search results since their data bases include not only key words in the text description, but also words from the contents of the entire site and pages contained therein. Dir.bg, one of the first and largest web portals in Bulgaria launched a standalone service – Diri.bg. "Diri" (in Bulgarian "дири") is an old word for "search" ("tarsi" – "търси"). This new service is in direct competition with the existing Jabse and claims to have in the order of 50 million pages within its index. It is still to be seen whether Jabse or Diri.bg will develop sufficiently to become a significant factor in the Bulgarian Internet sphere.

The automatic categorisation of documents (in the Internet and specialised archives) can be performed on the basis of various criteria, for example the specific nature of the text, with the help of key words and phrases, but usually these phrases are not sufficiently reliable in themselves. Language processing can be used in automatic categorisation as a basic classification mechanism by providing semantic interpretation. Recently automatic categorisation of documents is provided in the scope of the Atlas[22] project aiming at the development of a platform combining three separate solutions: i-Publisher, that will provide a powerful web-based instrument for creating, running and managing content-driven web sites; i-Librarian that will allow its users to store, organize and publish their personal works, to locate similar documents in different languages, and to obtain easily the most essential texts from large collections of unfamiliar documents, and EUDocLib – a publicly accessible repository of EU documents.

In contrast to information extraction systems the purpose of which is to provide users with an approximate list of search coincidences, a question-answering system must be able to provide its users with specific information relevant to the question asked, rather than a list of close coincidences. Socrates (Tanev 2004) is an online system for question answering in Bulgarian. It searches for definitions, authors, inventors and discoverers, geography, maps, family links and dates. It also offers online demonstration of the functionality of the question answering system.

---

22 http://kms.atlasproject.eu/index.

There are many areas of communication in which machine translation can be successfully used: for example access to multi-lingual data bases, the creation of search systems, extraction of information and translation of documents, foreign language training – both in traditional forms and in new forms of distance or electronic learning, in communications: for the translation of electronic messages or other documents wherein the rapid transfer of information is of vital importance, in working with the contents of documents aimed at the automatic definition of the text theme, localisation of description of products for the needs of national and regional markets through the creation of the necessary documentation, and last but not least, in professional translation through the use of translation memory technologies in systems to assist translators, in order to improve and increase the speed of their work, as well as to automate the basic part of the translation process.

Machine translation is particularly challenging for Bulgarian. The rather flexible word order which when combined with the lack of morphological distinction for nominal cases and subject omission is a real challenge for natural language processing of Bulgarian and especially for machine translation.

One of the good examples is WebTrance by SkyCode[23] – a machine translation (MT) system which automatically translates texts, help files, menus, windows and Internet pages from English, German, French, Spanish, Italian and Turkish into and from Bulgarian. Meaning-based translation, rather than word-for-word translation, is a challenge for many people studying a foreign language. The aim of WebTrance is to provide meaningful translation of texts. Provided good adaptation in terms of user-specific terminology and workflow integration, the use of MT can increase productivity significantly.

Bultra[24] is a translation system which translates from English into Bulgarian. The original English texts can be sourced from various areas of knowledge. The advantages are: the creation of its own proprietary lexical data bases: the ability to work with several lexical bases; the inputting of words and expressions which do not need to be translated; and integrated electronic English-Bulgarian dictionary.

The ongoing project iTranslate4[25] will offer not only full coverage of EU languages, but also will provide for each language pair the best quality available at the time and mediates easy transfer to professional translators. Translation service is already available online (the translation will be available from any to any language, in many cases directly or if needed through English).

There also exist individual products with limited functionality in subfields such as speech synthesis and speech recognition. Ciela – a Bulgarian publisher of legal literature has its own system for Bulgarian speech recognition. The system was developed as an academic project based on a corpus of legal texts containing over 200 million words used to compile a dictionary of 450,000 word forms (Mitankin et. al. 2009). On the Bulgarian market, there are a few Bulgarian text-to-speech systems. One of these is SpeechLab 2.0[26] provid-

[23] http://webtrance.skycode.com/?lang=bg.

[24] http://transdict.com/translators/bultra.html.

[25] http://itranslate4.eu/project/index.html.

[26] http://www.bacl.org/speechlab.html.

ed free-of-charge to computer users with visual disabilities. SpeechLab 2.0 (Andreeva et al. 2005) allows non-sighted computer users to work in the Microsoft Windows 98/2000/XP/2003 environment. It has a synthesizing speed of approximately 108 words/sec. The speech synthesizing method used is diaphonic concatenation. The speech synthesizer works in Bulgarian and also provides for the correct pronunciation of English words.

6. Conclusions

Due to the volume restrictions of this submission it is not possible to list and compare in any detail the qualities of the existing language resources, technologies and software available for Bulgarian.

To sum up, the results indicate that Bulgarian stands reasonably well with respect to the most basic language technology tools and resources, such as tokenizers, POS taggers, morphological analyzers, reference corpora. However, such a study leads to the following general conclusions: a small number of research centres and companies are involved in the creation of language resources and programmes for their use, but they lack sufficient coordination between them. This has led to the parallel creation of language resources and programmes of one and the same type, such as morphological dictionaries and taggers. But even this fact can be viewed positively as there can be no absolute duplication, i.e. there are variations in the completeness, quality and application. However, there needs to be reliable documentation, accessible results from validation tests, in such a way that future users will be able to choose resources or programmes depending on the specific needs of their developments. The results would be even better if there were capabilities for the standardisation and convertibility of the resources, as well as the link between commercial products and research developments.

From this it is clear that more effort needs to be directed towards the development of resources for Bulgarian as well as into research, innovation, and development. It is also to be hoped that Bulgaria's participation in CESAR[27] and META-NET will make it possible to develop, standardise and make available several important Language resources and thus contribute to the growth of Bulgarian language technology.

7. References

Andreeva, M./Marinov, I./Mihov, S. (2005): SpeechLab 2.0 – A high-quality text-to-speech system for Bulgarian: In: *Proceedings of the RANLP 2005, Borovets, September 2005*. Borovets, 52-58.

Chanev, A./Krushkov, H. (2006): A simple part-of-speech-tagger for Bulgarian. In: *Research and Applied Conference in Mathematics, Informatics and Comuter Science*. Veliko Tarnovo, 195-198.

Dimitrova, L./Ide, N./Petkevic, V./Erjavec, T./Kaalep, H.J./Tufiş, D. (1998): Multext-East: parallel and comparable corpora and lexicons for six Central and Eastern European languages. In: Boitet, C./Whitelock, P. (eds.): *Proceedings of the Joint 17th International Conference on Computational Linguistics, Montréal, Canada, August 1998*. Montréal: Université de Montréal, 315-319.

[27] http://ec.europa.eu/information_society/apps/projects/factsheet/index.cfm?project_ref=271022.

Dimitrova, L./Koseska, V./Roszko, D./Roszko, R. (2009): Bulgarian-Polish-Lithuanian Corpus – Current Development. In: *Proceedings of the RANLP 2009. Borovets, Bulgaria, 17 September 2009*. Borovets.

Ghouli, V./Simov, K./Glaros, N./Osenova, P. (2009): A web-enabled and speech-enhanced parallel corpus of Greek-Bulgarian cultural texts. In: *EACL 2009 Workshop on Language Technology and Resources for Cultural Heritage, Social Sciences, Humanities, and Education*. 35-42.

Grønn, A./Marijanovic, I. (2010): Russian in contrast. In: *Oslo Studies in Language* 2, 1, 1-24.

Doychinova, V./Mihov, S. (2004): High performance part-of-speech tagging of Bulgarian. In: *Proceedings of Eleventh International Conference on Artificial Intelligence: Methodology, Systems, Applications* (*AIMSA-2004*). (= LNAI 3192). 246-255.

EAGLES (1996) = *EAGLES: Recommendations for the morphosyntactic annotation of corpora* (1996). (= *EAGLES Document EAG-TCWG-MAC/R*). Pisa: Consiglio Nazionale delle Ricerche. Istituto di Linguistica Computazionale.

Fellbaum, C. (ed.) (1998): *Wordnet: An electronic lexical database*. Cambridge, MA: MIT Press.

Koeva, S. (1998): Gramatichen rechnik na balgarskiya ezik. Opisanie na koncepciyata za organizaciyata na lingvistichnite danni. In: *Bulgarian Language*.5, 49-58.

Koeva, S./Leseva, S./Stoyanova, I./Tarpomanova, E./Todorova, M. (2006): Bulgarian tagged corpora. In: *Proceedings of the Fifth International Conference Formal Approaches to South Slavic and Balkan Languages, 18-20 October 2006, Sofia, Bulgaria*. 78-86.

Koeva, S. (2007): Multi-word term extraction for Bulgarian, ACL 2007. In: *Proceedings of the Conference on Balto-Slavic NLP*. 59-66.

Koeva, S. (2010a): Bulgarian Wordnet – current state, applications and prospects. In: Miltenova, A.L. (ed.): *Bălgaro-amerikanski dialozi* (*Bulgarian-American Dialogues*). Sofia: Prof. Marin Drinov Academic Publishing House, 120-132.

Koeva, S. (2010b): Balgarskiyat semantichno anotiran korpus – teoretichni postanovki. In: Koeva, S. (ed.): *Balgarskiyat semantichno anotiran korpus*. Sofia: Institute for Bulgarian Language, 7-42.

Koeva, S. (2010c): Lexicon and grammar in Bulgarian FrameNet. In: Calzolari, N./Choukri, K./Maegaard, B./Mariani, J./Odjik, J./Piperidis, S./Rosner, M./Tapias, D. (eds.): *Proceedings of the Seventh International Conference on Language Resources and Evaluation* (*LREC '10*), *Valletta*. Valletta: European Language Resources Association (ELRA), 3678-3684.

Koeva, S./Blagoeva, D./Kolkovska, S. (2010): Bulgarian National Corpus project: In: Calzolari, N./Choukri, K./Maegaard, B./Mariani, J./Odjik, J./Piperidis, S./Rosner, M./Tapias, D. (eds.): *Proceedings of the Seventh International Conference on Language Resources and Evaluation* (*LREC '10*), *Valletta*. Valletta: European Language Resources Association (ELRA), 3678-3684.

Krauwer, S. (2003): The Basic Language Resource Kit (BLARK) as the first milestone for the Language Resources Roadmap. In: *Proceedings of SPECOM 2003*. Moscow, 8-15. www.elsnet.org/dox/krauwer-specom2003.pdf.

Leech, G. (1997): Introducing corpus annotation. In: Garside, R./Leech, G./McEnery, A.M. (eds.): *Corpus annotation: linguistic information from computer text corpora*. London: Longman.

Mitankin, P./Mihov, S./Tinchev, T. (2009): Large vocabulary continuous speech recognition for Bulgarian. In: *Proceedings of the RANLP 2009. Borovets, Bulgaria, 17 September 2009.* Borovets, 246-250.

Osenova, P./Simov, K. (2004): *BTB-TR05: BulTreeBank Stylebook.* (= BulTreeBank Project Technical Report No. 05).

Paskaleva, E. (1997): Bulgarian language resources and tools in joint European initiatives. In: Marcinkevičienė, R./Volz, N. (eds.): *Proceedings of the Second European Seminar of TELRI.* Kaunas: Institut für Deutsche Sprache/VDU, 99-109.

Ruppenhofer, J./Ellsworth, M./Petruck, M.R.L./Johnson, C.R. (2006): *FrameNet II: extended theory and practice.* Berkeley: Unpublished manuscript. http://framenet.icsi.berkeley.edu/book/book.html.

Steinberger, R./Pouliquen, B./Widiger, A./Ignat, C./Erjavec, T./Tufiş, D. (2006): The JRC-Acquis: A multilingual aligned parallel corpus with 20+ languages. In: *Proceedings of the Fifth International Conference on Language Resources and Evaluation (LREC '06), Genoa.* Genoa, 2142-2147.

Tanev, H.T. (2004): Socrates – a question answering prototype for Bulgarian. In: Nicolov, N./Bontcheva, K./Angelova, G./Mitkov, R. (ed.): *Recent advances in Natural Language Processing: selected papers from RANLP 2003.* Vol. 3. Amsterdam: John Benjamins, 377-385.

Totkov, G./Krushkov, H./Krushkova, M. (1988): Formalization of the Bulgarian Language and development of a linguistic processor (morphology). In: *Travaux scientifiques* 26, 3,1, 988 – Mathematique, 301-310.

Tufiş, D./Koeva, S./Erjavec, T./Gavrilidou, M./Krstev, C. (2009): ID 10503 Building language resources and translation models for machine translation focused on south Slavic and Balkan languages. In: Machačová, J./Rohsmann, K. (eds.): *Scientific results of the SEE-ERA. NET Pilot Joint Call.* Vienna: Centre for Social Innovation (ZSI), 37-48.

Uszkoreit, H. (2000): *What is Computational Linguistics?* www.coli.uni-saarland.de/~hansu/what_is_cl.html.

Waldenfels, R. (2006): Compiling a parallel corpus of slavic languages. Text strategies, tools and the question of lemmatization in alignment. In: Brehmer, B./Zdanova, V./Zimny, R. (eds.): *Beiträge der Europäischen Slavistischen Linguistik (POLYSLAV) 9.* München: Sagner, 123-138.

Eiríkur Rögnvaldsson

Icelandic language technology: an overview

Abstract

We describe the establishment and development of Icelandic language technology since its very beginning ten years ago. The ground was laid with a report from an Expert Group appointed by the Minister of Education, Science and Culture in 1998. In this report, which was delivered in the spring of 1999, the group proposed several actions to establish Icelandic language technology. This paper reviews the concrete tasks that the group listed as important and their current status. It is shown that even though we still have a long way to go to reach all the goals set in the report, good progress has been made in most of the tasks. Icelandic participation in Nordic cooperation on language technology has been vital in this respect. In the final part of the paper, we speculate on the cost of Icelandic language technology and the future prospects of a small language like Icelandic in the age of information technology.

1. Introduction

At the turn of the century, Icelandic language technology (henceforth LT) was virtually non-existent.[1] There was a relatively good spell checker, a not-so-good speech synthesizer, and that was all. There were no programs or even individual courses on language technology or computational linguistics at any Icelandic university, there was no ongoing research in these areas, and no Icelandic software companies were working on language technology.

All of this has now changed and Icelandic language technology has been firmly established. In the fall of 1998, the Minister of Education, Science and Culture, Mr. Björn Bjarnason, appointed an Expert Group to investigate the situation in language technology in Iceland. Furthermore, the group was supposed to come up with proposals for strengthening the status of Icelandic language technology. The members of the group were Rögnvaldur Ólafsson, Associate Professor of Physics, Eiríkur Rögnvaldsson, Professor of Icelandic Language, and Þorgeir Sigurðsson, electrical engineer and linguist.

The Expert Group handed its report to the Minister in April 1999 (Ólafsson et al. 1999). It took a while to get things going, but in 2000, the Icelandic Government launched a special Language Technology Program (Arnalds 2004; Ólafsson 2004), with the aim of supporting institutions and companies to create basic resources for Icelandic language technology work. In the report, four types of actions were proposed in order to establish Icelandic language technology:

- The development of common linguistic resources that can be used by companies as sources of raw material for their products.
- Investment in applied research in the field of language technology.
- Financial support for companies for the development of language technology products.
- Development and upgrading of education and training in language technology and computational linguistics.

[1] This paper is a revised and updated version of material in Rögnvaldsson (2008); cf. also Rögnvaldsson et al. (2009).

This has all been done, to some extent at least (Arnalds 2004; Ólafsson 2004; Rögnvaldsson 2005), and this initiative resulted in several projects which have had profound influence on Icelandic LT. In this paper, we will give an overview of this work and other activities in the field during the past ten years, and then speculate on the prospects of language technology in Iceland and the future of the language in the age of information technology.

2. Priority tasks and their implementation

In this section, we give an overview of the most important resources, research projects and language technology products that the LT program initiated. The Expert Group report stated the following (Ólafsson et al. 1999, 33):

> For Icelanders, the main aim must be that it should be possible to use Icelandic, written with the proper characters, in as many contexts as possible in the sphere of computer and communication technology. Naturally, however, they will have to adjust their expectations to practical considerations. To make it possible to use Icelandic in all areas, under all circumstances, would be an immense task. Therefore, the main emphasis must be put on those areas that touch on the daily life and work of the general public, or are likely to do so in the near future.

Following this statement, the LT Expert Group proposed a list of priority tasks for Icelandic language technology during the following five years. Those tasks are listed here in italics at the beginning of each subsection, and in the text that follows, we try to estimate to what extent each task has been fulfilled (cf. also Arnalds 2004; Ólafsson 2004; Rögnvaldsson 2005).

2.1 Software translation

The main computer programs on the general market (Windows, Word, Excel, Netscape, Internet Explorer, Eudora,...) should be available in Icelandic.

In 2004, Icelandic versions of Windows XP (including Internet Explorer) and Microsoft Office 2003 came on the market. These versions do not seem to suffer from any technical bugs, as was the case with the first translation of Windows (Windows 98) into Icelandic a few years earlier. However, the translations have not met with great success, and most people, except perhaps the older generation, seem to prefer the English version. The reason is probably that people had grown used to having these programs in English and saw no reason for adopting the Icelandic version. An Icelandic translation of Windows 7 and Microsoft Office 2010 has just been finished, and it will be interesting to see whether these versions gain more popularity than their predecessors.

In addition to this, special interest groups have been formed in order to translate open-source software for GNU/Linux. Thus, there exists an Icelandic version of the KDE (K Desktop Environment; www.is.kde.org/), and the Ubuntu operating system (www.ubuntu.com/) is currently being translated. The Firefox browser has also been translated into Icelandic, together with the interfaces of popular websites such as Facebook.

2.2 Icelandic characters

It should be possible to use the Icelandic non-ASCII characters (áéíóúýðþæöÁÉÍÓ ÚÝÐÞÆÖ) in all circumstances: in computers, mobile telephones, teletext and other applications used by the public.

When this was written, the ISO 8859-1 standard, which includes all the above-mentioned characters, had already been in existence for a number of years. However, many TV sets lacked special Icelandic characters in teletext pages, and mobile phones could not show any non-ASCII characters since they used a 7-bit character table. Nowadays, most TV sets and mobile phones can show all Icelandic characters although there seem to be some exceptions. Thus, the situation has improved considerably during the last decade.

2.3 Morphological and syntactic parsing

Work should proceed on the parsing of Icelandic, with the aim that it should be possible to use computer technology to analyze Icelandic texts grammatically and syntactically.

The LT Program funded three major projects in this area. The Institute of Lexicography received a grant for building a full-form morphological database of Icelandic (Bjarnadóttir 2005). This database is still growing and now contains around 260,000 lexemes and 5.6 million inflectional forms (http://bin.arnastofnun.is). In another project at the Institute of Lexicography, three data-driven taggers of different types (TnT, MXPOST and fnTBL) were trained and evaluated on a manually tagged Icelandic corpus of 500,000 words (Helgadóttir 2005).

A commercial company, Frisk Software (http://frisk.is/), also received a grant for developing an HPSG-based parser with the future aim of building grammar and style checking software for Icelandic (Albertsdóttir/Stefánsson 2004). Unfortunately, this project has not been finished.

After the LT Program ended, Hrafn Loftsson, Assistant Professor in Computer Science at Reykjavik University, developed a rule-based PoS tagger, *IceTagger* (Loftsson 2006). Loftsson is also the main author of a shallow syntactic parser, *IceParser* (Loftsson/Rögnvaldsson 2007). A mixed method lemmatizer for Icelandic, *Lemmald*, has been developed by Anton Karl Ingason, a Language Technology student (Ingason et al. 2008). These three programs make up the IceNLP package which is online at http://nlp.cs.ru.is.

Furthermore, the LT Expert Group (Ólafsson et al. 1999) mentioned two prerequisites for further progress in this field, which are listed in 2.3.1 and 2.3.2.

2.3.1 A balanced corpus

A large computerized text corpus including Icelandic texts of a wide variety of types should be established.

In 2004, the Institute of Lexicography received a grant from the LT Program for building a balanced morphosyntactically tagged corpus of Modern Icelandic (Helgadóttir

2004). This corpus will contain 25 million words of different genres, including transcribed spoken language, and shall be finished in 2011. A preliminary version is online at http://mim.hi.is.

2.3.2 A semantically annotated lexicon

A grammatically and semantically annotated lexicon should be established.

This lexicon was meant to be something similar to the PAROLE/SIMPLE lexicon (www.ub.es/gilcub/ SIMPLE/simple.html). No such lexicon has been built yet. However, many types of raw material for building a lexicon of this type do exist, especially in various collections and databases at the Institute of Lexicography, such as the ISLEX database which comprises 50,000 entries for Icelandic and their equivalents in Danish, Norwegian, and Swedish (www.arnastofnun.is/page/arnastofnun_ord_islex) and will be finished in late 2011.

2.4 Spelling and grammar checkers

Good auxiliary programs should be developed for textual work in Icelandic, i.e. for hyphenation, spell-checking, grammar correction, etc.

When this was written (Ólafsson et al. 1999), we had the spell-checking program *Púki* from Frisk Software (http://frisk.is), which has now been improved with support from the LT Program (Skúlason 2004). In 2002, the Dutch company Polderland (http://www.polderland.nl/) developed a spell-checking program for the Microsoft Office package. Furthermore, there exists an open source spell checker for Icelandic based on Aspell (http://aspell.net/) which can be used with GNU/Linux applications. These programs (as most spell checkers) are word-based, and hence cannot cope with many common spelling errors.

No grammar checking or style checking programs exist, but a prototype of a context-sensitive spell checker has been developed which could hopefully lay the ground for a basic grammar checker (Ingason et al. 2009). This prototype has been integrated into LanguageTools (www.languagetool.org) and works with OpenOffice (www.openoffice.org).

2.5 Text-to-speech system

A good Icelandic speech synthesizer should be developed. It should be capable of reading Icelandic texts with clear and comprehensible pronunciation and natural intonation that is understandable without special training.

A formant-based Icelandic speech synthesizer was originally made around 1990 (Carlson et al. 1990) and improved around 2000. Even though this synthesizer was very useful for blind and visually impaired people, its quality was far from being satisfactory for use in commercial applications for the general public.

The last project that the LT Program supported was a new text-to-speech system, which was made in cooperation between the University of Iceland, Iceland Telecom, and Hex Software. The system was trained by Nuance and uses their technology. For several reasons, the system has not been put to use in commercial applications and many users, especially among the blind, do not find the voice quality of the system satisfying.

As a result, the Icelandic Organization of Blind and Partially Sighted is now planning to develop a new text-to-speech system in cooperation with the University of Iceland, Reykjavik University, and the Ivo software company (www.ivona.com/). If everything goes as planned, this system will be finished in 2012.

2.6 Speech recognition

Work should be done on speech recognition for Icelandic, the aim being to develop programs that can understand normal Icelandic speech.

In 2003, the University of Iceland and four leading companies in the telecommunication and software industry joined efforts to build an isolated word speech recognizer for Icelandic, with support from the LT Program and in cooperation with ScanSoft (now Nuance) (Rögnvaldsson 2004). The performance of the system has turned out to be quite satisfying; the recognition rate appears to be at least 97% (Rögnvaldsson 2004). However, no attempts have been made to develop a system for recognizing continuous speech.

2.7 Machine translation

Work should be done on the development of translation programs between Icelandic and other languages, one of the aims being to simplify searches in databases.

The development in this area has been limited, although some isolated experiments have been made. In 2008, Stefán Briem, an independent researcher, launched a free web-based service, which offers translations between Icelandic and three other languages (English, Danish, and Esperanto; http://tungutorg.is/). Hrafn Loftsson and his associates have been developing a rule-based shallow transfer translation system from Icelandic to English (Brandt et al. 2011), based on the Apertium platform (http://www.apertium.org/). A preliminary version of the system is available online at http://nlp.cs.ru.is/ApertiumISENWeb/.

Since 2009, Google Translate (http://translate.google.com) has offered translation to and from Iclandic. The quality of the translation was rather poor in the beginning, but is constantly getting better.

3. The current status of Icelandic LT

After the LT Program ended six years ago, LT researchers from three institutes (University of Iceland, Reykjavik University and the Árni Magnússon Institute for Icelandic Studies), who had been involved in most of the projects funded by the LT Program, decided to join forces in a consortium called the Icelandic Centre for Language Technology (ICLT), in order to follow up on the tasks of the Program. The main roles of the ICLT are to:

- serve as an information centre on Icelandic LT by running a website (http://iclt.is);
- encourage cooperation on LT projects between universities, institutions and commercial companies;

- organize and coordinate university education in LT;
- participate in Nordic, European and international cooperation within LT;
- initiate and participate in R&D projects in LT;
- keep track of resources and products in the field of Icelandic LT;
- hold LT conferences with the participation of researchers, companies and the public;
- support the growth of Icelandic LT in all possible manners.

Over the past six years, the ICLT researchers have initiated several new projects which have been partly supported by the Icelandic Research Fund and the Icelandic Technical Development Fund. The most important product of these projects is the IceNPL package (IceTagger, IceParser and Lemmald) mentioned in section 2.3 above. In 2009, the ICLT received a relatively large three year Grant of Excellence from the Icelandic Research Fund for the project "Viable Language Technology beyond English – Icelandic as a test case" (http://iceblark.wordpress.com). Within that project, three types of LT resources are being developed:

- a database of semantic relations (a pilot WordNet; Nikulásdóttir/Whelpton 2010);
- a prototype of a shallow-transfer machine translation system (Brandt et al. 2011);
- a treebank with a historical dimension (Rögnvaldsson et al. 2011).

These resources were chosen because they were considered central to current LT work and prerequisites for further research and development in Icelandic LT.

For a small language community and a small research environment like the Icelandic one, it is vital to cooperate, not only on the national level but also internationally. Since 2000, Icelandic researchers and policy makers have taken an active part in Nordic cooperation on language technology. This has been of major importance in establishing the field in Iceland. The Nordic Language Technology Research Programme 2000-2004 was instrumental in this respect. Icelandic researchers also take part in the Northern European Association for Language Technology (NEALT, http://omilia.uio.no/nealt/), and the bi-annual Nordic-Baltic conferences of computational linguistics (NODALIDA). In 2003, the 14th NODALIDA conference was held at the University of Iceland in Reykjavík.

Iceland has just recently entered the CLARIN consortium (http://clarin.eu), and takes part in the EU-funded META-NORD project which starts February 1st, 2011, and aims to establish an open linguistic infrastructure in the Baltic and Nordic countries. We sincerely hope that our participation in these projects will help us to develop, standardize and make available several important LT resources and thus contribute to the growth of Icelandic language technology.

4. The price and prospects of Icelandic LT

Twelve years ago, the LT Expert Group estimated that it would cost around one billion Icelandic krónas (which then amounted to about ten million Euros) to make Icelandic language technology self-sustained. After that, the free market should be able to take over, since it would have access to public resources that would have been created by the LT Program, and that would be made available on an equal basis to everyone who was going to use these resources in their commercial products.

However, the total budget of the government-funded LT program over its lifespan (2000-2004) was only 133 million Icelandic krónas – that is, around ⅛ of the sum that the Expert Group estimated would be needed. It should therefore come as no surprise that we still have a long way to go. There are only 320,000 people speaking Icelandic, and that is not enough to sustain costly development of new products. At present, no commercial companies are working in the LT area because they don't see it as profitable. It is thus extremely important to continue public support for Icelandic language technology for some time, but given the current financial situation, it does not seem likely that such support will come from the state budget in the near future.

When we try to estimate the importance of Icelandic language technology we must realize that ICT has become an important and integrated feature of the daily life of almost every single Icelander. If Icelandic cannot be used within ICT, speakers will be faced with a completely new situation, without parallels earlier in the history of the language. We will have an important area of the daily life of ordinary people where they cannot use their native language. How is that going to affect the speakers and the language community? What will happen when the native language is no longer usable within new technologies and in other new and exciting areas; in fields of innovation and creativity; and in areas where new job opportunities are offered? We don't have to think long about this scenario to see the signs of imminent danger.

In 2009, the Icelandic Parliament (Alþingi) unanimously approved an official language policy which had been prepared by the Icelandic Language Council (Íslenska til alls 2009). The policy document contains a section on ICT and the Icelandic language, where it is explicitly stated that Icelandic should be useable – and used – in all areas within information and communications technology that touch upon the daily life of the public. It remains to be seen what the government is going to do in order to implement this policy.

But the need for native language technology is not, and should not be, only driven by people's wish to protect and preserve their language. It is equally – or even more – important to look at this from the user's point of view. Ordinary people should not be forced to use foreign languages in their everyday lives. They have the right to be able to use their native language anytime and anywhere within their language community, in all possible contexts. Otherwise, they will be linguistically oppressed in their own language community.

5. References

Albertsdóttir, M./Stefánsson, S.E. (2004): Beygingar- og málfræðigreinikerfi [A system for morphological and syntactic parsing]. In: *Samspil tungu og tækni*. Reykjavík: Ministry of Education, Science and Culture, 16-19.

Arnalds, A. (2004): Language technology in Iceland. In: Holmboe, H. (ed.): *Nordisk Sprogteknologi. Årbog 2003*. Copenhagen: Museum Tusculanums Forlag Københavns Universitet, 41-43.

Bjarnadóttir, K. (2005): Modern Icelandic inflections. In: Holmboe, H. (ed.): *Nordisk Sprogteknologi. Årbog 2005*. Copenhagen: Museum Tusculanums Forlag Københavns Universitet, 49-50.

Brandt, M.D./Loftsson, H./Sigurþórsson, H./Tyers, F. (2011): Apertium-IceNLP: a rule-based Icelandic to English machine translation system. In: Forcada, M.L./Depraetere, H./Vandeghinste, V. (eds.): *EAMT 2011: Proceedings of the 15th Conference of the European Association for Machine Translation, 30-31 May 2011*. 217-224.

Carlson, R./Granström, B./Helgason, P./Thráinsson, H./Jensson, P. (1990): An Icelandic text-to-speech system for the disabled. In: *STL-QPSR* 31, 4, 55-56.

Helgadóttir, S. (2004): Mörkuð íslensk málheild [A tagged Icelandic corpus]. In: *Samspil tungu og tækni*. Reykjavík: Ministry of Education, Science and Culture, 67-71.

Helgadóttir, S. (2005): Testing data-driven learning algorithms for PoS tagging of Icelandic. In: Holmboe, H. (ed.): *Nordisk Sprogteknologi. Årbog 2004*. Copenhagen: Museum Tusculanums Forlag Københavns Universitet, 257-265.

Ingason, A.K./Helgadóttir, S./Loftsson, H./Rögnvaldsson, E. (2008): A mixed method lemmatization algorithm using a Hierarchy of Linguistic Identities (HOLI). In: Nordström, B./Ranta, A. (eds.): *Advances in natural language processing*. (= Lecture Notes in Computer Science 5221). Berlin: Springer, 205-216.

Ingason, A.K./Jóhannsson, S.B./Rögnvaldsson, E./Loftsson, H./Helgadóttir, S. (2009): Context-sensitive spelling correction and rich morphology. In: Jokinen, K./Bick, E. (eds.): *Proceedings of the 17th Nordic Conference of Computational Linguistics NODALIDA 2009*. (= NEALT Proceeding Series 4). Tartu: NEALT, Tartu University Library, 231-234.

Íslenska til alls [Icelandic for all purposes] (2009): Tillögur íslenskrar málnefndar að íslenskri málstefnu samþykktar á Alþingi 12. mars 2009. Reykjavík: Ministry of Education, Science and Culture.

Loftsson, H. (2006): Tagging a morphologically complex language using heuristics. In: Salakoski, T./Ginter, F./Pyysalo, S./Pahikkala, T. (eds.): *Advances in natural language processing, 5th International Conference on NLP, FinTAL 2006, Proceedings.* (= Lecture Notes in Computer Science 4139). Berlin: Springer, 640-651.

Loftsson, H. (2007): *Tagging and parsing Icelandic text*. Doctoral dissertation. Sheffield: Department of Computer Science, University of Sheffield.

Loftsson, H./Rögnvaldsson. E. (2007): IceParser: an incremental finite-state parser for Icelandic. In: Nivre, J./Kaalep, H.-J./Muischnek. K./Koit, M. (eds.): *Proceedings of the 16th Nordic Conference of Computational Linguistics NODALIDA-2007*. Tartu: University of Tartu, 128-135.

Nikulásdóttir, A.B./Whelpton, M. (2010): Extraction of semantic relations as a basis for a future semantic database for Icelandic. In: *Proceedings of 7th SaLTMiL Workshop on Creation and Use of Basic Lexical Resources for Less-Resourced Languages*. Valetta: SALTMIL, 33-39.

Ólafsson, Rögnvaldur (2004): Tungutækniverkefni menntamálaráðuneytisins [The Language Technology Program of the Ministry of Education, Science and Culture]. In: *Samspil tungu og tækni*. Reykjavík: Ministry of Education, Science and Culture, 7-13.

Ólafsson, Rögnvaldur/Rögnvaldsson, E./Sigurðsson, Þ. (1999): *Tungutækni. Skýrsla starfshóps* [Language Technology. Report of an expert group]. Reykjavík: Ministry of Education, Science and Culture.

Rögnvaldsson, E. (2004): The Icelandic speech recognition project *Hjal*. In: Holmboe, H. (ed.): *Nordisk Sprogteknologi. Årbog 2003*. Copenhagen: Museum Tusculanums Forlag Tusculanums, 239-242.

Rögnvaldsson, E. (2005): Staða íslenskrar tungutækni við lok tungutækniátaks [The Status of Icelandic Language Technology at the End of the Language Technology Program]. In: *Tölvumál* 24-2. www.sky.is/index.php?option=com_content&task=view&id=55&Itemid=85).

Rögnvaldsson, E. (2008): Icelandic Language Technology ten years later. In: *Collaboration: Interoperability between People in the Creation of Language Resources for Less-resourced Languages. SALTMIL workshop, LREC 2008*. Marrakech: SALTMIL, 1-5.

Rögnvaldsson, E./Ingason, A.K./Sigurðsson, E.F. (2011): Coping with Variation in the Icelandic Diachronic Treebank. In: Johannessen, J.B. (ed.): *Language variation infrastructure. Papers on selected projects*. (= Oslo Studies in Language 3.2). Oslo: University of Oslo, 97-111.

Rögnvaldsson, E./Loftsson, H./Bjarnadóttir, K./Helgadóttir, S./Nikulásdóttir, A.B./Whelpton, M./Ingason, A.K. (2009): Icelandic language resources and technology: status and prospects. In: Domeij, R./Koskenniemi, K./Krauwer, S./Maegaard, B./Rögnvaldsson, E./de Smedt, K. (eds.): *Proceedings of the NODALIDA 2009 workshop Nordic Perspectives on the CLARIN Infrastructure of Language Resources*. Tartu: NEALT, Tartu University Library, 27-32.

Skúlason, F. (2004): Endurbætt tillögugerðar- og orðskiptiforrit Púka [Improved suggestions and hyphenations in the Púki Spell Checker]. In: *Samspil tungu og tækni*. Reykjavík: Ministry of Education, Science and Culture, 29-31.

6. Acknowledgements

As working at the University of Iceland as Professor of Icelandic Language, I would would like to thank the University and especially the Faculty of Icelandic and Comparative Cultural Studies for providing infrastructural assistance to my work and this text.

Andreas Witt / Oliver Schonefeld

Informationsinfrastrukturen am Institut für Deutsche Sprache

Abstract

This paper describes the effort of the Institut für Deutsche Sprache (IDS), the central research institution for the German language, connected with Information and Communications Technology (ICT). Use of ICT in a language research institute is twofold. On the one hand, ICT provides basic services for researches to accomplish their daily work. On the other hand, several national and international institutions have a strong interest in ICT. Therefore, ICT can also be seen as an amplifier for language research. The first part of this paper reports on the activates of the IDS in internal and external ICT-related projects and initiatives. The second part describes a general strategy towards an ICT strategy that could be useful both for the IDS and other national language institutes. We think such a general strategy is necessary to create a strong foundation not only for the ICT-related projects, but as a basis for a modern research institute.

1. Einleitung

Informations- und Kommunikationstechnologie ("Information and Communications Technology (ICT)") ist in den letzten Jahren in den Geisteswissenschaften bzw. der geisteswissenschaftlichen Forschung zu einem festen Bestandteil der Arbeitswelt geworden und wird in vielfältiger Weise eingesetzt. Dabei können grob zwei verschiedene Bereiche unterschieden werden: Auf der einen Seite finden sich IT-Systeme nahezu überall im Alltag eines (Geistes-)Wissenschaftlers. Forschungsinstitute müssen daher heutzutage eine Reihe von IT-Basisdiensten bereitstellen. Am Institut für Deutsche Sprache (IDS) sind daher verschiedene IT-Systeme etabliert und akzeptiert. Auf der anderen Seite ist die IT-Infrastruktur auch für grundlegende wissenschaftliche, am IDS natürlich sprachwissenschaftliche, Forschungen ein Motor. Dies zeigt sich am IDS unter anderem auch daran, dass in den letzten Jahren eine Vielzahl von Infrastrukturforschungsprojekten mit sprachwissenschaftlichem Fokus institutionalisiert worden sind.

Am 31.01.2011 veröffentlichte der Wissenschaftsrat Empfehlungen für Forschungs- und Informationsinfrastrukturen für die Geistes- und Sozialwissenschaften. Das IDS fühlt sich durch diese Veröffentlichungen aus unterschiedlichen Gründen angesprochen: direkt, da die IDS-Aktivitäten im Bereich Forschungsinfrastrukturen mehrfach explizit erwähnt wurden, aber auch indirekt, da die sich das IDS bestätigt fühlt, in den vergangenen Jahren seine Forschungs- und Entwicklungsaktivitäten so intensiv in diesem Bereich vorangetrieben zu haben. Zu diesen Aktivitäten gehören nicht nur genuine IDS-Projekte, die sich im Kontext der neuen Forschungsumgebungen positioniert haben, sondern auch Aktivitäten die im Rahmen nationaler oder internationaler Verbünde durchgeführt werden.

Aus der Sicht des IDS sind die nachfolgend aufgeführten Empfehlungen des Wissenschaftsrats besonders relevant:

- Das Engagement insbesondere für die von Forschungsfragen getriebenen Infrastrukturentwicklungen muss aus den wissenschaftlichen Gemeinschaften kommen, und entsprechende Projektvorschläge müssen sich in einem Ideenwettbewerb auszeichnen. (Wissenschaftsrat 2011a, S. 8)

- [Um] Infrastrukturbedarfe der disziplinären Grundversorgung [...] unabhängig von konkreten Projekten auf der Ebene einer Fachgemeinschaft [zu ermitteln, ist es] eine notwendige Voraussetzung [...], dass die entsprechende Fachgemeinschaft über eine für Infrastrukturfragen sensibilisierte und gegenüber den Zuwendungsgebern artikulationsfähige Organisationsstruktur verfügt. [...] Das Problembewusstsein und die Artikulationsfähigkeit insbesondere der Geisteswissenschaften [...] [sind] im Infrastrukturbereich vergleichsweise gering ausgeprägt. Hier besteht auch angesichts des erwartbaren nationalen Roadmap-Prozesses, der zu einer disziplinübergreifenden Priorisierung von Forschungsinfrastrukturen führen soll, noch Verbesserungsbedarf. (ebd., S. 42f.)
- Den Infrastruktur tragenden Einrichtungen empfiehlt der Wissenschaftsrat, sich bereits in der Konzeptionsphase für neue Infrastrukturprojekte in den Geistes- und Sozialwissenschaften mit anderen nationalen und internationalen Einrichtungen abzustimmen. (ebd., S. 82)
- Öffentlich finanzierte Informationsinfrastrukturen sollten externen Nutzerinnen und Nutzern aus dem In- und Ausland für wissenschaftliche Zwecke grundsätzlich zugänglich sein. (Wissenschaftsrat 2011b, S. 49)
- Informationsinfrastrukturen sollten eine zentrale Rolle bei der Entwicklung von sowohl national als auch international ausgerichteten Kooperations- und Vernetzungsstrategien der verantwortlichen Einrichtung einnehmen. In kooperativen Forschungsprojekten ist darauf zu achten, dass die entsprechenden Einrichtungen nicht ausschließlich oder überwiegend auf Servicefunktionen wie beispielsweise die Bereitstellung von Daten beschränkt bleiben, sondern sich mit eigenen Forschungsbeiträgen beteiligen. (ebd., S. 49)

Die bereits etablierten und in diesem Beitrag skizzierten forschungsinfrastrukturbezogenen Aktivitäten des IDS können im Kontext dieser Empfehlungen betrachtet werden.

Der Artikel ist dergestalt gegliedert, dass in der ersten Hälfte ein Vielzahl von IDS-Aktivitäten mit starkem Bezug zu ICT aufgeführt sind. Diese sind entweder reine Hausprojekte, die zum Teil seit mehreren Jahrzehnten erfolgreich laufen, oder nationale und internationale Verbundprojekte an denen sich das IDS beteiligt. Der zweite Teil des Beitrags skizziert eine Gesamtstrategie zum Umgang mit Informations- und Kommunikationstechnologie im IDS. Eine derartige Strategie ist unabdingbar um eine moderne und zukunftssichere Basis für den Umgang mit ICT am IDS zu schaffen und bildet damit nicht nur Grundlage für die Durchführung der im ersten Teil beschriebenen Projekte, sondern ist vielmehr die Basis für den Betrieb einer geisteswissenschaftlichen Institution, die sich der Erforschung und Dokumentation der Sprache widmet. Wir sehen daher die beschriebenen Aktivitäten des IDS in diesem Kontext auch als mögliches Modell für andere EFNIL-Einrichtungen.

2. Grundständige hausintere Projekte des IDS und interne Vernetzung

Das IDS führt seine Forschungsarbeiten in sogenannten Programmbereichen durch, die innerhalb einzelner Abteilungen oder im Bereich Zentrale Forschung angesiedelt sind. Nachfolgend werden exemplarisch aus zwei Programmbereichen einige Projekte, die insbesondere auf eine moderne informationstechnologische Infrastruktur angewiesen sind, vorgestellt.

2.1 Korpuslinguistik

Der Programmbereich Korpuslinguistik widmet sich seit mehreren Jahrzehnten u.a. dem Aufbau, der Pflege und dem Zugang zu Korpora geschriebener Sprache. Die empirische

Basis der Forschungsarbeiten der Korpuslinguistik bildet das Deutsche Referenz Korpus (DeReKo), das kontinuierlich weiter ausgebaut wird. Es ist bereits seit vielen Jahren weltweit eines der größten Sammlungen geschriebener deutscher Sprachdaten. Anfang des Jahres 2011 umfasste es etwa 4 Milliarden Wörter. Das Design des Korpus orientiert sich an dem im IDS konzipierten Ansatz der Urstichprobe. Dieser Ansatz steht im Kontrast zu den repräsentativen, ausgewogenen oder auch gewichteten Korpora, deren Design eine finale Ausbaustufe, meist definiert bezüglich Größe und Texttypverteilung, definiert, die dann beim Korpusaufbau angestrebt wird. Eine Urstichprobe dagegen wächst kontinuierlich und umfasst alle Texte, die akquiriert werden können. Die tatsächlichen Arbeitskorpora, die als virtuelle Korpora bezeichnet werden (Kupietz et al. 2010a), sind eine Teilmenge der Urstichprobe und die Auswahl der Texte basiert auf den Metadaten, die den einzelnen Texten zugeordnet sind.

Aufgrund von urheber- und lizenzrechtlichen Restriktionen ist es nicht möglich, die (virtuellen) Korpora frei, z.B. zum Download, zur Verfügung zu stellen. Vielmehr erfolgt der Zugriff mit spezialisierter Software. Derzeit steht hierfür das Korpusrecherche- und -analysesystem COSMAS (Corpus Search, Management and Analysis System) zur Verfügung. In seiner ersten Fassung (COSMAS I; vgl. al-Wadi 1994) wurde es 1991 der wissenschaftlichen Öffentlichkeit zur kostenlosen Benutzung zur Verfügung gestellt. Das Nachfolgesystem COSMAS II (Bodmer 2005) wurde 2003 in Betrieb genommen und hat sich seitdem im Dauerbetrieb bewährt. Es können u.a. über eine WWW-Schnittstelle Suchanfragen zu Wörtern, Wortfolgen und grammatischen Mustern eingegeben werden, nach denen die Korpustexte durchsucht werden sollen. Die Ergebnisse können gemäß unterschiedlichen Kriterien, u.a. nach Entstehungszeit, Erscheinungsland und Thematik, sortiert werden. Die gefundenen Belege zeigen die gesuchten Wörter im Kontext ihrer textuellen Umgebung gemeinsam mit den bekannten bibliographischen Angaben, wie Verlag, Autor, Entstehungszeit, Seitenangabe. Derzeit hat COSMAS II ca. 17.000 registrierte Benutzer.

Da COSMAS I und II bereits Anfang der 90er Jahre konzipiert wurden und die darauffolgenden softwaretechnischen Umsetzungen auf dem damaligen Stand der Informationstechnologie erfolgte, steigt heutzutage der Arbeitsaufwand diese Software zu pflegen und zu erweitern überproportional an. Zwischenzeitlich haben sich sowohl die technischen als auch die wissenschaftlichen Rahmenbedingungen derart stark verändert, dass die Entwicklung eines neuartigen Analyse-Tools erstrebenswert wurde. Mit dem Projekt "Korpusanalyseplattform der nächsten Generation" (KORAP) gelang es dem IDS in einem kompetitiven Auswahlverfahren der Leibniz Gemeinschaft ein Projekt einzuwerben, in dem eine neuartige Korpusanalyseplattform entwickelt werden wird, die eine Grundlage für den methodisch validen Umgang mit *very large corpora* insbesondere im Bereich der empirischen germanistischen Sprachwissenschaft schafft.

Um die eindeutige und nachhaltige Referenzierbarkeit von Sprachressourcen, z.B. auch der virtuellen Korpora, sicherzustellen, hat sich der IDS-Programmbereich Korpuslinguistik gemeinsam mit dem Programmbereich Forschungsinfrastrukturen auch im Bereich der Standardisierung eines persistenten Identifikationsmechanismus für Sprachdaten engagiert. Die Relevanz dieser Aufgabe ist auch in dem Wissenschaftsratsempfehlungen hervorgehoben: "Für die Langzeitarchivierung von Forschungsprimärdaten empfiehlt der Wissenschaftsrat den Ausbau von Referenz- und Zitationsmöglichkeiten für Datensätze" (Wissenschaftsrat 2011a, S. 9). Die international abgestimmte Standardisierungsaktivität mündete in dem vor seiner endgültigen Verabschiedung stehenden Standard ISO 24619 "Language resource management – persistent identification and sustainable access (PISA)".

© Cyril Belica: Modelling Semantic Proximity - Self-Organizing Map (version: 0.32, init tau: 0.04, dist: u, iter: 5000)

Sprache

Tschechisch	Italienisch	Fremdsprache	Rechnen
Niederländisch	Spanisch	gelehrt	Grundkenntnis
Ungarisch	Latein	pauken	Kulturtechnik
Schwedisch	Griechisch	büffeln	Einmaleins
Russisch	Französisch	Sprachunterricht	Lautsprache
Finnisch	Slowenisch	Unterrichtsfach	Landeskunde
Dänisch	Unterrichtssprache	Erdkunde	Philologie
Rumänisch	Sprachkenntnisse	unterrichten	Naturwissenschaft
Portugiesisch	Muttersprache	Gebärdensprache	Grammatik
Amtssprache	Landessprache	Konversation	Grundbegriff
Jiddisch	Hebräisch	rudimentär	Rechtschreibung
Hindi	Polnisch	Muttersprachler	Sprechen
Hochdeutsch	Englisch		Lesen
fließend	Chinesisch		Metier
Schweizerdeutsch	Türkisch		Lese
akzentfrei	Japanisch		Handwerk
Idiom	Schriftsprache	slawisch	Mentalität
Umgangssprache	Vokabel	Diktion	Bauchtanz
abfassen	übersetzt	linguistisch	Kulturraum
Mundart	übersetzen		Ausdrucksweise
Dialekt	Hochsprache		Ausdrucksmittel
abgefasst	Fachsprache		Kultur
Originalsprache	Blindenschrift		Bildsprache
gesprochen	verfasst		Stilelement
phonetisch	hebräisch	Literatur	Abstammung
Wort	Übersetzung	Dichtung	Herkunft
jiddisch	lateinisch	Lyrik	Staatsbürger
Alltagssprache	Text	Kalligraphie	Nationalität
hochdeutsch	kyrillisch	Ursprung	Folklore
Fachausdruck	Wörter	Sprachraum	Provenienz
plattdeutsch	Schriftzeichen	germanisch	Intellektueller
Redewendung	Alphabet	Einsprengsel	Lebensart

Abb. 1: Kookkurenzprofil des Wortes "Sprache" visualisiert als Selbstorganisierende Karte (SOM)

Ein weiteres in der Korpuslinguistik entwickeltes Werkzeug bildet die Kookkurrenzdatenbank (CCDB; Keibel/Belica 2007). Die CCDB wird beschrieben als eine "korpuslinguistische Denk- und Experimentierplattform für die Erforschung und theoretische Begründung von systemisch-strukturellen Eigenschaften von Kohäsionsrelationen zwischen den Konstituenten des Sprachgebrauchs" (http://corpora.ids-mannheim.de/ccdb/). In Abbildung 1 findet sich beispielhaft die Anzeige der Kookkurenzprofile des Wortes "Sprache". In unterschiedlichen Feldern, die in der Online-Fassung farbig angezeigt werden, sind verschiedene Lemmata aufgeführt, die sich, basierend auf statistischen Analysen in den Textkorpora, gruppieren lassen. Es kann beobachtet werden, dass die Wörter in den einzelnen Feldern gewisse semantische Eigenschaften teilen, obwohl keine manuelle Bearbeitung der Ergebnisse erfolgte.

Das Beispiel der CCDB zeigt ein weiteres Charakteristikum sowohl des Instituts für Deutsche Sprache als auch der Einsatzgebiete der Informations- und Kommunikationstechnologie in der sprachwissenschaftlichen Forschung: die Schnittstellen zwischen den einzelnen Bereichen und Abteilungen sind nicht immer trennscharf beschreibbar. So basiert die Kooperationsdatenbank zwar auf den Korpora und wurde konsequenterweise im Programmbereich Korpuslinguistik entwickelt, die Ergebnisse dieser Forschungsarbeiten sind aber auch für den Programmbereich Lexik äußerst nützlich und werden in bestimmte Onlineangebote der Lexik integriert.

2.2 Lexik

Im Programmbereich Lexik wird seit mehreren Jahren das Online-Wortschatz-Informationssystem Deutsch (OWID) entwickelt. Dieses Webportal (www.owid.de) ermöglicht den Zugang zu verschiedenen im Bereich Lexik entwickelten Angeboten. Hierbei handelt es sich um “elexiko” (Müller-Spitzer 2008), das digitale “Neologismenwörterbuch”, eine digitale Sammlung “Fester Wortverbindungen” und das elektronisch verfügbare “Diskurswörterbuch 1945-1955”. Diese digitalen Ressourcen haben zum Teil auch ein analoges Äquivalent, z.B. wurden die Neologismenwörterbücher des IDS auch auf Papier veröffentlicht (Herberg et al. 2004). Des Weiteren hat der Bereich Lexik eine Online-Bibliografie zur elektronischen Lexikografie (OBELEX) erarbeitet, die über das World Wide Web zur Verfügung gestellt wird.

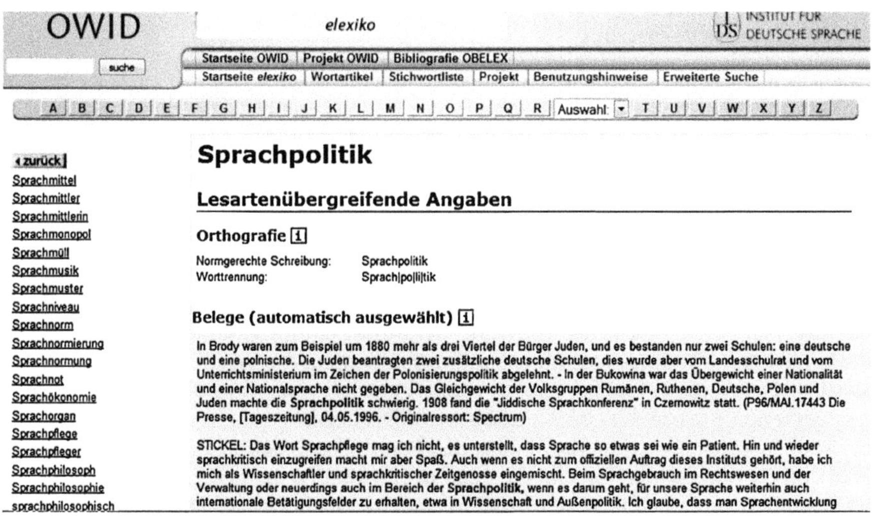

Abb. 2: Das elektronische Wörterbuch “elexiko”

Abbildung 2 zeigt einen Screenshot des elektronischen lexikalischen Informationssystems “elexiko”. Da es über das Portal OWID aufgerufen wurde, befinden sich in der Kopfzeile die Logos von OWID, elexiko und dem IDS. Die Basisinformation, die für ca. 300.000 Wörter über elexiko bereitgestellt wird, bildet den Hauptteil der Webseite. Zum Einen werden für die Wörter die korrekte Schreibung oder gegebenenfalls die normgerechten Schreibvarianten sowie die Grenzen für die Silbentrennung aufgeführt. Zum Anderen werden Vorkommen des Wortes in den IDS-Sprachkorpora angezeigt. Dies ist ein weiteres Beispiel für eine programmbereichsübergreifende Nutzung digitaler Sprachressourcen. Zu diesen Belegen werden zusätzlich die entsprechenden Metadaten angezeigt. So kann man beispielsweise sehen, dass der erste angezeigte Beleg aus der Tageszeitung “Die Presse” vom 4.5.1996 stammt.

Zusätzlich zu diesen Informationen werden für ausgewählte Lemmata detaillierte Wortartikel in elexiko angezeigt. Derzeit sind bereits ca. 1.600 Wortartikel verfasst worden. Für das in der Abbildung angezeigte Lemma steht ein derartiger Wortartikel bisher nicht zur Verfügung, so dass in dem Screenshot nur die Basisinformationen zu sehen sind.

Die starke Integration unterschiedlicher elektronischer Angebote ist in dem Portal auch an der Einbettung eines Verweises auf die Online-Bibliografie zur elektronischen Lexikografie sichtbar. Die Integrationsmöglichkeit für verschiedene elektronische Angebote stellt einen besonderen Mehrwert gegenüber traditionellen Arbeitsweisen dar. Bei der Aufbereitung von Informationen für das WWW haben sich in den vergangenen zwei Jahrzehnten hierbei sehr elaborierte Techniken entwickelt, die häufig genutzt werden. Eine neue Entwicklung besteht darin, die Integration und Interoperabilität von digitalen Sprachressourcen auch für über Web-Präsentationen hinausgehende Anwendungen zu ermöglichen. Dies ist ein Ziel von verschiedenen Verbundprojekten an denen auch das IDS beteiligt ist.

3. Externe Vernetzung

Das IDS ist mit dem Programmbereich Forschungsinfrastrukturen an einer Reihe von nationalen und internationalen Kooperationsprojekten beteiligt. Weiterhin wirkt das IDS in Standardisierungsgremien mit und beteiligt sich als aktiver Partner im Kompetenznetzwerk für Langzeitarchivierung (nestor). Diese Aktivitäten sollen in den nachfolgenden Abschnitten kurz vorgestellt werden.

3.1 CLARIN / D-SPIN

Das europäische Verbundprojekt CLARIN (Common Language Resource Infrastructure) hat das Ziel, ein europäisches Netzwerk von Infrastrukturzentren für den Zugang und die kollaborative Nutzung von digitaler Sprachressourcen aufzubauen. In verschiedenen an CLARIN beteiligen Ländern gibt es zudem nationale Verbünde, die die Netzwerke in den einzelnen Staaten auf- bzw. ausbauen. In Deutschland arbeitet an dieser Aufgabe das vom Bundesministerium für Bildung und Forschung (BMBF) geförderte Verbundprojekt D-SPIN (Deutschen Sprachressourcen-Infrastruktur), das seit 2011 als CLARIN-D weitergeführt wird. D-SPIN bzw. CLARIN-D hat das Ziel in Deutschland diese Infrastruktur und entsprechende spezialisierte Software interoperabel und nachhaltig verfügbar bereitzustellen. Um dies zu erreichen werden dedizierte Zentren aufgebaut, in denen Primärdaten, wie Textkorpora oder Sprachaufnahmen, und Metadaten zu derartigen Ressourcen dergestalt bereitgehalten werden, dass sie von Forschungseinrichtungen oder auch von Einzelpersonen insbesondere für die sprachwissenschaftliche Forschung genutzt werden können. Das IDS hat das Ziel im Rahmen von D-SPIN ein Sprachressourcenzentrum aufzubauen und in diesem Verbundprojekt den Standort Mannheim als wichtigen Partner zu etablieren.

Des Weiteren arbeitet das IDS in diesem Rahmen auch an Rechtefragen beim Umgang mit Sprachressourcen, wobei insbesondere Urheber-, Verwertungs- und Persönlichkeitsrechte von Bedeutung sind. Konkret erarbeitet das IDS u.a. Modelle für Lizenzvereinbarungen und für den Umgang mit Sprachdaten, die datenschutzrechtlichen Auflagen unterliegen. Außerdem werden weitergehende Fragestellungen betrachtet. Genannt sei hier exemplarisch die Problematik des Konflikts der im Grundgesetz verankerten Grundrechte zum Schutz des Eigentums und zur Freiheit der Forschung und Wissenschaft, da die freie Verfügbarkeit von Sprachressourcen den Rechten der Besitzer der Verwertungsrechte, z.B. der Verlage, entgegenstehen kann.

Ebenfalls im Kontext von D-SPIN und CLARIN-D wird in Mannheim an der Implementierung von Katalogen und Registraturen für virtuelle Kollektionen von Datenressourcen, wie z.B. für die bereits oben erwähnten virtuellen Korpora, gearbeitet, deren Bestandteile auch über verschieden Standorte verteilt sein können sollen. Um hierbei keine Insellösungen zu produzieren, war das IDS auch der Konzeption des bereits erwähnten ISO-Standards für die persistente Referenzierbarkeit von Sprachressourcen (ISO/DIS 24619) beteiligt.

3.2 TextGrid

Die nationalen, ebenfalls vom BMBF geförderten Forschungsverbünde TextGrid und WissGrid, an denen das IDS beteiligt ist, widmen sich der Grid-Technologie, einem informationstechnologischen Ansatz, der auf einer – auch räumlich – verteilten Rechnerarchitektur basiert. Die Computer können sowohl als distribuierte Datenspeicher als auch als Ansammlung einer großen Menge von Rechenprozessoren genutzt werden. Letzteres hat in den Naturwissenschaften zu Erfolgen geführt, da z.B. die Verwendung einer Vielzahl von Arbeitsplatzrechnern zu Problemen führte, deren Lösungsalgorithmen parallelisiert werden können und teure Supercomputer ersetzen können. In den digitalen Geisteswissenschaften, in denen sich das Projekt TextGrid verorten lässt, ist der Bedarf an sehr großen Rechenkapazitäten derzeit noch nicht so stark ausgeprägt. Der Einsatz der Grid-Technologie ist dennoch auch für TextGrid sehr sinnvoll, da die damit verbundene Rechnerarchitektur für die verteilte Datenhaltung genutzt werden kann, wodurch die Lastverteilung bei hohen Nutzerzahlen ermöglicht wird. Des Weiteren wird die Ausfallsicherheit erheblich verbessert, da z.B. bei einem Defekt eines Rechners die Nutzer auf den anderen Rechnern weiterarbeiten können.

Das Ziel von TextGrid besteht darin, eine *virtuelle Forschungsumgebung* (engl. Virtual Research Environment, VRE) für die Geisteswissenschaften aufzubauen. Eine VRE wird vom britischen Joint Information Systems Committee (JISC; www.jisc.ac.uk) u.a. dadurch charakterisiert, dass sie den Forscher/innen und ihren Forschungsprozessen die größtmögliche Unterstützung während der zunehmend komplexer werdenden Arbeitsabläufe bietet und hierfür Werkzeuge und Technologien bereitstellt, die benötigt werden, um kollaborativ, disziplinübergreifend, international und institutionell unabhängig interagieren zu können. Das Projekt TextGrid implementiert für diese Zwecke eine Software, die Module für verscheidende geisteswissenschaftliche Disziplinen unter einer gemeinsamen Benutzeroberfläche zusammenbringt. Diese Module wurden entweder neu entwickelt oder es erfolgte ein Integration existierender Dienste in das TextGrid-System. Zu den beteiligten Fachwissenschaften, für die die Software insbesondere entwickelt wurde, gehören neben der Sprachwissenschaft auch die Musikwissenschaft, die Editionsphilologie und die Kunstgeschichte.

Das Projekt WissGrid hat die Aufgabe, den Einsatz der Grid-Technologie in verschiedene Wissenschaften zu unterstützen und nachhaltig zu etablieren. Beteiligt sind neben der Sprachwissenschaft, die durch das IDS vertreten ist, u.a. auch Klimaforschung und medizinische Informatik. Zu den Zielen von WissGrid gehört die Erstellung von Konzepten für die Langzeitarchivierung im Grid, die Erarbeitung langfristiger Betriebsmodelle, die es ermöglichen die auch kostenaufwändige Infrastruktur langfristige zu betreiben, und das Verfassen von Leitfäden für Fachdisziplinen, die die Grid-Technologien neu nutzen möchten.

3.3 Standardisierung

In den eingangs erwähnten Empfehlungen des Wissenschaftsrates wird auch die Wichtigkeit von Standards hervorgehoben:

> Mit Blick auf die Bereitstellung und externe Nutzung bereits erhobener Daten und fertig gestellter Digitalisate ist ebenfalls eine verstärkte Koordination unter den dezentral verteilten Anbietern anzumahnen. Der Wissenschaftsrat empfiehlt hier nachdrücklich den Trägern von Infrastrukturen, sich bei disziplinär und thematisch verwandten Daten auf gemeinsame Standards der Aufbereitung und auf ein gemeinsames – von einer federführenden Einrichtung zentral bereitgestelltes – Portal zu verständigen, das den interessierten Nutzerinnen und Nutzern eine "one-stop-shopping"-Option ermöglicht. Das heißt, dass dezentral gesammelte, aufbereitete und angebotene Daten den Forscherinnen und Forschern über eine gemeinsame Anlaufstation zur Verfügung stehen müssten, auf die sie mit der ihnen gewohnten Terminologie zugreifen könnten. (Wissenschaftsrat 2011a, S. 83)

Das IDS ist sich der Bedeutung von Standards seit längerer Zeit bewusst. Dies zeigt sich nicht nur daran, dass die zusammengetragenen Sprachressourcen, wenn immer möglich, gemäß existierender internationaler Standards aufbereitet werden, sondern auch an der aktiven Mitwirkung von IDS-Mitarbeitern in den Standardisierungsorganisationen DIN und ISO sowie in der Text Encoding Initiative (TEI).

3.4 Langzeitarchivierung

Die Thematik Langzeitarchivierung digitaler Daten, der sich auch das Projekt WissGrid widmet, ist seit einigen Jahren für viele Institutionen hoch relevant. Von 2003 bis 2008 wurde daher vom BMBF das Netzwerk nestor gefördert, in dem Bibliotheken, Archive, Museen und führende Experten Strategien und Lösungen zu dieser Thematik arbeiten.

Nach dem Auslaufen der finanziellen Projektförderung durch das BMBF wurde dieser Verbund nicht nur von den meisten Projektpartnern weitergeführt, sondern wurde sogar erweitert. Das IDS stieß 2009 zu diesem Netzwerk dazu, da die dauerhafte Aufbewahrung digitaler Sprachdaten für das Institut von höchster Wichtigkeit ist, um seinen Auftrag der Dokumentation der deutschen Gegenwartssprache auch weiterhin so erfolgreich wie bisher erfüllen zu können.

4. Grundüberlegungen für eine IT-Gesamtstrategie am Institut für Deutsche Sprache

Die Anforderungen an Umfang und Qualität der IT-Dienste sind in den letzten Jahren stark gestiegen und diese Entwicklung wird sich auch in der Zukunft fortsetzen. Weiterhin sind eine Reihe neuer Anforderungen durch die notwendige externe Vernetzung in verteilen Infrastrukturen hinzugekommen (CLARIN, TextGrid, föderierte Authentifikations- und Autorisierungs-Infrastrukturen, wie z.B. DFN-AAI).

Um diesen zusätzlichen, bereits bestehenden oder antizipierbaren Anforderungen optimal gerecht zu werden und dabei eine Ausuferung von Insellösungen zu vermeiden, ist es sinnvoll, für das gesamte Institut Ziele für eine IT-Infrastruktur im IDS zu definieren und eine entsprechende IT-Gesamtstrategie zu entwerfen, die sich an diesen Zielen ausrichtet und die vorhanden Ressourcen berücksichtigt. Eine umfassende Strategie zum Aufbau von IT-Infrastrukturen setzt sich hierbei aus unterschiedlichen Komponenten zusammen.

Benutzer kommen hauptsächlich mit der Komponente der "Dienste" der IT-Infrastruktur in Kontakt, d.h. Nutzung von E-Mail, Internet-Zugang, VPN etc. Diese Dienste bilden das Dach der IT-Infrastruktur, das auf den Säulen "Identitätsmanagement", "Wartung und Betrieb" und "Sicherheit" ruht (vgl. Abbildung 3).

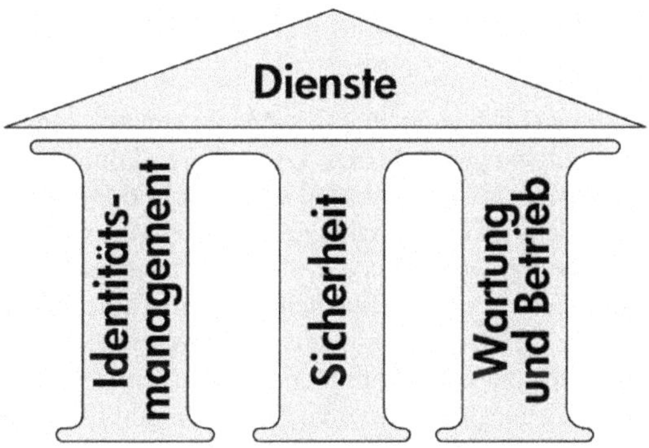

Abb. 3: Säulen der IT-Infrastruktur

4.1 Dienste

Die wichtigste Aufgabe innerhalb der IT-Infrastruktur ist das Bereitstellen von Diensten für den Benutzer. Diese umfassen beispielsweise den Zugriff auf das Internet zu Recherchezwecken, E-Mail, zentrale Datensicherung, zentrale Netzwerkfreigaben für Projekte,

Bereitstellung des Content-Management-Systems (CMS) für den Webauftritt des Instituts sowie Projekt- und personal-bezogenen Webseiten und das Intranet. Hinzu kommen auch noch Dienste der Bibliothek wie der Online Public Access Catalogue (OPAC) oder die Publikationsliste.

Insbesondere durch die zunehmende Mobilität der Mitarbeiter (Konferenzen etc.) oder Heimarbeit ist es weiterhin notwendig, dass die Mitarbeiter bequem auf notwendige Dienste zugreifen können. Für den E-Mail-Verkehr sollte daher die Möglichkeit bestehen, beispielsweise über eine Web-Mail-Schnittstelle E-Mails abrufen und versenden zu können. Der Zugang zu Systemen innerhalb des Instituts oder internen Informationen wie dem Intranet sollte weiterhin über ein Virtual-Private-Network (VPN) gewährleistet sein, wie er bereits erfolgreich im Testbetrieb angewandt wird. Weiterhin sollte über eine Teilnahme am Dienst eduROAM, der unterschiedliche teilnehmende Institutionen zu einer Föderation zusammenschließt, nachgedacht werden. Mitgliedern dieser Föderation wird es ermöglicht, an allen teilnehmenden Institutionen (das sind z.B. nahezu alle Universitäten in Deutschland) mit einer eigenen Benutzerkennung sich am W-LAN anzumelden und so das Internet zu nutzten. Besonders für Besucher des Instituts im Rahmen von Konferenzen oder Workshops bietet dies eine bequeme und einfache Möglichkeit um das Internet zu nutzen. Weiterhin profitieren auch Institutsmitarbeiter von der Teilnahme an eduROAM, da sie, wenn sie bei anderen Institutionen, die an eduROAM teilnehmen, zu Gast sind, ebenso einfach Zugriff auf das Internet haben.

4.2 Identitätsmanagement

Verschiedene Dienste, wie z.B. E-Mail oder VPN, sind auf personenbezogenen Daten angewiesen, um ordnungsgemäß zu funktionieren. Jeder Dienst verwaltet jedoch standardmäßig seine eigenen Stammdatensätze. Wenn sich daher beispielsweise durch eine Heirat der Namen eines Mitarbeiters ändern sollte, müssten diese Änderungen auf allen beteiligten Systemen einzeln durchgeführt werden. Dies führt schnell zu Fehlern und Inkonsistenzen.

Ein Identitätsmanagement (IdM, auch "Identity-Management") ermöglicht eine zentrale Verwaltung von personenbezogenen Daten. Diese Daten können von den zuständigen Stellen, z.B. der Personalverwaltung, aktuell gehalten und Diensten für ihren Betrieb notwendigen Daten aus dem Identitätsmanagement bereitgestellt werden. Über entsprechende Schnittstellen können Daten aus den Personaldatenbanken mit dem Identitätsmanagement synchronisiert werden. Mitarbeiter des Instituts können über eine Web-Schnittstelle die über sie im Identitätsmanagement gespeicherten Daten einsehen und gegebenenfalls ändern. Beispielsweise könnten sie so an einer zentralen Stelle ihr Passwort für die verschiedene Dienste ändern oder Einstellungen für Dienste, wie Abwesenheitsnotizen bei E-Mails, einrichten bzw. anpassen.

Das Identitätsmanagement dient so für verschiedene Dienste als Quelle für personenbezogene Daten, z.B. E-Mail oder die Telefonliste auf der Instituts-Webseite. In Zukunft sind zudem weitere Verknüpfungen mit dem Identitätsmanagement notwendig. Beispielsweise durch den Beitritt des Instituts zu den AAI-Föderationen des DFN bzw. CLARIN ist das IDS die Verpflichtungen eingegangen, Benutzerdaten innerhalb eng angelegter

Zeitrahmen auf dem neuesten Stand zu halten und ausgeschiedene Mitarbeiter zeitnah zu sperren. Weiterhin ist auch eine zentrale Verwaltung von Unix-Accounts, z.B. für Pool-Arbeitsplätze von Hilfskräften oder Zugriff von Mitarbeitern auf verschiedene interne Server, wünschenswert.

4.3 Betrieb und Wartung

Der Betrieb einer modernen IT-Infrastruktur ist eine anspruchsvolle Aufgabe und erfordert sorgfältige Planung, um einen robusten und störungsfreien Betrieb zu gewährleisten. Die Komponenten der Infrastruktur lassen sich grob in grundlegende Netzwerkinfrastruktur (Internet-Verbindung, lokales Netzwerk, zugehörige Dienste wie DHCP, DNS und WINS), Server (intern, sowie extern), allgemeine Infrastruktur (Drucker etc.), Arbeitsplatzrechner, Telefonanlage und weitere Anlagen (wie z.B. Video-Konferenz-Systeme) einteilen.

Die Komponenten der Infrastruktur sollten entsprechend ihrer Wichtigkeit nach bewertet und Konzepte für Ausfälle entworfen werden. Besonders kritische Komponenten (wie z.B. Internet-Verbindung, oder zentrale Netzwerkdienste) sollten durch redundante Systeme gesichert werden (z.B. Hot-Standby).

Besonders wichtig für einen robusten Betrieb sind Monitoring und Backup. Das Monitoring dient dazu, verschiedene Dienste und Systeme zu überwachen und bei Problemen entsprechende Warnmeldungen zu generieren. So kann z.B. der ordnungsgemäße Betrieb der Internet-Anbindung oder zentrale Server und Dienste (wie der Web-Auftritt des Instituts) kontrolliert werden. Des Weiteren kann ein Monitoring-System Warnungen versenden, wenn Störungen auftreten, die jedoch nicht unmittelbar zum Ausfall eines Systems führen und so oft, auch über einen längeren Zeitraum, übersehen werden könnten, wie beispielsweise der Ausfall einer Festplatte in einem RAID-Verbund eines Storage-Subsystems oder die Notwendigkeit des Austauschs von Batterien in einer Unterbrechungsfreien Stromversorgung (USV). Eine weitere Schlüsselkomponente für den sicheren Betrieb ist ein Backup-System. Zum einen dient ein Backup dazu, um im Falle eines schwerwiegenden Hardware-Defekts die Daten des betroffenen Systems wieder herstellen zu können. Zum anderen ist ein Backup unerlässlich, um bei fehlerhafter Bedienung eines Systems, z.B. versehentliches Löschen wichtiger Dateien oder Beschädigung von Daten durch eine Fehlfunktion eines Programms, einen Datenverlust zu vermeiden. Wichtige zentrale Systeme bzw. Daten sollten daher täglich gesichert werden. Ein Backup aller Arbeitsplatzrechner ist aus verschiedenen Gründen problematisch, da nicht alle Rechner nachts, wenn normalerweise das Backup durchgeführt wird, in Betrieb sind. Daher sollte beispielsweise für Mitarbeiter jeweils ein Netzlaufwerk angeboten werden, auf dem sie eigenverantwortlich Daten ablegen können. Der Server, auf dem die Daten der Netzlaufwerke vorgehalten werden, wird in das reguläre Backup eingebunden und so die Daten täglich gesichert.

Um den administrativen Aufwand zu minimieren, ist die Einführung einer an die Bedürfnisse des Instituts angepassten, standardisierten Softwareplattform für Serversysteme und Arbeitsplatzrechner unerlässlich. Besonders für Serversysteme ist dies relevant, da auf diese Weise ein “Wildwuchs” von verschiedenen, nicht-konsistenten

Software-Installationen vermieden und der Aufwand für die Pflege der Systeme reduziert wird. Eine zentrale Verteilung von Software-Updates für das Betriebssystem als auch Anwendungssoftware ist auch für die Arbeitsplatzrechner ermöglicht es, beispielsweise besonders kritische Software, wie z.B. Internet-Browser, zeitnah zu aktualisieren. Wünschenswert wäre auch die Unterstützung einer modernen Linux-Distribution als alternatives Betriebssystem für Arbeitsplatzrechner wie etwa für Pool-Arbeitsplätze von Hilfskräften.

Weitere Aufgaben bestehen in der zentralen Hardware-Beschaffung und der Planung des Lebenszyklus von Systemen. Hierzu gehören sowohl die Einführung, der Betrieb und die Wartung, als auch die Außerbetriebnahme inklusive der eventuellen Migration von Diensten auf die neuen Systeme. Hierdurch kann die aufwändige Wartung und Pflege von Altsystemen und der Betrieb parallelen Infrastrukturen vermieden werden. Des Weiteren ermöglicht eine langfristige Planung der Hardwarezyklen eine größere Planungssicherheit bei der Beschaffung und ermöglicht die Aushandlung von längerfristigen Rahmenverträgen mit Lieferanten. Aus der Sicht der Verwaltung ist insbesondere der letztgenannte Punkt essentiell, um einerseits bessere finanzielle Konditionen mit den Händlern aushandeln und andererseits die vom Geldgeber geforderte Transparenz auf unkomplizierte Weise sicherstellen zu können.

In den letzten Jahren sind die Energiekosten, insbesondere die Kosten für Strom, signifikant gestiegen. Da der Anteil der IT-Infrastruktur am Gesamtstromverbrauch des Instituts nicht unerheblich ist, können Einsparungen dort auch erhebliche finanzielle Einsparungen nach sich ziehen. Im Rahmen der Klimaschutzdebatte ist unter anderem der Begriff *Green IT* geprägt worden. Green IT gliedert sich grob in zwei Themenbereiche: zum einen die Verwendung von energieeffizienten Geräten und Arbeitsmitteln und zum anderen die Einsparung von Energie durch die Nutzung von IT, z.B. durch das Durchführen von Videokonferenzen zur Vermeidung von Dienstreisen. Bei der Neuanschaffung von IT-Systemen sollte zukünftig vermehrt auf deren Energieeffizienz geachtet und die bestehende Infrastruktur auf mögliches Einsparungspotential untersucht werden. Beispielsweise durch Konsolidierung von Systemen als virtuelle Server kann die Anzahl der physikalischen Rechner verringert und dadurch unter anderem auch die Kühlung des Rechenzentrums optimiert werden. Im Rahmen einer IT-Gesamtstrategie sollte daher auch die IT-Infrastruktur im Hinblick auf Green IT untersucht und entsprechenden Maßnahmen ergriffen werden, denn der positiven Außenwirkung in Hinblick auf Nachhaltigkeit gibt es finanzieller Seite ein signifikantes Einsparpotentialen bei den Energiekosten für das Institut.

4.4 Sicherheit

Die Aufrechterhaltung eines angemessenen Sicherheitsniveaus wird beim Betrieb von IT-Infrastruktur leider häufig vernachlässigt. Dies kann vielfältige Gründe haben, wie z.B. fehlende Ressourcen, knappe Budgets, fehlendes bzw. unzureichendes Sicherheitsbewusstsein und nicht zuletzt die steigende Komplexität der Systeme. Auch wenn ein geisteswissenschaftliches Institut auf den ersten Blick ein eher "unattraktives" Ziel für einen Angriff zu sein scheint, sollte man sich nicht in falscher Sicherheit wiegen. Botnet-Betreibern geht es hauptsächlich um Quantität, d.h. möglichst viele Rechner zu infizieren, um beispielsweise mehr Spam versenden zu können. Aber auch gezielte Angriffe sind nicht auszuschließen. Weiterhin besitzt das Institut eine Reihe von Ressourcen, die aus verschiedensten Gründen (z.B. Datenschutz, Urheberrechte Dritter, ...) insbesondere vor unberechtigtem Kopieren oder Vandalismus zu schützen sind.

Durch die in den letzten Jahren gewachsene Infrastruktur und auch aufgrund Anforderungen externer Projekte, wie CLARIN oder TextGrid, ist es notwendig, die bestehenden Maßnahmen zur IT-Sicherheit am IDS zu überprüfen und gegebenenfalls zu überarbeiten. Dazu könnte nach den Empfehlungen zum IT-Grundschutz des Bundesamts für Sicherheit in der Informationstechnik (BSI) vorgegangen werden. Entsprechend an die Gegebenheiten im IDS angepasst, können nach einer initialen Gefahrenabschätzung identifizierte Probleme zusammen mit den betroffenen Stellen gezielt angegangen und Maßnahmen schrittweise umgesetzt werden. Weiterhin sollte über die Schaffung der Funktion eines IT-Sicherheitsbeauftragen nachgedacht werden, die, analog zum Datenschutzbeauftragen, die Evaluation und Umsetzung von Sicherheitsmaßnahmen begleitet. Des Weiteren könnte das Institut auch eine Zertifizierung für die Umsetzung des IT-Grundschutzes anstreben. Dies könnte einerseits das Institut bei der sachgerechten Umsetzung des Grundschutzes unterstützen und sich anderseits auch positiv auf die Außenwahrnehmung des Instituts aus der Sicht von Kooperationspartnern oder Drittmittelgebern auswirken.

5. Referenzen

Wissenschaftsrat

Wissenschaftsrat (2011a): *Empfehlungen zu Forschungsinfrastrukturen in den Geistes- und Sozialwissenschaften.* Drs. 10465-11. Berlin: Wissenschaftsrat.

Wissenschaftsrat (2011b): *Übergreifende Empfehlungen zu Informationsinfrastrukturen.* Drs. 10466-11. Berlin: Wissenschaftsrat.

DeReKo

Belica, C. et al. (2011): The morphosyntactic annotation of DEREKO: Interpretation, opportunities and pitfalls. In: Konopka, M./Kubczak, J./Mair, C./Šticha, F./Wassner, U. (eds.): *Grammatik und Korpora 2009. Dritte Internationale Konferenz. Mannheim, 22.-24.9.2009.* (= Korpuslinguistik und interdisziplinäre Perspektiven auf Sprache 1). Tübingen. Gunter Narr, 451-469.

Kupietz, M. et al. (2010a): The German Reference Corpus DeReKo: A primordial sample for linguistic research. In: Calzolari, Nicoletta et al. (eds.): *Proceedings of the Seventh Conference on International Language Resources and Evaluation* (*LREC 2010*), 1848-1854. Internet: www.lrec-conf.org/proceedings/lrec2010/pdf/414_Paper.pdf.

Kupietz, M. et al. (2010b): The German Reference Corpus: New developments building on almost 50 years of experience. In: *Proceedings of the LREC 2010 Workshop "Language Resources: From Storyboard to Sustainability and LR Lifecycle Management"*. Valetta, Malta, 39-43.

CCDB

Belica, C. (2007): *Kookkurrenzdatenbank CCDB – V3. Eine korpuslinguistische Denk- und Experimentierplattform für die Erforschung und theoretische Begründung von systemisch-strukturellen Eigenschaften von Kohäsionsrelationen zwischen den Konstituenten des Sprachgebrauchs*. Mannheim. Institut für Deutsche Sprache. Internet: http://corpora.ids-mannheim.de/ccdb/.

Keibel, H./Belica, C. (2007): CCDB: A Corpus-Linguistic Research and Development Workbench. In: *Proceedings of Corpus Linguistics 2007, Birmingham*. Internet: http://corpus.bham.ac.uk/corplingproceedings07/paper/134_Paper.pdf.

COSMAS

al-Wadi, D. (1994): *COSMAS – Ein Computersystem für den Zugriff auf Textkorpora. Version R.1.3-1. Benutzerhandbuch*. Mit einem Geleitwort von Prof. Dr. Gerhard Stickel. Mannheim: Institut für deutsche Sprache.

Bodmer, F. (2005): COSMAS II. Recherchieren in den Korpora des IDS. In: *Sprachreport* 3/2005, 2-5.

D-SPIN

Bankhardt, C. (2009): D-SPIN – Eine Infrastruktur für deutsche Sprachressourcen. In: *Sprachreport* 1/2009, 30-31.

Geyken, A./Klein, W. (2009): Deutsche Sprachressourcen-Infrastruktur. In: Berlin-Brandenburgische Akademie der Wissenschaften (Hg.): *Berlin-Brandenburgische Akademie der Wissenschaften – Jahrbuch 2008*. Berlin: Akademie Verlag, 336-337.

Lexik

Herberg, D,/Kinne, M./Steffens, D. (2004): *Neuer Wortschatz. Neologismen der 90er Jahre im Deutschen*. Unter Mitarbeit von Elke Tellenbach und Doris al-Wadi. (= Schriften des Instituts für Deutsche Sprache 11). Berlin/New York: de Gruyter.

Müller-Spitzer, C. (2008): The lexicographic portal of the IDS. Connecting heterogeneous lexicographic resources by a consistent concept of data modelling. In: *Proceedings of the 13th EURALEX International Congress. Euralex 2008*. Barcelona: Universitat Pompeu Fabra, 457-461.

Müller-Spitzer, C. (2010): OWID – A dictionary net for corpus-based lexicography of contemporary German. In: Dykstra, A./Schoonheim, T. (Hg.): *Proceedings of the XIV Euralex International Congress. Leeuwarden, 6-10 July 2010*. Leeuwarden: Fryske Akademy, 445-452.

Standards

ISO/FDIS 24619-2011: *Language resource management – persistent identification and sustainable access* (*PISA*). Genf: International Organization for Standardization (ISO).

TextGrid

Kerzel, M./Mittelbach, J./Vitt, T. (2009): TextGrid – Virtuelle Arbeitsumgebung für die Geisteswissenschaften. In: *Künstliche Intelligenz* 4/November 2009 (Themenheft "Kulturerbe und Künstliche Intelligenz"), 36-39.

Zielinski, A./Pempe, W./Gietz, P./Haase, M./Funk, S./Simon, C. (2009): TEI Documents in the grid. In: *Literary and Linguistic Computing* 24 (3), 267-279.

WissGrid

Enke, H. (2010): Grid: user perspectives. In: *Proceedings of SwissGrid Day 2010, November 30, 2010*. Internet: www.wissgrid.de/publikationen/presentations/SwissGrid-Day2010-WissGrid.pdf.

Ludwig, J. (2009): Long-term preservation of digital research data. In: *Proceedings of DESY Computing Seminar (DVSEM), November 23, 2009, Hamburg*. Internet: www.desy.de/dvsem/WS0910/ludwig_talk.pdf.

Ludwig, J. (2010): Diversity and interoperability of repositories in a grid curation Environment. In: *Proceedings of Open Repositories Conference, July 6, 2010, Madrid*. Internet: www.wissgrid.de/publikationen/presentations/2010-07-06--or2010-DiversityandInteroperabilityofRepositoriesinGridCurationEnvironment.pdf.

nestor

Neuroth, H./Oßwald, A./Scheffel, R./Strathmann, S./Jehn, M. (Hg.): *Nestor-Handbuch: eine kleine Enzyklopädie der digitalen Langzeitarchivierung*. Version 2.0, Juni 2009. Boizenburg: Hülsbusch.

BSI Grundschutz

Bundesamt für Sicherheit in der Informationstechnik (2008a): *BSI-Standard 100-1: Managementsysteme für Informationssicherheit* (*ISMS*).

Bundesamt für Sicherheit in der Informationstechnik (2008b): *BSI-Standard 100-2: IT-Grundschutz-Vorgehensweise*.

Bundesamt für Sicherheit in der Informationstechnik (2008c): *BSI-Standard 100-3: Risikoanalyse auf der Basis von IT-Grundschutz*.

Bundesamt für Sicherheit in der Informationstechnik (2008d): *BSI-Standard 100-4: Notfallmanagement*.

d) Panel discussion

Bessie Dendrinos / Jean-François Baldi / Pietro G. Beltrami /
Walery Pisarek / Maria Theodoropoulou

Panel discussion: The symbolism of the notion of national language

1. Introduction (by Bessie Dendrinos)

The invitation sent to the panel participants contained an explanation that the starting point for this event was a paragraph of the Dublin Declaration (see Appendix) which initially was articulated as follows:

> The "one nation, one language" ideology is still very strong in politics, the media and indeed public opinion in many countries. However, it is largely invisible, and its acceptance is taken for granted. Thus the use of other languages is nearly always socially marked. Such an ideology is at variance with the demands of the processes of globalisation in general and European integration in particular. EFNIL is resolved to promote a debate to overcome this situation.

This statement disturbed most EFNIL delegates. After several edited versions which were still annoying to some, I rephrased it as follows:

> Most European states still view the 'one nation-one language' construct as the norm, whereas in many instances the social reality is different. This reality often does not surface due to lack of reliable, recent statistics on the actual regional and minority languages. Given today's conditions of social plurality in European states, and the need for social cohesion, EFNIL is committed to promoting plurilingual citizenry and to working together with other European organisations, in order to collect and disseminate reliable data and best practice in this field.

Still, however, there were a few delegates disturbed by the very idea that 'one nation-one language' may be viewed as a construct or an ideologically loaded notion. Therefore, based on the comments received, the next version was edited as follows:

> In some European countries there are more than one official or national language, and in several countries certain minority languages are recognised but others not. However, the linguistic reality is not always visible due to lack of reliable, recent statistics which would give us a valid linguistic map of Europe. Yet, we recognize today's conditions of social plurality in European member states, and because of the need for social cohesion, EFNIL is committed to promoting plurilingual citizenry and to working together with other European organisations, in order to collect and disseminate reliable data and best practice in this field.

Finally, because even the immediately above was disturbing to some delegates, we arrived at the more or less unanimous version of paragraph 6, included in the Dublin Declaration as follows:

> In most European countries today there is a rather complicated linguistic reality which is not always visible due to lack of reliable, recent statistics. As EFNIL recognises the conditions of social plurality in Europe and the need for social cohesion, it is committed to promoting plurilingual citizenry and to working together with other European organisations, in order to collect and disseminate reliable data and best practice in this field.

The 'history' of the Dublin Declaration, as concerns this paragraph in particular, is the context of the present discussion during which each panellist presented a five minute position paper. Indeed, the discussion that followed the position papers included in this article was a heated one, since issues related to one's language create divergent and deeply felt beliefs, as one's language is often deeply tied to questions of identity, nationhood and power.

Below, there are the position papers by the four panelists and this article concludes with a fifth position statement by me, as chair of the panel.

2. The symbolism of "national language" (by Jean-François Baldi)

Une petite partie de la déclaration de Dublin – dans sa version initiale – a suscité des réserves de notre part. Il s'agissait de ces quelques mots qui s'en prenaient à l'assimilation d'une langue à une nation, et considéraient ce couple "une langue, une nation" comme, je cite, "une vieille idéologie".

Nous avons bien conscience du mouvement historique qui a conduit à "déterritorialiser" les langues. De nombreux facteurs y contribuent, et la conférence de Thessalonique a mis en évidence l'importance des technologies dans cette "déterritorialisation".

Les langues ne sont pas, ne sont plus, enfermées dans un territoire: elles ne sont pas l'apanage exclusif d'une nation. Nous avons nous-même coutume de dire que le français n'appartient pas à la France: il appartient à ceux qui le parlent.

Pour autant, c'est dans un rapport étroit avec la nation et son émanation politique, l'Etat, que s'est construite la politique du français. Et c'est dans un rapport étroit avec la langue française que l'Etat-nation s'est développé en France, notamment depuis que l'ordonnance de Villers-Cotterêts en 1539 visa à faire du français la langue officielle du droit et de l'administration, en lieu et place du latin et des autres langues du pays.

Nous sommes désormais une "République indivisible", selon l'article 1er de notre Constitution. Constitution qui précise également, dans son article 2, que "la langue de la République est le français".

Ces dispositions constitutionnelles ont des conséquences très directes sur la politique de la langue de notre pays.

D'une part, à travers la loi du 4 août 1994, nous sommes dotés d'un cadre légal auquel nos concitoyens sont très attachés et qui vise à leur garantir un "droit au français" dans un grand nombre de circonstances de la vie sociale, économique et culturelle.

D'autre part, c'est à l'Etat, en collaboration avec un réseau de partenaires, qu'échoit la responsabilité de conduire cette politique et d'en rendre compte devant le Parlement. Ainsi, le gouvernement est officiellement tenu chaque année de produire un rapport sur l'emploi du français à l'attention des parlementaires.

Cependant, si la langue de la République est le français, le français n'est pas la seule langue parlée sur le territoire de la République.

En effet, rien ne s'oppose à l'usage et à la promotion d'autres langues que le français dès lors que ne sont pas conférés des droits spécifiques à des groupes de locuteurs, à l'intérieur de territoires dans lesquels ces langues sont pratiquées. C'est cette limite que la Constitution fixe à l'emploi des langues régionales dans notre pays.

Des évolutions récentes se font jour. Ainsi, depuis la révision constitutionnelle de juillet 2008, l'article 75 de la Constitution prévoit que "les langues régionales appartiennent au patrimoine de la France". Là encore, c'est bien dans une référence à un patrimoine national que s'inscrivent les langues régionales. Le breton, l'alsacien, l'occitan, le basque... ne sont pas l'affaire des seuls locuteurs de ces langues et des territoires sur lesquels elles sont parlées, même si ceux-ci ont une responsabilité particulière dans leur développement et leur promotion, mais de la nation toute entière.

Voilà pourquoi, en France, malgré l'internationalisation des échanges, l'intégration européenne, et leur corollaire, le développement des identités locales, la nation constitue un cadre de référence encore actuel à la conception et à la mise en oeuvre de la politique de la langue.

3. The symbolism of "national language" (by Pietro G. Beltrami)

Prenderò lo spunto dalla situazione italiana. Nel 1861, quando l'Italia è stata unificata, coloro che parlavano italiano erano una modesta percentuale della popolazione, dal 2,5% al 10% secondo le diverse stime.[1] Nella vita quotidiana si parlavano i cosiddetti dialetti, che sono in realtà lingue derivate dal latino indipendentemente. L'italiano era una lingua quasi solo scritta, una costruzione letteraria, ma rappresentava, e da alcuni secoli, un simbolo dell'unità culturale del Paese e, in questo senso, era la sua lingua nazionale. Con l'unificazione politica la lingua nazionale diventò anche la lingua del nuovo stato, cioè la lingua ufficiale, anche se nessuna legge lo stabilì esplicitamente. Da allora esiste una stretta relazione fra italiano e nazione italiana, e una spia di ciò può essere vista oggi nel fatto che i movimenti autonomistici cercano di ottenere l'uso o l'insegnamento del dialetto nella scuola accanto all'italiano, o al suo posto. In effetti, poiché i dialetti non derivano dall'italiano, la distinzione fra dialetti e lingue di minoranza può diventare opinabile.

La prima e unica dichiarazione dell'italiano come 'lingua ufficiale della Repubblica' si trova infatti precisamente nella legge del 1999 sulle lingue di minoranza,[2] mentre prima di questa legge l'italiano è stato niente di più (ma anche niente di meno) che una 'lingua ufficiale di fatto'. La scelta di parole è significativa: l'italiano è detto 'lingua ufficiale', non 'lingua nazionale'. 'Lingua ufficiale' è un concetto amministrativo e politico, men-

[1] Il numero preciso di coloro che parlavano italiano nel 1861 è controverso. La stima più bassa, di De Mauro, è il 2,5% della popolazione; la più alta, di Castellani, è il 10% (non c'è accordo sul punto se coloro che parlavano i dialetti toscani si debbano considerare parlanti dell'italiano o no). Ancora nel 1950 la percentuale della popolazione che parlava normalmente italiano non era superiore al 18%; un 18% era in grado di parlare italiano oltre il proprio dialetto locale, e il restante 64% parlava solo un dialetto o una lingua di minoranza. Secondo i dati disponibili più recenti, oggi il 44% della popolazione parla solo italiano, il 51% italiano e il proprio dialetto o la propria lingua di minoranza, e il 5% non parla italiano per niente (De Mauro, T. (2004): *Cari italiani, come state parlando*? In: LId'O – Lingua italiana d'oggi I, 55-70).

[2] Legge 482, 15 dicembre 1999, art. 1: "la lingua ufficiale della Repubblica è l'italiano". Le lingue di minoranza di cui si occupa la legge sono il sardo, il ladino e il friulano (che appartengono al sistema italo-romanzo, ma hanno un'identità linguistica e storica distinta dall'italiano e dai dialetti italiani); il tedesco; il francese, il franco-provenzale e l'occitano; il catalano; il greco; l'albanese; lo sloveno e il croato.

tre 'lingua nazionale' è un concetto culturale. Come lingua nazionale, si può dire che l'italiano è la lingua parlando la quale come parlanti nativi ci si sente italiani, anche se non si deve dimenticare che nella realtà questa lingua non è la stessa per tutti.

Oggi, tuttavia (e questa può essere un'affermazione, o una domanda), non è più realistico pensare che solo coloro che parlano la stessa lingua possano sentirsi parte della stessa nazione. In effetti, quali che siano state le motivazioni del legislatore italiano, la scelta della parola 'ufficiale', non 'nazionale', implica che una legge che protegge le lingue di minoranza non nega che l'Italia sia una nazione, e non tante nazioni quante sono le lingue protette. Una nazione, o meglio una società, della quale oggi fanno parte non solo comunità storiche di lingua diversa dall'italiano, ma anche nuove comunità originate dall'immigrazione, alle quali si deve chiedere di saper usare la lingua ufficiale, ma si deve anche riconoscere il diritto di mantenere l'uso delle loro lingue di origine (come dice anche la Dichiarazione di Dublino della EFNIL). La lingua nazionale, dunque (e anche questa può essere una domanda), dovrebbe essere considerata, piuttosto che un simbolo di unità politica, un patrimonio culturale.

Questo porta a dire che il problema di cui discutiamo non è linguistico, ma politico; non è il concetto di 'lingua nazionale', ma quello di 'nazionalità'. È palese che la globalizzazione, nel mondo, e in Europa il processo di integrazione dell'Unione Europea, hanno acuito ovunque il senso dell'identità e il timore dell'assimilazione, e ciò riguarda sia gli stati nazionali, come gli stati europei nel loro rapporto con l'Unione, sia tutti i popoli grandi o piccoli che possono identificare se stessi per storia, tradizioni, costumi, lingua, all'interno di uno stato o in regioni a cavallo di più stati e così via. Il nome di lingua nazionale, o ufficiale, o altro che uno stato dà alla propria lingua è di fatto in relazione con tutti gli altri aspetti dei rapporti di potere e con l'ideologia. Sono i conflitti che nascono di qui che rendono l'uso dell'espressione 'lingua nazionale' una materia delicata, ed è per questa ragione che, a mio parere, una politica linguistica rivolta ad appianarli deve superare il concetto di nazione per quello di cittadinanza.

4. National and/or official language (by Walery Pisarek)

Since the first glimpse at one of the paragraphs of the *original* version of the Dublin Declaration, I was convinced that it is, to me, formally and ideologically unacceptable. Almost each word and expression it contained awakened negative emotions in me; almost each judgment and proposition it contained has provoked my determined opposition. To quote this paragraph:

> The "one nation, one language" ideology is still very strong in politics, the media and indeed public opinion in many countries. However, it is largely invisible, and its acceptance is taken for granted. Thus the use of other languages is nearly always socially marked. Such an ideology is at variance with the demands of the processes of globalization in general, and European integration in particular. EFNIL is resolved to promote a debate to overcome this situation.

Let's start from the very beginning, i.e. from the phrase *one nation, one language ideology*. Maybe it is a question of my age, but I am not able to hear, to read, or to use this phrase without thinking of the slogan *ein Volk, ein Reich...* and so on. Even the slogan *one state, one nation, one language*, shortened to version *one nation, one language* looks a bit manipulative: more or less widespread antipathy to its conjectural full version is transferred to the shortened one. Hence – in my opinion – this phrase is rhetorically marked and, as such, it may be used today exclusively for the overtly persuasive purposes and for this reason it is not suitable for use in a non-militant declaration.

What is a *nation* in English? According to the Oxford Advanced Learner's Dictionary it is (1) *a country considered as a group of people with the same language, culture and history, who live in a particular area under one government* or (2) *all the people in a country.* And according to the Oxford Dictionaries Online *nation* is *a large body of people united by common descent, history, culture or language, inhabiting a particular state or territory.*

As a Pole, I find it hard to accept unreservedly these definitions of the word *nation* (and especially the first one of them), because according to them, the Poles in the nineteenth century, divided into three parts to the three neighbouring countries, ceased to be a nation. On the other hand, I do realize that the word *nation* is used internationally according to the Oxford Dictionary definitions, i.e. in the names of the UN and UNESCO.

What is a *nation* (*naród*) in Polish? According to the dictionary of the Polish language (Słownik języka polskiego, t. 2, PWN, Warszawa 1995), *nation* (*naród*) is a *stable community of people formed historically, founded on the basis of community of the historical fate, culture, language, territory and economic life as reflected in the national consciousness of its members.* An important element of the definition of the nation as a group of people is, in my opinion, the national consciousness of its members. It means that for instance the Polish nation is a community of people who view themselves as Poles. The same applies to other nations and their members. This self-awareness is sometimes reinforced by a common territory, common State, common religion and/or common language.

I don't need to remind anyone here that there are nations without common state, territory, religion or language, and nations whose national awareness is strengthened first of all by one or two of the factors just mentioned. According to my deepest conviction the national self-awareness of the Poles is based mainly on their language. My conviction is supported by various old (historical) and new (contemporary) arguments. Already in the fifteenth and sixteenth century, the population of the then Polish Kingdom was described as *gens linguae polonicae* – people of Polish language – thanks to their common language. The Poles, partitioned for more than 100 years into three parts by three neighboring states, remained Poles.

In 1985, in a national opinion poll the adult population of Poland answered the question "What above all makes us Poles?" Respondents were asked to assess the validity of each of seven factors. (Numbers in parentheses indicate the percentage of respondents who considered this factor as very important.)

1. Common history (87)
2. Common territory (80)
3. Common culture (81)
4. Common fate today and tomorrow (63)

5. Common religion (63)
6. Common state (55)
7. Common language (92)

Common language appeared to be the most important factor, more important than common territory and common state.

The Polish language is the national language of all the Poles. Of course it is – as are most judgments relating to the social sphere – a statistical truth. Of course there are people who consider themselves to be Poles and do not speak Polish.

What does *national* mean in English and in Polish (*narodowy*)? Etymologically or rather structurally, it is 'that of nation, belonging to nation' etc. And thus the difference between the English *national* and Polish *narodowy* boils down to the difference between the English *nation* and Polish *naród*. Hence *national language* is a language of some nation; e.g. the Polish language is national language of the Polish nation. Just like the Czech language is the national language of the Czechs and the German language the national language of the Germans. Some Czechs, Slovaks, Germans and Lithuanians live in Poland. Some of them have Polish citizenship, but despite this, they consider themselves Czechs, Slovaks, Germans and Lithuanians, and they state that their national language (national mother language) is Czech, Slovak, German or Lithuanian. At the same time dealing with public administration institutions, they use (yes, they have to use) Polish as the official language in Poland. In this way the Polish language, being the national language of the Poles, serves, as the official language in Poland, the needs of the Poles, of Polish citizens of other nationality and of other people living in Poland. As the official language it should be to all of them primarily a means of communication but – thanks to its phatic function – also a means of communion.

"Terms such as 'minority language' and 'regional language' are – as one can read in our Dublin Declaration – usually charged with ideological meanings, as are terms such as 'national language', 'official language' and many others used to indicate the condition or status of a language (e.g. indigenous, autochthonous, ethnic, lesser-used, co-official, dialect, non-territorial, dominant language)." Certainly we should use these terms very carefully, but the indigenous, lesser-used, non-territorial and dominant languages do exist and we need the terms to be able to refer to them. And, on the other hand, we should remember, that many languages have in some countries status of the official or state language and in other (usually neighboring) countries they are minority languages. Simply speaking, the same language may be dominating in one country and dominated in some others.

Most of us here, or maybe even all of us, represent "national institutions" in EFNIL and we are obliged according to our Federation statutes to support our national/official languages. Moreover, we represent 23 national languages of 27 countries on the general principle of one country one language. Some politically correct observers of the scene of EFNIL and of EU could say that this principle is quite apparent symptom of the "one nation – one language ideology". I don't share such an accusation with them.

5. The symbolism of "national language" (by Maria Theodoropoulou)

My position statement begins with reference to historical facts, one of which is that to identify a nation with a specific language is the basic characteristic of the nation-state and its politics. Prior to the development of nation-states, the notion of "national language" did not exist. Also, it is widely recognized that, the promotion of a standard form of a single language, adopted as the national language, was required for the sake of homogenization. This type of homogenization was one of the main objectives of the nation-state in the socio-historical context of its formation: the pursuit of linguistic and cultural homogenization was a requisite for the creation of a homogenized labour force in the service of mass production. The consequence is also well known: the endorsement of a hegemonic – for historical reasons – linguistic variety as a standard language, which resulted in the elimination of the other varieties by means first of devaluating those varieties while re-evaluating at the same time the standard language with the added prestige of guaranteed social mobility.

Language was considered to be a constitutive part of a nation since the era of European romanticism by means of its identity with the nation's "Geist" ("spirit") or "genius". In the new socio-historical context, language was attributed with the role of defining the dividing line between "us" – that has a unifying function – and "the others" – which has a discriminating function. This happens irrespective of the fact that different nations can share the same language or that various multilingual nations consider multilingualism as a basic constituent of their identity. In other words, regardless of whether linguistic reality around the globe offers strong evidence that identifying a nation with a specific language is not an objective "truth" of some sort, this connection remains strong in our consciousness through an imaginary. The term *imaginary* is used here in order to emphasize the fact that the relation between language and nation is invested with a symbolic load, which not only lies outside the field of science but which is a social construct, deeply rooted in issues related to the formation of a national identity, as well as to the challenges that a nation faces vis a vis other nations.

By qualifying a language as *national* the identity of a language as a means of communication is transcended: thus language is converted into a subject-matter of symbolisms. Purity, continuity and origin become the main issues on which these symbolisms are anchored. I shall try to outline this line of thought using the Greek language as an example, but clearly it is not limited to this. With regard to purity, it is well known that the process of standardization is inevitably connected to a linguistic "cleansing" aiming to ensure a "unified" and homogeneous language. However, what is cleansed and by what it is replaced, entails a series of political and ideological decisions. Let me bring an example from the history of the Greek language: In the process of its standardization a high variety of Greek was opted for – in the 19th century – as the standard national language, validating thus in an institutional manner a diglossia which lasted until the second part of the 20th century. This process was marked by two acts: on the one hand, the massive elimination of the Turkish loan words, a result of the coexistence between Greeks and Turks during the 400 years of Turkish occupation in Greece. On the other hand it was marked by the massive adoption of loan words from the French and Italian languages or from older versions of Greek. From one point of view this was certainly legitimate since this was what the society wished – and perhaps also needed – at that time. What is significant, however, is that borrowing from the West had to do both with the implicit and explicit claims of the new established Greek state concerning its European identity: it was an explicit claim in so far as it accommodated that historical conjuncture, that is, borrowing from a western language; it was an implicit claim as it appealed to the roots of its symbolic capital, the ancient Greek civilization, which was at that time "managed" by the West.

Coming now to the second point that brings forth the symbolic with regard to language: it is to be noted that the history of a language is the central space where the issue of continuity occurs. In the history of the Greek language, symbolisms became so forceful that they erased historical factuality, even for a number of linguists. In this complex context of claims that the newly established Greek nation pursued towards its European identity, and under the threat of theories that argued its "barbarization", the continuity of the modern with the ancient Greek language was argued in favour of an "intrinsic" conservatism of Greek; a view which, of course, renounced linguistic change as a basic characteristic of language. Furthermore, the histories of the Greek language were written with an emphasis on the learned form of the language, which was conservative in its evolution, rather than the everyday language that the common people spoke. Of course, the existence of dialects, the field of linguistic change, was hushed. Finally, it should be noted that the historic orthography [spelling] is another field in which the continuity with older forms of language is asserted on a symbolic level. A debate, taking place in Greece at present, meets with two opposing views: the first one argues in favour of an archaic orthography that strictly follows the rules of etymology; the second one argues in favour of a rationally simplified spelling, more user-friendly and in accordance with the new social conditions that are continuously changing in Greece and other countries. The first one – an unscientific argument – is strongly supported and brings forth predictions of incurring dangers for the Greek language, and specifically its loss of "Greekness".

I shall finish suggesting that, on one hand, these attitudes are founded in socio-historical reasons that lie deeply in the roots of ethnogenesis, as was mentioned before. On the other hand, these attitudes are intertwined with unconscious collective wishes and fantasies that elevate a language as the richest, the oldest, the most important one etc., which is of course spoken by a "privileged" nation. Such a stance, as far as I know, is not particular to Greece alone.

6. Final remarks on the notion "national language" (by Bessie Dendrinos)

From the discussion that followed the position papers, we understand that language is still tightly linked to social identity. It is one of the most important forms of human symbolic behaviour and is a key component of a group's social identity. Since people belong to different groups and have many potential identities, different codes serve as markers or tools to forge these identities. A separate, national language, for example, is often perceived as a necessary condition for a nation to exist.

Of course we also understand that definitions of languages can be very *subjective*. Seemingly identical linguistic codes can be identified as separate languages if distinct identities need to be established for two, otherwise similar, ethnic groups. An example of this is that until the 1991 war in the former Republic of Yugoslavia, Serbian and Croatian were treated as a single language (Serbo-Croat). The main difference between the two varieties was that they were written in two alphabets, Cyrillic and Roman respectively. After the war, however, linguists and non-linguists in the country went to considerable lengths to establish the varieties as separate languages by asserting how much the two codes differ structurally. If, say, British English and American English were to undergo similar political 'theorizing', one could imagine claims being made that they are radically different languages, whereas currently we think of them as varieties of a common code, distinguished by minor matters of vocabulary, pronunciation and orthography. Through this example, it becomes more apparent that what was at stake in the former Yugoslavia was not a linguistic reality but a set of political and social realities.

There are, of course, noteworthy exceptions to the generalization that national or ethnic identity is tied to a *national* or *ethnic* language. For example, the Irish have largely lost the autochthonous language – Irish Gaelic, but not a sense of nationhood.

Other peoples have lost the indigenous languages, but have not necessarily lost their ethnic identity or cultural vitality. In some of these cases, language can be a source of national or ethnic identity, but in a rather negative way – through a sense of loss. For example, when asked about their linguistic and cultural heritage, many Welsh monoglot English speakers invoke their Welshness in terms of a national language which has been denied to them. For other Welsh people, and particularly those whose learning of Welsh halted the decline in the overall numbers of Welsh speakers at the 1991 census, a Welsh identity is likely to be linked to the language in a less abstract way.

There are several political and moral questions surrounding language and ethnic identity and many sociolinguists have been investigating them extensively. For example, the well-known American sociolinguist, Joshua Fishman, has spoken of the myth of 'one nation, one state, one language' as a damaging and dangerous (Eurocentric?) construct, which became well established in the 19th century. We have seen through the position papers and the discussion that followed this panel, and then we have seen how deeply disturbing it is still for most Europeans to speak of this construct negatively. In Europe it is part of the political and popular conception of nationhood. On the other hand, most of us have been witnesses to how such an ideology can easily be a tool of reactionary propaganda, in the rhetoric of such groups as 'English Now' in the USA. This movement calls for the linguistic cleansing of America by imposing English as the official language in the country. Such legislation may lead to a ban on bilingual education and might also spark off some version of ethnic cleansing, on the grounds of the supposed superiority of English over other languages spoken in America; that is, racism.

In contrast to the view of a nation as an ethnic and linguistic monolith, ethnic and linguistic diversity is proposed today by the European Commission that calls for a new kind of politics which does not favour monolingualist ideals or homogenization through assimilation. It promotes multilingualism not only as a universal and normal condition, but as a necessary and desirable one. In this context "ethnicity is a non-discriminatory, value-free notion, which we may oppose theoretically to racism —the prejudicial, essentially hierarchical, value-laden notion that one group and its language is inferior to another." This is due to the fact that European countries have ethnic and linguistic minorities within their boundaries. To construe them as a problem is to assert a divisive monocultural and purist ideal. Against this, the primary goal of sociolinguistics has been to assert principles of linguistic and cultural pluralism, to which EFNIL, in accordance with the policies of the European Union, the European Commission in particular, ascribes.

7. Contributors

- Bessie Dendrinos, Consultant of the Centre for the Greek Language and Professor of the University of Athens (Chair);
- Jean-François Baldi, Délégue adjoint, Délégation générale à la langue française et aux langues de France;
- Pietro Beltrami, Direttore, CNR Opera del Vocabolario Italiano;
- Walery Pisarek, Honorary President of the Polish Language Council;
- Maria Theodoropoulou, Centre for the Greek Language [Kentro Ellenikis Glossas] and Lecturer at the Department of Greek Studies, Aristotle University of Thessaloniki.

8. Appendix

THE DUBLIN DECLARATION

The relationship between official, regional and minority languages in Europe

1. The linguistic reality varies considerably from one country to another across Europe, as a result of differing historical, social, and political conditions. EFNIL members, as national or central institutions of the EU member states, are dedicated to supporting their official, standard language(s) through language research, status/corpus planning, documentation, and policy. In addition, they have a responsibility to monitor closely the development of language use and linguistic diversity in each of their countries.

2. Terms such as 'minority language' and 'regional language' are usually charged with ideological meanings, as are terms such as 'national language', 'official language' and many others used to indicate the condition or status of a language (e.g. indigenous, autochthonous, ethnic, lesser-used, co-official, dialect, non-territorial, dominant language). The use of such a range of terms is itself indicative of the fact that the relationship between languages and between language and society is very complex. EFNIL intends to contribute to awareness-raising regarding the use of such terms and to promote their careful use in official documents and language policies.

3. EFNIL views all languages as equal in cultural value, and this of course includes minority languages. EFNIL makes no distinction between autochthonous, immigrant and minority languages when it comes to their rights for access to knowledge and language education. To this end, EFNIL advocates the inclusion of as many languag-

es in school curricula as possible, and urges state authorities to take a proactive approach to the inclusion of minority migrant languages in school programmes and/or to offer opportunities for accessing education in these languages whenever possible.

4. Language groups living outside their 'kin-state(s)' or without a 'kin-state' should be reassured (for instance by bilateral agreements as regards groups with 'kin-state(s)' or by adequate legal acts regarding other groups) that the country of which they are citizens respects and indeed values linguistic rights. Such practices might contribute to improved international relations, exchange, and trade.

5. Citizens are typically expected to have a command of a particular language (usually termed the 'national' or 'official' language). Those wishing to acquire citizenship have to provide evidence of their competence in this language. In a few countries this requirement is applicable to one of several official languages. Nevertheless, this should not mean that other autochthonous languages, as constituent languages of the country and part of its cultural heritage, should not be valued. The rapid decline of speakers of some of these languages in recent times is a cause for great concern. EFNIL urges state authorities and the general public to recognise the cognitive, social, and indeed political and economic advantages for the national community of the bi- or multilingualism of all its members.

6. In most European countries today there is a rather complicated linguistic reality which is not always visible due to lack of reliable, recent statistics. As EFNIL recognises the conditions of social plurality in Europe and the need for social cohesion, it is committed to promoting plurilingual citizenry and to working together with other European organisations, in order to collect and disseminate reliable data and best practice in this field.

Contacts

Jean-François Baldi	jean-francois.baldi@culture.gouv.fr
Pietro Beltrami	beltrami@ovi.cnr.it
Guy Berg	guy.berg@europarl.europa.eu
Linde van den Bosch	lvandenbosch@taalunie.org
Manuel Casado Velarde	mcasado@unav.es
Sean Ó Cearnaigh	socearnaigh@forasnagaeilge.ie
Catia Cucchiarini	ccucchiarini@taalunie.org
Anna Dąbrowska	aniadab@poczta.onet.pl
Bessie Dendrinos	vdendrin@enl.uoa.gr
Maria Gavrilidou	maria@ilsp.athena-innovation.gr
Tibault Grouas	thibault.grouas@culture.gouv.fr
Anna Maria Gustafsson	anna-maria.gustafsson@focis.fi
John Nikolaos Kazazis	jkazazis@gmail.com
Sabine Kirchmeier-Andersen	sabine@dsn.dk
Svetla Koeva	svetla@dcl.bas.bg
Dimitrios Koutsogiannis	dkoutsog@lit.auth.gr
Penny Labropoulou	penny@ilsp.gr
Einar Meister	einar@ioc.ee
Pirkko Nuolijärvi	pirkko.nuolijarvi@kotus.fi
John C. Paolillo	paolillo@indiana.edu
Tadeusz Piotrowski	tad46ster@gmail.com
Stelios Piperidis	spip@ilsp.gr
Walery Pisarek	uwpisare@cyf-kr.edu.pl
Antonios Rengakos	antonios.rengakos@gmail.com
Eiríkur Rögnvaldsson	eirikur@hi.is
Fernando Sánchez León	fsanchez@rae.es
Oliver Schonefeld	schonefeld@ids-mannheim.de
Gerhard Stickel	stickel@ids-mannheim.de

Toni Suutari	toni.suutari@kotus.fi
Maria Theodoropoulou	mtheod@lit.auth.gr
Tamás Váradi	varadi@nytud.hu
Andreas Witt	witt@ids-mannheim.de

European Federation of National Institutions for Language (EFNIL): Members and associate member institutions

For detailed information on EFNIL and its members see www.efnil.org

Member institutions grouped by country

Austria	***Österreichisches Sprachen-Kompetenz-Zentrum***, Graz Austrian Centre for Language Competence ***Bundesministerium für Unterricht, Kunst und Kultur***, Wien Federal Ministry for Education, Art, and Culture
Belgium	***Service de la langue française***, Bruxelles French Language Service ***Nederlandse Taalunie***, Den Haag Dutch Language Union (Flanders and The Netherlands)
Bulgaria	***Българска академия на науките, Институт за български език***, Sofia Bulgarian Academy of Sciences, Institute for Bulgarian Language
Cyprus:	***Πανεπιστημίου Κύπρου***, Nicosia University of Cyprus
Czech Republic	***Ústav Českého národního korpusu Univerzity Karlovy***, Praha Institute of Czech National Corpus, Charles-University
Denmark	***Dansk Sprognævn***, København Danish Language Council
Estonia	***Eesti Keelenõukogu***, Tallin Estonian Language Council ***Eesti Keele Instituut***, Tallin Institute of the Estonian Language
Finland	***Kotimaisten kielten tutkimuskeskus / Forskningscentralen för de inhemska språken***, Helsinki/Helsingfors Research Institute for the Languages of Finland
France	***Délégation Générale à la langue française et aux langues de France***, Paris General Delegation for the French Language and the Languages of France

Germany	***Institut für Deutsche Sprache***, Mannheim Institute for the German Language
	Deutsche Akademie für Sprache und Dichtung, Darmstadt German Academy for Language and Literature
Greece	***Κέντρο Ελληνικής Γλώσσας***, Thessaloniki Centre for the Greek Language
Hungary	***Magyar Tudományos Akadémia, Nyalvtudományi Intézet***, Budapest Hungarian Academy of Sciences, Research Institute for Linguistics
	Oktatási és Kulturális Minisztérium, Budapest Ministry for Education and Culture
Ireland	***Foras na Gaeilge***, Dublin (the all-island body for the Irish language)
Italy	***Accademia della Crusca***, Firenze (the central academy for the Italian language)
	CNR – Opera del Vocabolario Italiano, Firenze The Italian Dictionary
Latvia	***Valst valodas komisija***, Riga State Language Commission
	Valsts valodas aģentūra, Riga State Language Agency
Lithuania	***Lietviu Kalbos Institutas***, Vilnius Institute of the Lithuanian Language
	Valstybine Lietuviu Kalbos Komisija, Vilnius State Commission for the Lithuanian Language
Luxembourg	***Institut Grand-Ducal, Section de linguistique***, Luxembourg Grand Ducal Institute, Linguistic Section
	Conseil permanent de la langue luxembourgeoise, Luxembourg Permanent Council of the Luxembourgish language
Malta	***Kunsill Nazzjonali ta'l-Ilsien Malti*** National Council of the Maltese language
Netherlands/Belgium	***Nederlandse Taalunie***, Den Haag Dutch Language Union
Poland	***Rada Jezyka Polskiego***, Warszawa Council for the Polish Language

Portugal	***Instituto Camões***, Lisbõa (the institution for the promotion of Portuguese language and culture)
Romania	***Academia Română, Institutul de Lingvistica***, Bucureşti Romanian Academy, Institute of Linguistics
Slovakia	***Jazykovedný ústav Ĺudovíta Štúra Slovenskej***, Bratislava Slovak Academy of Sciences, Ludovit Stúr Institute of Linguistics
Slovenia	***Ministrstvo za kulturo - Sektor za slovenski jezik***, Ljubljana Ministry of Culture, Section for the Slovenian language
Spain	***Real Academia Española***, Madrid Royal Spanish Academy
Sweden	***Språkrådet***, Stockholm The Swedish Language Council
United Kingdom	***Oxford English Dictionary***, Oxford ***The British Council***

Associate member institutions

Croatia:	***Institut za hrvatski jezik i jezikoslovlije,*** Zagreb Institut of Croatian Language and Linguistics
Iceland	***Íslensk málnefnd***, Reykjavik Icelandic Language Council
Norway	***Språkrådet***, Oslo Norwegian Language Council

DUISBURGER ARBEITEN ZUR SPRACH- UND KULTURWISSENSCHAFT
DUISBURG PAPERS ON RESEARCH IN LANGUAGE AND CULTURE

Herausgegeben von
Ulrich Ammon, René Dirven und Martin Pütz

Band 1 René Dirven / Yvan Putseys (Eds.): A User's Grammar of English: Word, Sentence, Text, Interaction - Part A. The Structure of Words and Phrases. 1989.

Band 2 René Dirven / Richard A. Geiger (Eds.): A User's Grammar of English: Word, Sentence, Text, Interaction - Part B. The Structure of Sentences. 1989.

Band 3 René Dirven / Wolfgang Zydatiß / Willis J. Edmondson (Eds.): A User's Grammar of English: Word, Sentence, Text, Interaction - Parts C & D. The Structure of Texts / The Structure of Interaction. 1989.

Band 4 René Dirven: (Ed.): A User's Grammar of English: Word, Sentence, Text, Interaction - Compact Edition. 1989.

Band 5 Martin Pütz / René Dirven (Eds.): Wheels within Wheels. Papers of the Duisburg Symposium on Pidgin and Creole Languages. 1989.

Band 6 Ulrich Schmitz / Rüdiger Schütz / Andreas Kunz (Eds.): Linguistic Approaches to Artificial Intelligence. 1990.

Band 7 Friedrich Lenz: Organisationsprinzipien in mündlicher Fachkommunikation. 1989.

Band 8 Luc Van Doorslaer (Hrsg.): Niederländische Literatur im Spiegel niederländischer Kultur. Aufsätze zur Gastprofessur von Prof. Dr. Marcel Janssens (Universität Löwen) in Duisburg, Sommersemester 1988. 1990.

Band 9 Frank Lüschow / Marita Pabst-Weinschenk (Hrsg.): Mündliche Kommunikation als kooperativer Prozeß. Sprechwissenschaftliche Arbeitsfelder. Festschrift für Elmar Bartsch. 1991.

Band 10 Susanne Niemeier: Ein Fall im Medienvergleich: Film- und Fernsehversion von "A Streetcar Named Desire". Beitrag zur Annäherung an eine Mediensemiotik. 1990.

Band 11 Paul Kent Andersen: A new look at the passive. 1991.

Band 12 Richard Kremer: The efficiency of English language teaching in smaller countries: Denmark. Basic English language teaching in Denmark and its wider context. 1991.

Band 13 Frank Lüschow: Sprache und Kommunikation in der technischen Arbeit. 1992.

Band 14 Günter Kellermann / Michael D. Morrissey (Eds.): Diachrony within Synchrony: Language History and Cognition. Papers from the International Symposium at the University of Duisburg 26-28 March 1990. 1992.

Band 15 Wim Waumans (Hrsg.): Mit fremden Augen. Niederländisch: eine Sprache, verschiedene Kulturgemeinschaften. 1993.

Band 16 Eberhard Klein: Konditionalität in didaktischen und pädagogischen Grammatiken des Englischen. Prinzipien zur Erstellung von Lehr- und Lerngrammatiken. 1993.

Band 17 Xiaoan Zhu: "Wenn sich das Gras bewegt, dann muß auch der Wind blasen!" Studien zur Metapher in der deutschen politischen Pressesprache – unter besonderer Berücksichtigung der China-Berichterstattung. 1993.

Band 18 Fritz Ponelis: The Development of Afrikaans. 1993.

Band 19 Martin Pütz: Sprachökologie und Sprachwechsel. Die deutsch-australische Sprechgemeinschaft in Canberra. 1994.

Band 20 Heiner Pürschel (Ed.); Co-Editors: Elmar Bartsch, Peter Franklin, Ulrich Schmitz, Sonja Vandermeeren: : Intercultural Communication. Proceedings of the 17th Inter- national L.A.U.D. Symposium. Duisburg, 23-27 March 1992. 1994.

Band 21 Dominiek Sandra: Morphology in the reader's mental lexicon. 1994.

Band 22 René Dirven: Metaphor and Nation. Metaphors Afrikaners live by. 1994.

Band 23 Ralph Bisschops: Die Metapher als Wertsetzung. Novalis, Ezechiel, Beckett. 1994.

Band 24 René Dirven / Johan Vanparys (Eds.): Current Approaches to the Lexicon. A Selection of Papers Presented at the 18th LAUD Symposium, Duisburg, March 1993. 1995.

Band 25 Michael Schloßmacher: Die Amtssprachen in den Organen der Europäischen Gemeinschaft. Status und Funktion. 1996. 2., durchges. Aufl. 1997.

Band 26 Johan Vanparys: Categories and Complements of Illocutionary Verbs in a Cognitive Perspective. 1996.

Band 27 Hideaki Takahashi: Die richtige Aussprache des Deutschen in Deutschland, Österreich und der Schweiz nach Maßgabe der kodifizierten Normen. 1996.

Band 28 Angela Heidemann: The visualization of foreign language vocabulary in CALL. 1996.

Band 29 Kazuma Matoba: Referenzperspektive in Sprechakten. Ihre Funktion und Entwicklung in der deutschen und japanischen Sprache. 1997.

Band 30 Olaf Jäkel: Metaphern in abstrakten Diskurs-Domänen. Eine kognitiv-linguistische Untersuchung anhand der Bereiche Geistestätigkeit, Wirtschaft und Wissenschaft. 1997.

Band 31 Birgit Smieja / Meike Tasch (Eds.): Human Contact through Language and Linguistics. 1997.

Band 32 Martin Pütz (Ed.): The Cultural Context in Foreign Language Teaching. 1997.

Band 33 Andrea Gerbig: Lexical and Grammatical Variation in a Corpus. A Computer-Assisted Study of Discourse on the Environment. 1997.

Band 34 Helga Bister-Broosen: Sprachkontakte und Sprachattitüden Jugendlicher im Elsaß und in Baden. Vergleichende soziolinguistische Untersuchungen in Colmar (Frankreich) und in Freiburg und Müllheim (Deutschland). 1998.

Band 35 Helga Bister-Broosen (Hrsg.): Niederländisch am Niederrhein. 1998.

Band 36 Alicja Sakaguchi: Interlinguistik. Gegenstand, Ziele, Aufgaben, Methoden. 1998.

Band 37 Benjamin Biebuyck / René Dirven / John Ries (Eds.): Faith and Fiction. Interdisciplinary Studies on the Interplay between Metaphor and Religion. A Selection of Papers from the 25th LAUD-Symposium of the Gerhard Mercator University of Duisburg on 'Metaphor and Religion'. 1998.

Band 38 Ulrich Ammon (Hrsg.): Sprachförderung. Schlüssel auswärtiger Kulturpolitik. 2000.

Band 39 El Hadj Ibrahima Diop: Das Selbstverständnis von Germanistikstudium und Deutschunterricht im frankophonen Afrika. Vom kolonialen Unterrichtsfach zu eigenständigen Deutschlandstudien und zum praxisbezogenen Lernen. 2000.

Band 40 Herman M. Batibo / Birgit Smieja (Eds.): Botswana: The Future of the Minority Languages. 2000.

Band 41 Harald Haarmann: Die Kleinsprachen der Welt – Existenzbedrohung und Überlebenschancen. Eine umfassende Dokumentation. 2001.

Band 42 Dirk Scholten: Sprachverbreitungspolitik des nationalsozialistischen Deutschlands. 2000.

Band 43 Riana Roos Paola: Pro-active Language Teacher Education in a Multicultural Society. 2001.

Band 44 Angelika Daniel: Lernerwortschatz und Wortschatzlernen im bilingualen Unterricht. 2001.

Band 45 Edel O'Halloran: Ist Mode englisch? Französische und englische Einflüsse auf die deutsche Mode- und Gemeinsprache im 20. Jahrhundert. 2001.

Band 46 Maya Khemlani David (Ed.): Methodological and Analytical Issues in Language Maintenance and Language Shift Studies. 2002.

Band 47 Martin Praxenthaler: Die Sprachverbreitungspolitik der DDR. Die deutsche Sprache als Mittel sozialistischer auswärtiger Kulturpolitik. 2002.

Band 48 Ulrich Ammon / Grant McConnell: English as an Academic Language in Europe. A Survey of its Use in Teaching. 2002.

Band 49 Birgit Smieja: Language Pluralism in Botswana - Hope or Hurdle? A sociolinguistic survey on language use and language attitudes in Botswana with special reference to the status and use of English. 2003.

Band 50 Carlos Inchaurralde / Celia Florén (Eds.): Interaction and Cognition in Linguistics. 2003.

Band 51 Andreas Ross: Europäische Einheit in babylonischer Vielfalt. Die Reform des Sprachenregimes der Europäischen Union im Spannungsfeld von Demokratie und Effizienz. 2003.

Band 52 Michael Anton Böhm: Deutsch in Afrika. Die Stellung der deutschen Sprache in Afrika vor dem Hintergrund der bildungs- und sprachpolitischen Gegebenheiten sowie der deutschen Auswärtigen Kulturpolitik. 2003.

Band 53 Martin Pütz / JoAnne Neff-van Aertselear / Teun A. van Dijk: Communicating Ideologies. Multidisciplinary Perspectives on Language, Discourse, and Social Practice. 2004.

Band 54 Yuko Sugita: Gesprächserwartungen. Eine kontrastive Studie über die Gesprächsführung in deutschen und japanischen Telefonaten. 2004.

Band 55 Eithne B. Carlin: A Grammar of Trio. A Cariban Language of Suriname. 2004.

Band 56 Maya Khemlani David (Ed.): Teaching of English in Second and Foreign Language Settings. Focus on Malaysia. 2004.

Band 57 Rita Brdar-Szabó / Elisabeth Knipf-Komlósi (Hrsg.): Lexikalische Semantik, Phraseologie und Lexikographie. Abgründe und Brücken. Festgabe für Regina Hessky. 2004.

Band 58 Claudia Kunschak: Language Variation in Foreign Language Teaching. On the Road to Communicative Competence. 2004.

Band 59 Allan Turner: Translating Tolkien. Philological Elements in *The Lord of the Rings*. 2005.

Band 60 Markus Motz (Hrsg.): Englisch oder Deutsch in Internationalen Studiengängen? 2005.

Band 61 Birte Kellermeier-Rehbein: Areale Wortbildungsvarianten des Standarddeutschen. Beiuntersuchung zum *Variantenwörterbuch des Deutschen*. 2005.

Band 62 Maya Khemlani David / Hafriza Burhanudeen / Ain Nadzimah Abdullah (Eds.): The Power of Language and the Media. 2006.

Band 63 Vít Dovalil: Sprachnormenwandel im geschriebenen Deutsch an der Schwelle zum 21. Jahrhundert. Die Entwicklung in ausgesuchten Bereichen der Grammatik. 2006.

Band 64 Sara Hägi: Nationale Varietäten im Unterricht Deutsch als Fremdsprache. 2006.

Band 65 Albert Weideman / Birgit Smieja (eds.): Empowerment through Language and Education. Cases and Case Studies from North America, Europe, Africa and Japan. 2006.

Band 66 Iraide Ibarretxe-Antuñano / Carlos Inchaurralde / Jesús-M. Sánchez-García (eds.): Language, Mind, and the Lexicon. 2007.

Band 67 Roswitha Reinbothe: Deutsch als internationale Wissenschaftssprache und der Boykott nach dem Ersten Weltkrieg. 2006.

Band 68 Fredericka van der Lubbe: Martin Aedler and the *High Dutch Minerva*. The First German Grammar for the English. 2007.

Band 69 Frank Polzenhagen: Cultural Conceptualisations in West African English. A Cognitive-Linguistic Approach. 2007.

Band 70 Augustin Simo Bobda (ed.): Explorations into Language Use in Africa. 2008.

Band 71 Johannes Eckerth / Sabine Siekmann (eds.): Task-Based Language Learning and Teaching. Theoretical, Methodological, and Pedagogical Perspectives. 2008.

Band 72 Laura Sicola: *No, they won't 'just sound like each other'*. NNS-NNS Negotiated Interaction and Attention to Phonological Form on Targeted L2 Pronunciation Tasks. 2009.

Band 73 Gerhard Stickel (ed.): National and European Language Policies. Contributions to the Annual Conference 2007 of EFNIL in Riga. 2009.

Band 74 Daniel Klaaß: Untersuchungen zu ausgewählten Aspekten des Konsonantismus bei österreichischen Nachrichtensprechern. 2009.

Band 75 Javier Herrero Ruiz: Understanding Tropes. At the Crossroads between Pragmatics and Cognition. 2009.

Band 76 Javier Valenzuela / Ana Rojo / Cristina Soriano (eds.): Trends in Cognitive Linguistics. Theoretical and Applied Models. 2009.

Band 77 Maya Khemlani David / James McLellan / Shameem Rafik-Galea / Ain Nadzimah Abdullah (eds.): Code Switching in Malaysia. 2009.

Band 78 Gerhard Stickel (ed.): Language Use in Business and Commerce in Europe. Contributions to the Annual Conference 2008 of EFNIL in Lisbon. 2010.

Band 79 Geert Brône: Bedeutungskonstitution in verbalem Humor. Ein kognitiv-linguistischer und diskurssemantischer Ansatz. 2010.

Band 80 Olga Martynova: Sprachwahl in der deutsch-russischen Unternehmenskommunikation. 2010.

Band 81 Gerhard Stickel (ed.): National, Regional and Minority Languages in Europe. Contributions to the Annual Conference 2009 of EFNIL in Dublin. 2011.

Band 82 Harald Haarmann: Writing as Technology and Cultural Ecology. Explorations of the Human Mind at the Dawn of History. 2011.

Band 83 Beate Höhmann: Sprachplanung und Spracherhalt innerhalb einer pommerischen Sprachgemeinschaft. Eine soziolinguistische Studie in Espírito Santo / Brasilien. 2011.

Band 84 Gabriele Schmidt: Motives for Studying German in Australia. Re-examining the Profile and Motivation of German Studies Students in Australian Universities. 2011.

Band 85 Michael Szurawitzki: Der thematische Einstieg. Eine diachrone und kontrastive Studie auf der Basis deutscher und finnischer linguistischer Zeitschriftenartikel. 2011.

Band 86 Azirah Hashim / Maya Khemlani David / James McLellan: Text, Discourse and Society. Functional and Pragmatic Approaches to Language in Use. 2011.

Band 87 Gerhard Stickel / Tamás Váradi (eds.): Language, Languages and New Technologies. ICT in the Service of Languages. Contributions to the Annual Conference 2010 of EFNIL in Thessaloniki. 2011.

www.peterlang.de

www.ingramcontent.com/pod-product-compliance
Ingram Content Group UK Ltd.
Pitfield, Milton Keynes, MK11 3LW, UK
UKHW021832100926
8556IPUK00004B/288

9 783631 635360